Divine Disorder *and the* Rescue of God

Divine Disorder *and the* Rescue of God

MARK CORNER

Foreword by Richard H. Roberts

CASCADE *Books* · Eugene, Oregon

DIVINE DISORDER AND THE RESCUE OF GOD

Copyright © 2024 Mark Corner. All rights reserved. Except for brief quotations in critical publications or reviews, no part of this book may be reproduced in any manner without prior written permission from the publisher. Write: Permissions, Wipf and Stock Publishers, 199 W. 8th Ave., Suite 3, Eugene, OR 97401.

Cascade Books
An Imprint of Wipf and Stock Publishers
199 W. 8th Ave., Suite 3
Eugene, OR 97401

www.wipfandstock.com

PAPERBACK ISBN: 978-1-6667-5051-5
HARDCOVER ISBN: 978-1-6667-5052-2
EBOOK ISBN: 978-1-6667-5053-9

Cataloguing-in-Publication data:

Names: Corner, Mark, author. | Roberts, Richard H., foreword.

Title: Divine disorder and the rescue of god / Mark Corner ; foreword by Richard H. Roberts.

Description: Eugene, OR : Cascade Books, 2024 | Includes bibliographical references and index.

Identifiers: ISBN 978-1-6667-5051-5 (paperback) | ISBN 978-1-6667-5052-2 (hardcover) | ISBN 978-1-6667-5053-9 (ebook)

Subjects: LCSH: MacKinnon, Donald M. (Donald MacKenzie), 1913-1994. | Philosophy and religion. | Philosophical theology.

Classification: BT1102 .C67 2024 (paperback) | BT1102 .C67 (ebook)

02/08/24

Unless otherwise noted, all scriptures are from the REVISED STANDARD VERSION, Grand Rapids: Zondervan, 1971. Used by permission. All rights reserved.

In memory of Donald MacKinnon

Contents

Foreword by Richard H. Roberts — ix
Introduction — xi

Part 1 | Uncertainty, the Handmaiden of Faith

Chapter 1: Doing without Proof — 3
Chapter 2: The Return to History — 13
Chapter 3: A Theological Justification of Uncertainty — 19
Chapter 4: The Limitations of Our Convictions — 27

Part 2 | Uncertainty in the Created Order

Chapter 5: The "Big Picture" People — 37
Chapter 6: God and the Nature of Chance — 50
Chapter 7: Quantum Mechanics and Divine Tampering — 64

Part 3 | Uncertainty in the Moral Order

Chapter 8: The Omnipotence of Divine Love — 79
Chapter 9: Hell and Divine Failure: The Hard Side of Kenoticism — 85
Chapter 10: The Strange Doctrine of the Fall — 102

Part 4 | The Nature of God

Introduction — 119
Chapter 11: Creation and Kenosis — 122
Chapter 12: God Transcendent and Immanent — 135
Chapter 13: God as Trinity — 154

Part 5 | The Uncertain Christ

Chapter 14: How the Logos Left Heaven Behind: The Unavoidable Focus? 169
Chapter 15: Avoiding the Skydive 182
Chapter 16: Beginning from the Human Subject 192
Chapter 17: The Mystery of God 207
Chapter 18: MacKinnon's Warning 218

Bibliography 237
Index 247

Foreword

Mark Corner has written a remarkable book; another of this writer's individual contributions to a British tradition of theological reflection that exhibited much vitality in the period following the Second World War and persisted into the first decade of this century. A central figure in this flowering of critical yet responsible thought was the redoubtable Professor Donald M. MacKinnon, whose lectures in the Old Divinity School in central Cambridge remain unforgettable for those who heard them. While there are a significant number of (mostly male and British) theologians who owe a debt to MacKinnon, Mark Corner's response is distinct and creative. Rather than merely own the psycho-spiritual impact of a charismatic man, Corner shows how core strands in his mentor's thinking were prescient and rich in their long-term implications. This comment does not, of course, do justice to Corner's own role as a highly informed and independent theologian. His achievement is to have sustained and repeatedly reasserted in a series of books the kind of wide-ranging, discursive argumentation that has now become problematic in the British higher education environment in which all research and publication has to be conceived and carried out with a view to scores that determine funding. The reader of *Divine Disorder* is led through an extended argument that accepts as axiomatic the inevitability of uncertainty, and is then built up step-by-step through consideration of the created and moral orders, the nature of God, which then culminates in Christology. The entire argument is infused by informed awareness of the much-discussed topic of kenosis, to which MacKinnon drew forceful yet critical attention. Mark Corner invigorates his argument with vivid and telling contemporary images in order to avoid, for example, the "sky-diving" Logos. In an era in which British postmodern theologians have extended theology into virtuosic abstraction, and sector theologians have asserted the right of every interest group to reify its own theology, by contrast Corner takes us back on to the path of a broad church in which disagreement was managed but not silenced by the regulation of thought and expression imposed by "Safe Space" policies. It was, in this reader's first-hand experience, never "safe" to be in proximity to Donald MacKinnon. Mark Corner continues this open tradition that asserts the will-to-truth, and he does this with clarity and a faithful integrity.

Richard H. Roberts (Prof.), Honorary Fellow, Faculty of Divinity, University of Edinburgh, September 15, 2023

Introduction

The central thesis of *Divine Disorder and the Rescue of God* is that theism can be plausible only where there is recognition of a deliberate act of self-limitation on the part of God. This act was made necessary by God's decision to create free and independent human beings. It produces disorder in terms of the self-willed inability of God to ensure that human society progresses toward a world of peaceful cooperation. Indeed, human beings may only manage to destroy themselves. But since the possibility of such self-destruction is a consequence of the freedom granted to us by God, even the complete obliteration of the human race can be viewed as being consistent with the existence of God. This perspective was reflected in the words of Austin Farrer at the end of his *Finite and Infinite*, published in 1943 but written during the dark days of 1940:

> As I wrote this, the German armies were occupying Paris, after a campaign prodigal of blood and human distress. Rational theology will not tell us whether this has or has not been an unqualified and irretrievable disaster to mankind and especially to the men who died. It is another matter, if we believe that God Incarnate also died, and rose from the dead. But rational theology knows only that whether Paris stands or falls, whether men die or live, God is God, and so long as any spiritual creature survives, God is to be adored.[1]

Farrer accepts God's willingness to stand by and allow "an unqualified and irretrievable disaster to mankind." It so happens that this was avoided in 1940–45, but there are still ways in which such a disaster can happen in our own day. It may be a product of human actions (a nuclear exchange, long-term erosion of the planet's capacity to sustain life) or a simple consequence of misfortune (for instance a collision with a meteorite).

---

1. Farrer, *Finite and Infinite*, 300.

It might seem that Farrer's claim that God should be adored so long as any "spiritual creature" remains alive, even in the face of complete catastrophe, is the sign of a credulous believer willing to maintain his belief in God at all costs. But the "rescue of God," even in the face of the sort of disaster that may well come our way in the next generation or two, is based on the fact that you cannot offer freedom with one hand and then take it back with the other. Farrer recognized, at a point where he faced the potential end of civilization, that God's gift of life could not be trivialized by the belief that she would intervene at any dangerous moments and prevent us from destroying ourselves or being destroyed. The nuclear exchange will be prevented; the asteroid will be diverted. Farrer recognized that this would not happen. And if his conclusion was that "God is God, and so long as any spiritual creature survives, God is to be adored," that was because the universe was not simply created as a suitable home for what are sometimes thought to be its only important members: human beings.

In its broad outline, there is nothing new in the approach of this book. Readers will at once recognize the contours of a kenotic theology, one based upon the famous self-emptying or kenosis referred to in the so-called christological hymn of Phil 2:5–11. The hymn, which is admittedly open to various interpretations, refers to Christ's act of self-emptying, a contrast between the first Adam, who counts equality with God as a "thing to be grasped," and the second Adam, who humbles himself and takes the form of a servant. But a kenotic theology takes this much further (theology is, after all, God-talk) and claims that the self-emptying of Christ is itself a revelation of the nature of God. God takes the form of a servant; God limits God's power, in some sense sheathes the sword and stands back in order to allow human beings the space to develop—and go wrong. The humble Jesus becomes the revelation of—the realization of—the humble God, in life as in death. Hence the title of a book written in the 1960s by Jürgen Moltmann and which had lasting significance, *The Crucified God*.

Kenoticism has, of course, had its critics and there are obvious difficulties with it that will be explored later. The idea of a crucified God is a powerful one, but Moltmann hardly meant the same as the "death of God" school in the 1960s[2] and he was hardly echoing the words of Nietzsche a century earlier, when the Madman takes to the streets and declares:

> God is dead. God remains dead. And we have killed him. How shall we comfort ourselves, the murderers of all murderers? What was holiest and mightiest of all that the world has yet owned has bled to death under our knives: who will wipe

2. See Altizer and Hamilton, *Radical Theology*.

this blood off us? What water is there for us to clean ourselves? What festivals of atonement, what sacred games shall we have to invent? Is not the greatness of this deed too great for us? Must we ourselves not become gods simply to appear worthy of it?[3]

It becomes necessary to qualify the death of God as a death within God, to pursue the idea that God's self-giving in Christ is so complete that Christ's death is also God's—but without claiming that God no longer exists. The advocate of a kenotic theology has to be clear about what they are saying and prevent what is undoubtedly a powerful and attractive image from leading them into claims that cannot be substantiated.

Why, then, another book along what might be considered familiar lines? After all, there are some who would consider kenoticism virtually mainstream nowadays. When David Brown published his *Divine Humanity: Kenosis and the Construction of a Christian Theology* in 2011, the cover quoted the well-known Cambridge theologian Brian Hebblethwaite, welcoming what he called "Brown's return to mainstream Christian theology and metaphysics" and spoke of "the prevalence of kenoticism in virtually all contemporary theologies of creation and incarnation."[4] The main reason for returning to the issue once more is that while I believe that a kenotic approach is the best one for making sense of the ways of God toward humanity, I still do not believe that the implications of that approach have been fully worked out, despite the impact of recent works like Bruce McCormack's *The Humility of the Eternal Son*, subtitled *Reformed Kenoticism and the Repair of Chalcedon*, which guaranteed to make it impossible to avoid the phrase "ontological receptivity" in any theological discussion.[5] Moreover, while the idea of a "crucified God" might be an example of taking such an approach too far, I believe that there are significant areas of theological thinking where it has not been taken far enough. They will be explored later in this book.

Brown points to a paradox in kenotic writing. On the one hand, it appears to have been taken up by theologians who would be considered orthodox in their thinking or were at least trying to rescue an orthodox position in the face of new challenges. Brown writes of how, for many nineteenth-century advocates,

> kenosis is advocated not as some new "liberal" idea to be valued for its own sake but rather as the best means for "orthodoxy" to

---

3. Nietzsche, *Gay Science*, para. 125.
4. D. Brown, *Divine Humanity*, cover.
5. The phrase helps to maintain its status through its elusive character. Ontological receptivity on the part of the Son is "not directly intuitable." See McCormack, *Humility of Eternal Son*, 272.

deal with the new challenges that are now being presented to faith from philosophy and historical studies alike.[6]

He says similar things of later writers in the same tradition. Frank Weston, for instance, is described as "a kenoticist who saw himself as fanatically loyal."[7] On the other hand, they are often unwilling to acknowledge where their own thoughts are leading them. In some cases, it is their determination to be faithful to the biblical text (and not particularly Phil 2:5–11; one could also point to Col 2:9, "In Him dwells all the fullness of the Godhead bodily") that seems to drive them where they do not necessarily wish to go. Brown describes the Scottish theologian Alfred Ernest Garvie as "the first example of many writers to follow who will base their reading of the New Testament on kenotic principles yet retreat from any elaboration of a corresponding metaphysics."[8] He sees a similar reluctance in the French biblical scholar Frederic Louis Godet, as he wrestled with the implications of John 1:14, "the Word became flesh," in his commentary on the Fourth Gospel. Even where one of the most powerful kenoticists of the twentieth century, John Austin Baker, is concerned, Brown argues:

> Perhaps, as with Weston, we have here yet another bishop who wants to endorse the basic kenotic approach but is frightened by some of the metaphysics employed by its advocates. So instead, like Weston, he claims to be saying something quite different when in fact all that is happening is reluctance to pursue questions beyond a certain artificial limit.[9]

Hence, Brown says of kenosis that "despite its radically new way of thinking about Christ it is not a movement of liberal but of essentially conservative thought."[10] And he goes on, "One major reason for adopting kenoticism, and for some the primary reason, was because it was seen as the best way of giving the scriptures a consistent voice."[11] A kenotic approach appears, for many "orthodox" commentators, to bring the humanity of Christ alive in a way that they find deeply attractive. It also helps them to come to terms with developments in biblical criticism and human psychology that brought out vividly what Wolfgang Friedrich Gess identified as the way "the Logos lives among men of flesh as their brother: a life of

6. D. Brown, *Divine Humanity*, 40.
7. D. Brown, *Divine Humanity*, 21.
8. D. Brown, *Divine Humanity*, 108.
9. D. Brown, *Divine Humanity*, 164.
10. D. Brown, *Divine Humanity*, 70.
11. D. Brown, *Divine Humanity*, 70.

continually unfolding struggle; a life of devotedly ethical work, and of both human joy and human sorrow."[12] Biblical criticism was arguably unleashing a more fully human Christ, freed from the constraints of a dogmatic orthodoxy that had removed some of the frailties and uncertainties of the human condition. But then theologians had to face the theological implications of this—in other words, they found themselves balking at what they must be saying about God if God is indeed in this Christ that they are laying bare through kenosis in his full humanity. This is another example of the apparent divine disorder from which God needs to be rescued.

Brown refers to the words attributed to the centurion in Mark 15:39 ("Truly this man was the son of God") as capable of being seen as "Scripture's most ringing endorsement of Thomasius's own account of divinity: God discovered in external powerlessness."[13] Yet this conclusion, with all its radical implications for the doctrine of God, is a consequence of an "orthodox" reading of the text. No attempt here to say "a" son of God (as in the same scene as described in Luke 23:47, where the centurion talks of "a good man"), thereby opening the door to a purely human interpretation of the nature of Christ. Truly this man was "the" son of God—really? Did that mean that "truly this man was God the Son"? And therefore that this expiring victim of painful asphyxiation, with or without the relief of the first century's equivalent of an anaesthetic, was part of the eternal life of God? What sort of a God do we end up with here? At once we see that the real challenge of kenoticism is to the doctrine of God, plunged by God's own decision into the disorder of human existence and needing to be rescued or at least—insofar as it is possible for human beings—understood.

Hence the kenoticists have found themselves—sometimes almost unexpectedly—forced to face the consequences of their own orthodoxy. It is as if kenosis is lurking behind a corner, waiting to leap out at them as they labor to make sense of their beliefs. It draws them on like some kind of Pied Piper until they fear that they are emptying themselves of all intellectual reasoning and disappearing over the cliff edge into the kenotic yonder. Their God, who according to a less orthodox reasoning would be safely in heaven blessing the best of servants from afar, is found instead (as Thomasius says[14]) in external powerlessness. If, as in the title of Donald Baillie's book, which became one of the classics of orthodoxy, God was in Christ, then God was in this helpless human suffering an agonizing death on the cross, and the

12. D. Brown, *Divine Humanity*, 68.

13. D. Brown, *Divine Humanity*, 54.

14. A key section of Gottfried Thomasius's *Christ's Person and Work*, "The Person of the Mediator," which encapsulates his kenotic approach, can be found in Welch, *God and Incarnation*, 31–101.

centurion's observation provides a suitable background for the title of *The Crucified God*, the book by Jürgen Moltmann mentioned earlier, published just over a decade after Baillie's.

The organization of this book is as follows.

Part 1, entitled "Uncertainty, the Handmaiden of Faith," suggests that God forces us to live in a state of uncertainty even about God's existence. However compelling the sense of God's presence may be or however intense the experience of God's love, religious experience cannot take away uncertainty about the source of that experience. Uncertainty is a part of the human condition, a condition of faith that is often misconstrued as the enemy of faith. This part of the book examines what has been neglected by Christian theology on account of a false demand for certainty, including a serious study of history where Christian origins are concerned.

Part 2 is entitled "Uncertainty in the Created Order." The Book of Genesis emphasizes the order brought by God when chaos was "upon the face of the deep" (Gen 1:2). But what exactly is the nature of that "order" and how much room does it give the created universe to develop in ways of its own? Is there some kind of built-in flexibility to the created universe and if so in what sense? Part 2 examines movements of thought over the last two hundred years, including evolution, chaos theory, and quantum theory, in order to assess how far they illustrate God's willingness to give a degree of independence to the created order. How far can one talk about "Creation as Kenosis," the subtitle of *The Work of Love*,[15] a famous collection of essays published in 2001?

Part 3 is entitled "Uncertainty in the Moral Order." By giving human beings freedom, God opens up the possibility of failure, including her own. Unlike the God whose power knows no limits, even self-imposed ones, human beings face the much more challenging prospect of a God who by her own choice is unable to save them from the consequences of their own actions, whether this is understood in terms of their own individual destinies or the future of the created universe that they have been "allowed" to blow up or burn up. The doctrine of the fall expresses the impossibility of empowering human beings without risking disaster. Such is the risk of tragic consequences that the biblical text presents these powers as stolen rather than adopted by divine fiat, and Christian tradition has often represented a war in heaven preceding creation, as if the divine plan was subject to intense internal debate before it was finally carried into being against the will of those angels who dissented and became themselves "fallen." A

---

15. See Polkinghorne, *Work of Love*.

kenotic approach, this section concludes, means that alongside the inherent instability of the created order is that of the moral order.

In Parts 4 and 5 the book turns to consider the nature of the God who embraces risk, suffering, and even failure through the work of creation. Clearly the focus in these sections of the book is upon the risk, suffering, and failure displayed in the life of Christ. From a christological perspective, this life of Christ is the life of a human being, but it is also internal to the life of God. It is to prepare for this christological perspective in part 5 that part 4 highlights the importance of God as Trinity, as transcendent and immanent, and of space and time as part of God's creation rather than an independent backdrop to the history of salvation. These are intended to provide the scaffolding that might permit the christological claims to make sense. Part 5 finally tackles the issues surrounding "ontological receptivity" in order to try to do this.

This book is an attempt to express some of the ideas that I first heard half a century ago in lectures by Professor Donald MacKinnon. They have never left me. He certainly had a particular interest in kenoticism, but whether this book goes any way toward conveying some of the things he wanted to say I do not know. In any case, I should like to dedicate the book to his memory. The ideas one can still chew upon. The pencil, perhaps not!

PART 1

Uncertainty, the Handmaiden of Faith

Now faith is the assurance of things hoped for, the conviction of things not seen.
(HEB 11:1)

I have therefore found it necessary to deny knowledge in order to make room for faith.
(IMMANUEL KANT, CRITIQUE OF PURE REASON)

Chapter 1

Doing without Proof

Theology sometimes suffers from claiming too much. Literally, it is talk about God, and God, if there is a God, is beyond our comprehension. Certainly, we have to say something about God, or we are left saying that there exists something of which we know nothing, doubtless a true statement but one which many things besides God could satisfy.

The theologian therefore has to tread carefully, saying enough to differentiate God from other things without attempting to define what cannot be defined.

In an earlier book, *Does God Exist?*, I made the claim that God does not want us to know that God exists. God hides. Why? Because to demonstrate beyond all doubt that God existed would be too easy. It would be like the miracle or "sign" that the Pharisees demanded from Jesus in order to give them proof. No such sign was given. People had—and have—to live by faith, which makes sense only on the basis of intellectual uncertainty. Doubting that God exists is compatible with there not being a God, but it is also compatible with there being a God who doesn't want us to be sure that God exists. Which is it? Maybe we die without knowing the answer to that question. But maybe we do so because not knowing the answer is the right way to ensure that we do the best in our lives on earth, understanding what we can and not claiming more than we can know.

Such an approach might seem to minimize the assurance brought by true faith. I do not see why it should. I want to challenge a view that has characterized a great deal of theological thinking, namely the presumption that the believer must be sure of God's existence. I would argue that a measure of intellectual uncertainty has to be accepted, not as antithetical to faith but as part of it—an uncertainty that can reach down even to the very bones of the discussion, namely whether God exists at all. Furthermore, I believe that theism has taken a lot of wrong directions, and has lost a great deal of credibility, by supposing that if God exists that fact must be known with absolute certainty, whether through irrefutable "proofs" of God's existence or through a blinding revelation that cannot be understood in any other terms.

The argument can be put by asking a simple question: Is it possible to believe in God and yet not be sure that there is one? Many people, whether theists or atheists, would answer that question with a no. This book argues the opposite. Not only is it possible not to be sure that there is a God, but a great deal more sense can be made of theology when such uncertainty is assumed. We can get a much better idea of what God is like and of what God is trying to do with us if we understand why God wants to be elusive.

We change our minds; we go in and out of convictions concerning God's existence and have no absolute assurance. But why is this so surprising? Why can't we accept that a God might exist who doesn't want us to be sure there is a God? Why can't God be subtler than the God presented in Shelley's poem:

> My name is Ozymandias, king of kings:
> Look on my works, ye Mighty, and despair![1]

If there is a God, must God be self-assertive enough to satisfy the desire for certainty? Christian tradition is wary of such a notion, putting so much emphasis as it does on a wandering Galilean preacher who can get lost in a crowd and who, despite his miracle-working capacities, refuses the Pharisees a sign. The same refusal is given to the devil who tempts him in the wilderness with the request that he throw himself from the top of the temple (Luke 4:9–12) and show the world how the angels would rush to hold him up, like a group of starstruck rock fans when their idol goes crowd-surfing at a concert.

In *Does God Exist?* I argued that there can be both too little *and too much* evidence for God's existence to make faith a tenable option. The whole religious vocabulary of faith makes sense only if there is intellectual uncertainty. It is for this reason that attempts to prove the existence of God are fruitless. There is a sense of "proved" that means tested or tried, and this is arguably the most appropriate meaning of "proof" in the context of belief in God. Our intellectual uncertainty isn't to be denied. Instead, it can be accepted and even welcomed as a way in which we are ourselves being tested and required to have faith.

---

1. "Ozymandias," in Shelley, *Selected Poetry and Prose of Shelley*, 194.

I would like to recall one or two arguments made in my earlier book, before developing them in a new way. I suggested that there have been many famous approaches to God's existence, whether from a theist or nontheist point of view, which have taken for granted that a person may be certain that God does (or does not) exist. One approach is considered in the next section.

The Presumption of Proof

In 1948 there was a discussion, first broadcast on *BBC Radio*, between the most famous atheist of the day, Bertrand Russell, and his nearest counterpart among theists, the Jesuit theologian F. C. Copleston. The debate was about the existence of God, and this is how it opened:

> Copleston: As we are going to discuss the existence of God, it might perhaps be as well to come to a provisional agreement as to what we understand by the term "God." I presume that we mean a supreme personal being—distinct from the world and creator of the world. Would you agree—provisionally at least—to accept this statement as the meaning of the term "God"?
>
> Russell: Yes, I accept this definition.

The debate then continued as follows:

> Copleston: Well, my position is the affirmative position that such a being actually exists, and that his existence can be proved philosophically. Perhaps you would tell me if your position is that of agnosticism or of atheism. I mean, would you say that the nonexistence of God can be proved?
>
> Russell: No, I should not say that. My position is agnostic.[2]

It seems to me that Russell's position is more defensible than that of Copleston, and even that it is more compatible with theism. I do not for one moment think that God's existence can be "proved philosophically." I agree with Russell that one has to remain agnostic about whether there is a God. Since I would consider myself a theist, it comes as some surprise to find that I am agreeing with one of the most renowned atheists of the twentieth century and disagreeing with one of the most renowned theists. But it seems to me that the idea of a philosophical proof of God is a will-o'-the-wisp. The Russell-Copleston debate soon got bogged down in a discussion

---

2. Philosophy Overdose, "Russell-Copleston." The whole debate is available on YouTube.

of necessary propositions, because Copleston wished to show Russell that the world was such that it *must* have had a Creator. But does theism have to make such a case? Isn't it making the mistake of claiming too much and raising the stakes to unnecessarily high levels? Do we really have to have God's existence proven before we believe in God? Mightn't it even be the case that it makes more sense to believe in God if God's existence *can't* be proven, if this subtle deity deliberately desires to conceal God's identity behind the ambiguities of the world? This is the first sense in which what appears to be divine disorder may prove to be a means of rescuing God.

Can we go further? Could it not even be that if what Copleston was claiming about the evidence for God's existence were true, then that would actually *undermine* rather than establish faith? If it were really possible to show that God "necessarily" existed, then surely faith is redundant. We may plunge through the intricacies of what, for instance, Alvin Plantinga had to say about formal logic in the hope of finding a proof of God's existence, but perhaps we should be more afraid of the consequences to faith if by chance Plantinga succeeded in his quest.[3] Moreover, to be fair to Plantinga, he was perfectly able to argue that we do not need a successful argument for God's existence in order to believe in God.[4]

The Presumption of Proof and the Possibility of Dialogue

There is another side to this, which is that accepting uncertainty provides an opportunity for discussion and for both sides in the debate about God to listen to one another. In *Does God Exist?* I talked about "no meaning" theists and "no meaning" atheists, who often enjoy the sort of empathy that the supporters of political extremes do, even though they are poles apart on the political spectrum. The empathy comes from the fact that both sides of the argument agree in ruling out any theological argument as a waste of time.

The first group that effectively rules out any theological discussion consists of "no meaning" atheists. By this I mean those who can make no sense whatsoever of God talk. It is all mumbo-jumbo. The question of whether God exists is irrelevant because the word "God" has no meaning. If you ask a "no meaning" atheist whether he or she thinks God exists, they will reply: "I don't know what you're talking about."

---

3. The matter of necessary propositions is taken further in Plantinga's *Nature of Necessity*.

4. See Plantiga's argument in *God and Other Minds*. In both cases (God and other minds) we believe in something without being able to prove its existence.

This is essentially the position that Professor Alfred Ayer took. Ayer did more than anyone else to familiarize the Anglo-Saxon world with the school of logical positivism in the early twentieth century, and his book *Language, Truth and Logic* rapidly became a bestseller. He wrote as follows about the word "god":

> If "god" is a metaphysical term, then it cannot even be probable that a god exists. For to say that "God exists" is to make a metaphysical utterance which cannot either be true or false. And by the same criterion, no sentence which purports to describe the nature of a transcendent god can possess any literal significance.[5]

It would seem that Ayer is making the rules so that the theist cannot win. He says in effect: You can't be a theist unless you use metaphysical terms. Metaphysical terms, however, are meaningless. Therefore, anything you say about God is bound to be meaningless.

The argument is to be found in the first chapter of *Language, Truth and Logic*, "The Elimination of Metaphysics." Ayer points out:

> Our charge against the metaphysician is not that he attempts to employ the understanding in a field where it cannot possibly venture, but that he produces sentences which fail to conform to the conditions under which alone a sentence can be literally significant.[6]

The argument against the theist is that he or she does not produce a meaningful sentence when talking about God. The conditions under which sentences can be literally significant are not met. And what are those conditions? Ayer proceeds to tell us:

> The criterion which we use to test the genuineness of apparent statements of fact is the criterion of verifiability. We say that a sentence is factually significant to any given person if, and only if, he knows how to verify the proposition which it purports to express—that is, if he knows what observations would lead him, under certain conditions, to accept the proposition as being true, or reject it as being false.[7]

This is the famous "verification principle," and Ayer very helpfully gives us an example of what he considers to be a meaningless theological

---

5. Ayer, *Language, Truth and Logic*, 114. The argument is developed on 114–20.
6. Ayer, *Language, Truth and Logic*, 35.
7. Ayer, *Language, Truth and Logic*, 35.

statement: "The Absolute enters into, but is itself incapable of, evolution and progress." Ayer claims that "one cannot conceive of an observation which would enable one to determine whether the Absolute did, or did not, enter into evolution and progress." Ayer says that he selected this sentence "at random" from F. H. Bradley's *Appearance and Reality*.[8] Thus, anyone making a theological statement like the one above "has made an utterance which has no literal significance even for himself."[9]

In one sense what Ayer says seems perfectly reasonable. If anyone claims to be making a factual statement, then they ought to be able to state what observations would be relevant to determining the truth or falsity of that statement.

But then, many theists would claim that theological statements filled this bill perfectly well. Take the statement "God is the creator of the universe" (this idea will be considered in detail in part 4). A theist might agree that there were a number of observations that were relevant to determining the truth or falsity of this statement. They might point to the beauty of the natural world or the intricacy of its design. They might cite, for instance, the very famous example given by William Paley in his *Natural Theology*:

> In crossing a heath, suppose I pitched my foot against a stone, and were asked how the stone came to be there; I might possibly answer, that, for anything I knew to the contrary, it had lain there forever: nor would it perhaps be very easy to show the absurdity of this answer. But suppose I had found a watch upon the ground, and it should be inquired how the watch happened to be in that place; I should hardly think of the answer I had before given, that for anything I knew, the watch might have always been there. . . . There must have existed, at some time, and at some place or other, an artificer or artificers, who formed [the watch] for the purpose which we find it actually to answer; who comprehended its construction, and designed its use. . . . Every indication of contrivance, every manifestation of design, which existed in the watch, exists in the works of nature; with the difference, on the side of nature, of being greater or more, and that in a degree which exceeds all computation.[10]

Paley compares tripping over a stone when out walking on the heath to tripping over a watch. Tripping over a stone, one would simply assume that it had always been there, but tripping over a watch, one would immediately

---

8. Ayer, *Language, Truth and Logic*, 36.
9. Ayer, *Language, Truth and Logic*, 49.
10. Paley, *Natural Theology*, 1–8.

recognize it as an artifice and would presume that someone had made it. The world in which we live, Paley argues, is just such a watch that we "trip over" in our daily lives and are led to suppose has some maker.

Now Paley's argument is certainly contentious and has come in for a great deal of effective criticism. To give one example of many, watches are often made by several people, so his argument is compatible with polytheism as well as monotheism. Even if the universe were a product of intelligent design, there is no reason to suppose that it has only one designer rather than being the result of a team effort. But though Paley's argument is open to argument and perhaps has been effectively undermined by the criticisms it has received, it would surely be odd to see it as meaningless. It is something that can be discussed. The theist can say: "There must be a designer of such an intricate world." The atheist can respond: "Why just one? Why not a dozen?" This is a debate between a "meaning theist" and a "meaning atheist." One side does not say to the other: "I don't understand what you're saying." Each side says to the other: "I understand what you're saying, but I think you're wrong." This is the stuff of honest argument such as goes on (hopefully) in seminar rooms or debating chambers around the world.

Of course, Ayer's own example is more complex and perhaps looks more off-putting to those searching for meaning in theological statements: "The Absolute enters into, but is itself incapable of, evolution and progress."[11] There would have to be a discussion of what "Absolute" meant. There would have to be a discussion of what "change" meant. But even here it is not immediately clear that the statement is meaningless. A Christian might suggest that the Absolute enters human history through Jesus of Nazareth. He or she would suggest that Jesus of Nazareth represents observable evidence of God's nature. Once again, no one denies that such a claim raises a host of contentious issues. Why this person in particular? How much do we really know about Jesus of Nazareth anyway? But it is not clear that the statement is meaningless.

The "no meaning" atheist might persist by returning to Ayer's chosen example and asking: "What sense does it make to say that God, who (at least according to Ayer's chosen sentence) is incapable of evolution and progress, can be identified with a human being who grows up and lives through all the changes of a short lifetime? Does this not bring us closer to contradiction rather than contentiousness, to having to throw up our arms and admit that we just don't know what is meant by this God who is both unchanging and subject to change?"

---

11. Ayer, *Language, Truth and Logic*, 36.

Yet even if we concede that the particular sentence chosen "at random" by Ayer is too full of contradictions to hold water, it surely does not follow that *all* theological statements are meaningless. We can surely argue that even if theologians *sometimes* make meaningless statements and dress up their contradictions as "paradoxes" (an essay by the late Bernard Williams entitled "Tertullian's Paradox" explored this tendency[12]), it does not follow that they always do this. After all, it is not difficult to find examples of meaningless statements across a range of respected academic disciplines. Our conclusion is therefore that although it is sometimes necessary to say that a theological statement simply makes no sense, we can easily provide examples of theological statements that do make sense, even though they may be hotly disputed (which is our whole point—the issue merits a good debate).

There is also a "no meaning" position that is adopted on the other side of the argument, by theists rather than atheists, and indeed the position of each throws light on that of the other. "No meaning" theists make particular use of theological terms that point to a special kind of knowledge delivered to the believer by God. Words like "revelation," "grace," and, in particular, "faith" are enlisted in order to justify the idea of an exclusive channel of communication between the deity and God's followers.

To a Christian, for instance, the word "faith" might recall the arguments of the Protestant Reformers about justification by faith, the idea that salvation was earned by faith and not by works—good deeds. But then the Christian has to contend with the argument that faith itself might be described as an inner work, a good deed of the mind. The Protestant Reformers met this criticism with the argument that faith was not a work because it was an act of God rather than of the human person. Whereas works were human actions, faith was a gift of grace, a divine action, something implanted in the believer by God.

This view of faith as a divine gift rather than the product of human effort then becomes a way of marking off the believers from the unbelievers. Some people are given faith; some people are not. To John Calvin, among others, it simply proved that God predestined some to eternal salvation and some to eternal damnation before they were born.

Ask a "no meaning" theist why he or she believes that God exists, and they may well reply, "It is a matter of faith." If the questioner persists by saying, "At least explain to me what it's like to believe in God," then the offer is refused. Faith can speak only to faith. To those outside it is all nonsense—an observation that Ayer would be the first to corroborate. In this respect

---

12. B. Williams, "Tertullian's Paradox."

we can see how "no meaning" theists and "no meaning" atheists stand side by side and support each other's ideas. The more the latter find theological statements nonsensical, the more the former feel justified in saying that the truth is only revealed to believers.

The famous Anglican preacher who later became the founder of Methodism, John Wesley, discussed faith in interesting terms when he compared it to a "spiritual sense" in his *Earnest Appeal to Men of Reason and Religion*:

> As you cannot reason concerning colors if you have no natural sight—because all the ideas received by your senses are of a different kind . . . so you cannot reason concerning spiritual things if you have no spiritual sight, because all your ideas received by your outward senses are of a different kind.[13]

Wesley offers an explanation of why the believer cannot offer the unbeliever an explanation of what he or she has learned through faith. It would be like explaining to someone blind what color is like. Once again, Ayer's position is convenient for such a theist. To Wesley, Ayer would be the blind man who cannot see, like many others described in the Christian Gospels. Of course, "color talk" (metaphysical statements) appears nonsense to someone like Ayer. It is outside the range of his experience. The unbeliever is simply someone who lacks the God-given capacity to understand—someone whose eyes haven't been opened by divine grace.

For the "no meaning" theist, those who *really* believe must confess to an unbridgeable gulf between themselves and unbelief. Therefore, hearing from the "no meaning" atheist that theology is all mumbo-jumbo is music to the "no meaning" theist's ears. Of course, they would say, it is mumbo-jumbo to those whose eyes have not been opened by faith! And so each of the two sides agrees never to understand what the other is saying. Each side is happily embedded in its own comfort zone.

But both sides are wrong. It is not possible to put an exclusion zone around belief, based on a claim to special enlightenment or to the implantation of some sixth sense enabling believers to perceive things concerning which the rest of the world remains blind. Nor is it possible to put an exclusion zone around all theological discourse and declare it meaningless, as the "no meaning" atheists do. The clash of ideas is unavoidable—and a good thing. Our argument is that God wants it that way. We would suggest that God neither relishes the way some atheists regard God's existence as beyond discussion, nor the way some theists cozy up to God in the assurance that

---

13. Wesley, *Earnest Appeal*, para. 34.

nothing anyone ever says in order to challenge God's existence can ever touch them.

Lack of Proof and the Kenotic Imperative

The traditional focus of kenoticism has been upon the nature of Christ, and whether he concealed or abandoned certain divine attributes in becoming incarnate. That is something that is examined in more detail in part 5. However, the kenotic imperative, traditionally seen in terms of the self-limitation of the Word in becoming incarnate, reflects the self-limitation inherent in the nature of God, in God's eternal being, and in the work of creation as well as of incarnation and reconciliation.

The kenotic imperative, in other words, runs through every aspect of theology, including the debate demanded by any academic discipline. Discussion of God's existence remains part of the ordinary language of academic discourse, where fashions change and disagreements abound. There is no escaping this, whether by claiming that the whole area of discussion is meaningless (Ayer) or that it is superfluous (because God is known only to those who have faith).

This realization strengthens the self-confidence of theology as a discipline, caught as it ever is between opponents who consider it academically weak (or at the very least not respectable) and opponents who see it as undermining the roots of religious belief by encouraging questioning where there should be only faith. And as the next chapter tries to point out, it strengthens theology's confidence in the insights of disciplines it has sometimes neglected, the neglect stemming from the fact that they don't deliver the equivalent of mathematical proof.

Chapter 2

The Return to History

Once it realizes that it is not obliged to deliver proof, theology is able to embrace the insights of a discipline like history that cannot ever give certainty. It is not faced by Gotthold Lessing's famous "ugly broad ditch" (*der garstige breite Graben*), which suggested an unbridgeable divide between what he called the accidental truths of history and the necessary truths of reason that were the proper realm of theology.[1] Lessing's ditch has had an unfortunate effect on theological thinking.

On the one hand it has made theologians insufficiently serious about the insights of history, dismissing or at least undervaluing attempts, for instance, to discover what sort of person Jesus was and what sort of society he lived in. Such historical inquiry is dismissed as nothing more than rummaging about in an uncertain past that offers no more than various shades of grey. This has led both to an academic failure to take into account the insights of two centuries of biblical criticism, and to a lack of social and political seriousness on the part of many Christians, since the sort of events with which anyone who reads the gospel story becomes familiar—conflict with the authorities, praise for the poor, persecution, suffering, and death— are all seen as part of this hazy and uncertain world of the past about which nothing is certain. The danger is that because history cannot offer certainty, it suddenly doesn't matter. This immediately removes the ethical seriousness surrounding what are believed to have been the crucial elements of the Christian narrative. Instead, everything to do with Christian belief and commitment is taken away from the detailed study of the past and is loaded

---

1. See Lessing, "On the Proof."

onto experience of "Jesus now," something that is all the more comforting in being infinitely malleable.

When the theologian Martin Kähler entitled his influential book *The So-Called Historical Jesus and the Christ of Faith* (*Der sogenannte historische Jesus und der geschichtliche, biblische Christus*), first published in 1892, the revealing title showed that Lessing's unbridgeable ravine was firmly in place over a century later. "Christian faith and a history of Jesus repel each other like oil and water," Kähler wrote,[2] and that message was passed down largely intact to many theologians in the twentieth century who were important in New Testament studies, such as Rudolf Bultmann. In an essay entitled "The Crisis of Belief," Bultmann declared, "In the Christian message . . . there is absolutely no question of man's being given an historical account of a section of the past, which he might put to the test, or critically confirm or reject."[3] At the core of Bultmann's skepticism about the value of a "historical account" was a conviction that only certainty would do, and certainty could come only from some transformative experience in the present. Historical research into Christian origins was seen as representing a failure to appreciate where the real significance of Jesus lay. The Anglican theologian John Knox summed the position up with admirable clarity in *The Church and the Reality of Christ*:

> Since even the best attested fact of the history of the past can possess no more than a very high degree of probability and since, by definition, Christian and indeed all religious faith must from the believer's point of view be absolutely certain and secure, can faith ever be said to depend upon an historical fact, no matter how well established? Faith must know its object in a way we cannot know an historical fact.[4]

Since even the best attested historical fact falls short of providing religious faith with what must from the believer's point of view (at least as John Knox saw things) be "absolutely certain and secure," the study of Christian origins becomes effectively an irrelevant thrashing around in the dark. But where did Knox get this idea that religious faith must be absolutely certain and secure? He clearly thought that such certainty is crucial to faith, but what if the opposite were the case? What if faith by definition has to be *uncertain*? What if we were forced to spend our lives thrashing about, not in the dark perhaps but at least in the half-light? Could that not nevertheless

---

2. Kähler, *So-Called Historical Jesus*, 74.
3. Bultmann, *Essays*, 18.
4. Knox, *Church and the Reality*, 16.

be a form of faith, indeed something closer to the sense of trust rather than certainty that the word "faithful" normally entails?

In an essay entitled "The Poverty of Historical Skepticism," Peter Carnley questioned the way in which so many theologians set out in search of a *sturmfreies Gebiet* (essentially a trouble-free zone)[5] where their convictions were untroubled by doubt. Ironically, at a time when classical scholars busied themselves uncovering far more about the ancient world than they had been able to do in the past, their theological counterparts, in many cases with historical evidence that was much fuller than that available to their colleagues in Departments of Ancient History, were refusing to draw any conclusions at all. I well remember colleagues in the Classics Departments of universities in the 1980s muttering to me about how ridiculously skeptical theologians were in their own dealings with the past. If they thought there was nothing much to be learned from the past about Jesus of Nazareth, they should try working on the evidence for Julius Caesar!

It was one of the lasting contributions of the theology of liberation in the second half of the last century that it encouraged a serious study of the social conditions within which the Jesus movement emerged. It is interesting how enduring the works of theologians like Gerd Theissen and Wayne Meeks proved to be. Theissen's *The First Followers of Jesus* was originally published by SCM Press in 1978, but a paperback reprint was produced in 2012. *The Shadow of the Galilean: The Quest of the Historical Jesus in Narrative Form* was first published by Fortress Press in 1987, but a new edition commemorating the twentieth anniversary of the book's publication was brought out in 2007. Wayne Meeks's *The First Urban Christians: The Social World of the Apostle Paul* was brought out in 1983 by Yale University Press, but then reprinted twenty years later in 2003. A *New York Times* book review by Robert McAfee Brown declared that "those with any historical bent will be intrigued by the way a story overlaid with thick layers of theological speculation is unravelled."[6] This theological speculation was seen as a source of the comforting certainties that historical unravelling could never guarantee. But the point is that there are no such guarantees. When that is accepted, the layers of theological dogma (rarely speculation) can indeed be peeled away.

Of course, that peeling away produces no comparable historical certainties. Liberation theology knew that recovering the text involved recognizing the presumptions and prejudices of both writers and readers. But something lasting happened in those last decades of the twentieth century.

---

5. See Sykes and Clayton, *Christ, Faith and History*, 186.
6. R. Brown, "Review," para. 7.

When Gerd Theissen produced *The Gospels in Context: Social and Political History in the Synoptic Tradition* or *Social Reality and the Early Christians* it was the socioeconomic context, not the dance of disembodied theological terms, that was being referred to. The abandonment of certainty was the price of admission to serious historical and sociological reflection about the world of the New Testament.

The New Testament scholar is in the same position as any other academic studying material about events taking place two millennia ago. This is accepted by any serious student of theology. It can certainly be argued that the documents available for trying to piece together something about the life of Jesus are as good as those other ancient historians have at their disposal for understanding the lives of other historical figures. But even so, every academic is in the same boat, dealing with often piecemeal and contradictory sources. A great deal can be learned nonetheless, and ancient historians of one kind or another rightly have a degree of confidence in what they can uncover of the past. At the same time, they know and accept that certainty about what happened is impossible.

We Live in Uncertainty Now

The last section argued that the impossibility of being certain about what happened in the past is no reason for denigrating the insights the past can yield. But precisely the same point can be made about events in the present. It is no more possible to be certain about a current event than about a past one. The uncertainty we have to live with in understanding the past does not vanish when it comes to contemporary events.

In an earlier book on miracles, I tried to outline a scenario where somebody who claimed that they were Christ returned two millennia on.[7] Let us imagine that this person claims to work miracles and that thousands claim to have witnessed these wonders while others condemn them as tricks. Let us suppose that this person has some kind of run-in with the authorities of our day, perhaps because of a radical social and political message that is extremely controversial. Then the person dies (we will presume in suspicious circumstances).

A great deal of media attention, let us say, has been focused on this "Christ." Some have become ardent followers, others are uninterested, a few point out that mental institutions are full of would-be Christs and a significant number of establishment figures see the persona of the "impostor" as

---

7. I outline this scenario in Corner, *Signs of God*, 188–93, in a section titled "The Return of Christ: An Imagined Account."

a front for social revolution. There are fears (and hopes) of a resurrection. There are suspicions on the part of the authorities that a fake resurrection will be carried out in order to support social revolution; there are equivalent fears on the part of followers convinced that a resurrection will indeed take place but will be covered up by the authorities. Perhaps the sentiments are not so very different from what they were two millennia back. But this is the twenty-first century, and we supposedly have "science" at our disposal.

I wrote in these terms about what I tried to imagine as the circumstances surrounding the death of a contemporary messianic claimant nearly two decades ago, before the advent of smartphones, social media, and other recent developments made the point I was trying to make even clearer. The point is that the technology may become ever more sophisticated, but it remains unable to deliver certainty, any more than the historian can deliver certainty about what happened at a graveside outside Jerusalem more than two millennia ago. If Christ came back and was killed all over again and rose from the dead again, observed by an array of smartphones, tablets, and other handheld devices, their findings immediately passed on through social media, this would not supply the proof that was unavailable to those living in a supposedly prescientific era two millennia ago. There would be an array of conspiracy theories about how new technology, rather than making it possible to confirm the authenticity of an event beyond doubt, makes it possible to create a forgery in a more sophisticated manner. The arguments would go on indefinitely. Nothing in modern technology or even in the absence of historical distance from the events taking place delivers us from a measure of uncertainty about what has happened. One need hardly enter into the arguments about "fake news" in the 2020s, or the debate, for instance, about what actually happened when the capitol was stormed in January 2021 by disconsolate supporters of President Trump, to know that technology is not the handmaiden of an indisputable account of events. Whether it was the resurrection of Jesus two millennia ago or the supposed resurrection of someone today, a few would believe that someone had risen from the dead, while for others the whole story would be an example of fake news. There is no way of putting either events in the distant past or those taking place in the present beyond doubt.

We can seek to make intelligent observations about past and present events—indeed, it is frequently said that in an age of fake news it is doubly important to understand what is really happening in the present. No one would deny in the context of current events in Ukraine that it is necessary to reach a judgment about what is really going on, whether in interpreting stories of "false flags" or trying to identify the real source of video footage or what exactly it is depicting. In all this there may well be an absence of certainty about what has been happening in the recent past, just as there is an absence of certainty about what was happening in the distant past. Yet the uncertainty we have to live with is no reason for thinking that our conclusions about past or contemporary events are unimportant or that they are not an essential part of the theologian's task. One cannot shunt aside the question of what the historical evidence suggests concerning the life and teaching of Jesus of Nazareth, simply by saying that we can never reach any certain conclusions about it. One cannot say that whatever conclusions we are able to reach have nothing to do with the faith that is built upon a rock, not upon the shifting sands of scholarly fashion. For it is in those shifting sands that we have been placed; it is in those sands that God placed God when making God both available and manipulable as a human being. Fake news came God's way, too, as when Jesus was accused of casting out devils by the prince of devils (Matt 9:34; 12:24). If God made God known in such a way that God could be taken to be the opposite of what God was, if God allowed disinformation to be woven around the story of God's own determination to be identified with the human condition, then those shifting sands are where we, too, are intended to find our way.

Chapter 3

A Theological Justification of Uncertainty

John Henry Newman, the famous Anglican theologian and leading light of the nineteenth-century Oxford Movement, who later converted to Catholicism and eventually became a cardinal, argued that religious belief was like other forms of belief in requiring commitment in the light of evidence that fell short of proof. In his *University Sermons* he suggests something like a quantitative scale, whereby the more important a particular belief may be to us, the more subtle and even ambiguous will be the evidence for it:

> Next let it be considered, that the following law seems to hold in our attainment of knowledge, that according to its desirableness, whether in point of excellence, or range, or intricacy, so is the subtlety of the evidence on which it is received.[1]

It is the beliefs of which we can be most certain, Newman suggests, that play the least significant part in our lives. We can possess a mathematical certainty that twenty-five multiplied by twenty equals five hundred, but this rarely matters to us. On the other hand, we can never possess such a certainty that someone loves us. There is always a possibility of deceit or self-deception. But it is precisely the possibility of being wrong in believing that someone loves us that makes it appropriate to talk in this context of trust. Where belief in God is concerned, Newman accepted that God's existence could be doubted and that there was no possibility of the mathematical certainty that can be achieved in the case of equations. But this

---

1. "Nature of Faith in Relation to Reason," sermon 11, para. 23, in Newman, *University Sermons*, 151.

he regarded as appropriate. The risk of faith is a willingness to venture into what in a later work, *Essay in Aid of a Grammar of Assent*, Newman called a "real assent" rather than a "notional assent," and which we might call a certainty of commitment rather than a certainty of understanding, another interesting anticipation of the theology of liberation. In his sermon, Newman continues:

> We are so constituted, that if we insist on being as sure as is conceivable, in every step of our course, we must be content to creep along the ground, and can never soar. If we are intended for great ends, we are called to great hazards; and, whereas we are given absolute certainty in nothing, we must in all things choose between doubt and inactivity, and the conviction that we are under the eye of One who, for whatever reason, exercises us with the less evidence when He might give us the greater.[2]

If we seek to protect ourselves from doubt in matters of belief, the result will be inactivity. The person who seeks to be protected from doubt in their beliefs is like the person who, in order to be protected from the risk of illness, never ventures from the home. Newman therefore insists in his sermon that faith is "a state in which we must assume something to prove anything, and we can gain nothing without venture."[3]

A further example, one to be found in the Victorian "age of doubt," comes from the poet Robert Browning in "Bishop Blougram's Apology." This is a small part of what Bishop Blougram has to say:

> All we've gained is, that belief,
> As unbelief before, shakes us by fits,
> Confounds us like its predecessor....
> All we have gained then by our unbelief
> Is a life of doubt diversified by faith,
> For one of faith diversified by doubt:
> We called the chess-board white,—we call it black.[4]

Blougram does not suggest that there is no difference between belief and unbelief. He suggests that each is more tempted by the other, and more alive to the nature of the other, than either one of them cares to admit. Both have some idea of how reality might appear if it was perceived as the other

---

2. "Nature of Faith in Relation to Reason," sermon 11, para. 22, in Newman, *University Sermons*, 151.

3. "Nature of Faith in Relation to Reason," sermon 11, para. 22, in Newman, *University Sermons*, 151.

4. Browning, "Bishop Blougram's Apology," 231.

perceives it ("meaning" theist and "meaning" atheist in terms of our earlier definitions). Both at times experience in themselves as an exception what the other experiences as a rule—a life of faith diversified by doubt, or a life of doubt diversified by faith. Is that not how many of us live, shaken at times by moments of doubt about the theism we have always found compelling—or the atheism that has always seemed to us a mere matter of common sense? Perhaps we cling too much to fixed positions precisely because we mistakenly think that any hint of uncertainty would indicate that we had never been honest in our convictions.

The eighteenth-century cleric Bishop Butler (one of many intellectual and controversial bishops of Durham) made a similar point in his famous *Analogy of Religion*. He tackles there the question of what sort of evidence one must possess in order to believe in God. His central principle is that "probability is the guide to life," and he applied this principle to those who found it hard to accept Christianity. His argument was that people expect to be certain, and therefore interpret any doubt as evidence of unbelief:

> They take for granted, that if Christianity were true, the light of it must have been more general, and the evidence of it more satisfactory.... If any of these persons are, upon the whole, in doubt concerning the truth of Christianity; their behavior seems owing to their taking for granted, through strange inattention, that such doubting is, in a manner, the same thing as being certain against it.[5]

What Butler is saying is that because we see doubt as the antithesis of faith rather than as an integral part of it, we suppose that those who doubt are by definition those who disbelieve. Once the slightest piece of doubt creeps into our own convictions, we see this as evidence that we aren't really believers at all, and therefore we are inclined to abandon our belief at the first tremor of uncertainty. Ironically, therefore, he is suggesting that we might be more prepared to keep our faith if we recognized that doubts were a part of faith and not a sign of its disappearance. Those who insist upon certainty are not so much demonstrating their own faith as inhibiting the faith of others.

The dialogue between Russell and Copleston showed that many atheists appear to be used to dealing with theists who adopt a position of unassailable certainty in their beliefs. This chapter has sought to argue that this is far from the only theistic position. Why can't the theist argue that faith in God is a form of trust? By definition, there will be facts and events that will count against this faith—but if nothing could count against it, would it any longer be faith? Why is it that the sort of certainty that parades its

---

5. Butler, *Analogy of Religion*, 322.

unassailable inner convictions on the basis of a directly implanted sixth sense is so often associated with "faith" when the word "faith" carries with it a sense of trust that is meaningless without *un*certainty? How can it be that this was one point on which the most famous atheist and one of the foremost theists of the last century felt that they could agree with each other? In the dialogue between the theist Copleston and the atheist Russell cited in the first chapter, Copleston asked, "Would you say that the nonexistence of God can be proved?" Russell replied, "No, I should not say that. My position is agnostic."[6] I would suggest that the atheist might ask the theist, "Would you say that the existence of God can be proved?" And the theist could perfectly well reply, "No, I should not say that. My position as a theist is that God's existence cannot be proved."

Are There Any Limits to Uncertainty? Ventures and Leaps

Blaise Pascal has a famous description of a "wager" in his pungently aphoristic and unfinished *Pensées* (*Thoughts*) written in the mid-seventeenth century.[7] Pascal accepts that the chances of God's existence might be slight—a possible God rather than a probable God. However, since the rewards of believing are so high (in fact, infinite) in proportion to the amount staked (a finite life), he suggests that the bet that God exists is worth taking even when, in all likelihood, it will be lost.

The view that one should always wager on the outsider if the odds are high enough is open to criticism. It is a favorite technique of lottery organizers to hide the punters' slim chance of winning behind a much-hyped huge first prize that they have less than a million-to-one chance of securing. More sensible gamblers prefer the horses or football, or even the roulette wheel. Pascal's commitment to the outsider would seem to entail that even if the possibility of God's existence were minuscule, the choice of belief should be made. His position could be summed up as saying that so long as it has not been established beyond doubt that God does *not* exist, we should believe in God.

Pascal's wager has its attractions in the way it compares belief in God with the kind of risk venture taken when making a bet. To Pascal religious belief was a commitment made in the context of obvious intellectual uncertainty. If God's existence is wagered upon in the way the outcome of a race is wagered upon, then by definition that existence cannot be certainly known until after the race is run (presumably after death). You make your

---

6. Philosophy Overdose, "Russell-Copleston."
7. Pascal, *Pensées*, sect. 3, "Of the Necessity of the Wager."

bet—essentially you make a commitment and live by it—but you do so without knowing for certain that your bet will be a winning one.

At the same time, it seems to me that the theist must be prepared to defend the idea that it is reasonable to believe in God, even though it cannot be certain. It must be a plausible explanation of the way things are, not a kind of wild surmise against all the odds. Moreover, the idea of the outsider's bet can easily decline into a position that almost relishes outsider status. From this point of view, however, the rewards of believing are: the less evidence there is for God's existence, the better. It is as if a faith that flies in the face of reason is more admirable than a faith that decides to commit itself to what seems reasonable but can never be certain (such as a particular interpretation of history).

The early nineteenth-century Danish theologian and so-called father of existentialism Søren Kierkegaard is in danger of adopting this position. It is as if in order to test the believer and evoke real trust, God ordains a world in which all the evidence points against God's existence. Kierkegaard has a famous example that takes precisely this approach, although it applies to the goodness of God rather than God's existence. He highlights the part of the Hebrew Bible where Abraham is told by God to kill his son Isaac (Gen 22:1–19). Abraham prepares to do so, and only when it is clear that Abraham will obey the divine command does God at the last moment spare Isaac and tell Abraham to sacrifice a sheep instead.[8] Kierkegaard interpreted the parable to mean that we should trust God unconditionally. Even when God appears evil, commanding actions universally regarded as bad, such as killing a son in order to satisfy the whims of a deity, we should nevertheless call God good and be prepared to do as God bids. In the same way we could argue that we must believe in the existence of God even when all the evidence for God's existence appears absurd. Such absurdity is there only to test our faith in the way that Abraham was tested with an "absurd" moral demand. The atheist is right—all the evidence points against God. But what the atheist fails to see is that this is precisely how God arranged things in order to ensure that we had true faith, which is not a reasoned commitment or even a dangerous venture but rather a "leap." The leap of faith is not a rational decision based on observing the way the universe is structured or even studying the odds at the bookmakers. It is a leap in the dark. It is taking the plunge. It is accepting the absurdity of belief in God and yet understanding that the absurdity of what is believed only strengthens the faith shown in believing it. Echoing a famous saying of the early Christian

---

8. Kierkegaard, *Fear and Trembling*; see the section "Eulogy on Abraham."

apologist Tertullian, the theist declares: *Certum est, quia impossibile* (It is certain, because it is impossible).

This book rejects the leap of faith approach as much as it opposes the certain proof approach. The idea that the more unlikely God's existence appears the more creditable it is to believe it, is as untenable as the idea that God's existence can be proved beyond any reasonable doubt. The position argued for here is that the existence of God has to be less than provable but more than highly improbable. True, this sounds like a position full of grey areas ("Exactly what percentage likelihood would you settle for?" one can imagine someone saying. "Is 35 percent too little? Is 95 percent too much?"). However, though there is no answer to this in terms of precise percentages, it seems to me a defensible position to take. A famous example will illustrate this.

The philosopher Antony Flew wrote the following in a symposium entitled "Theology and Falsification," later published in a set of essays entitled *New Essays in Philosophical Theology*:

> Now it often seems to people who are not religious as if there was no conceivable event or series of events the occurrence of which would be admitted by sophisticated religious people to be a sufficient reason for conceding "There wasn't a God after all" or "God does not really love us then." Someone tells us that God loves us as a father loves his children. We are reassured. But then we see a child dying of inoperable cancer of the throat. His earthly father is driven frantic in his efforts to help, but his Heavenly Father reveals no obvious sign of concern. Some qualification is made—God's love is "not a merely human love" or it is "an inscrutable love," perhaps—and we realize that such sufferings are quite compatible with the truth of the assertion that "God loves us as a father (but, of course, . . .)." We are reassured again. But then perhaps we ask: what is this assurance of God's (appropriately qualified) love worth, what is this apparent guarantee really a guarantee against? Just what would have to happen not merely (morally and wrongly) to tempt but also (logically and rightly) to entitle us to say: "God does not love us" or even "God does not exist"? I therefore put to the succeeding symposiasts the simple central questions, "What would have to occur or to have occurred to constitute for you a disproof of the love of, or of the existence of, God?"[9]

Once again, I find myself on the side of the atheist. It seems to me that Flew makes a fair point. "I believe because it is absurd" will not do. By focusing

9. Flew and MacIntyre, *New Essays*, 98–99.

on "falsification," Flew is asking the theist: Just what would have to happen to make you reject or even simply doubt the existence of God? Rather than asking what could prove the existence of God, he is asking what could *dis*prove it. To repeat his final sentence: "I therefore put to the succeeding symposiasts the simple central questions, 'What would have to occur or to have occurred to constitute for you a disproof of the love of, or of the existence of, God?'"

One of Flew's fellow symposiasts did indeed try to answer the question. The philosopher of religion Basil Mitchell offered the following example of his own.[10] In an occupied country during wartime, a member of the resistance meets a stranger who deeply impresses him, and who assures him that he is on the side of the resistance. The partisan feels that he can trust the stranger, although that trust is tested severely in future weeks. Sometimes the stranger appears in the uniform of the police handing over other partisans to the forces of occupation. At other times he engages in activities that help the resistance. The evidence for the stranger's allegiance is therefore ambiguous, and Mitchell makes clear that the partisan's trust in him, though real, is not unconditional and could be withdrawn if the evidence that he is a double agent, for instance, becomes too strong.

Mitchell's point is that it is of the nature of religious commitment to come to terms with what may count against one's own beliefs as well as for them. If we followed his example of trusting in the stranger, it would make no sense to say that the member of the resistance is "certain" that the stranger is on his side. He trusts him, but he also weighs the evidence from the stranger's activities, and he might in principle observe the stranger doing things that would take his trust away. It seems to me that this sort of trust fits perfectly well with Bishop Blougram's experience

> that belief,
> As unbelief before, shakes us by fits.[11]

For there are doubtless moments when the member of the resistance finds himself wondering whether the stranger is betraying him. But he retains a "certainty of commitment" to the partisan, even while he has doubts about his trustworthiness. He continues to help him, protect his cover, entrust other members of the resistance to his charge, etc. But this could end. Should the evidence of the partisan's activities point too much toward his being a double agent, he might well consent to having him shot.

Flew's harrowing example of the dying child doubtless describes occasions when a number of people have lost their faith (whether in the love of

---

10. Flew and MacIntyre, *New Essays*, 103–5.
11. Browning, "Bishop Blougram's Apology," 230.

God or the existence of God or both), while others have been able to continue believing. But we don't have to agree with what Flew implies, which is that those who believe in God do so because nothing could ever count against their belief. We can argue that like the member of the resistance the believer can have moments of doubt, encounter evidence that counts against belief, and even stop believing, for a time or for the rest of their lives. That is the precarious position we are always in, whether in our beliefs or in our lives themselves.

Conclusion

This chapter has tried to provide a theological justification for the uncertainty that must attend anyone trying to puzzle out the meaning of life. It has argued that the beliefs of which we can be most certain are the ones that play the least significant part in our lives (Newman). About the things we hold most dear there can be moments when we are tempted by the other side of the argument (Bishop Blougram's chessboard). Perhaps ironically, we might be more prepared to keep our faith if we recognized that doubts were a part of faith and not a sign of its disappearance (Butler).

If this chapter seems to have invited doubt in, it does not mean it thinks that the more improbable belief in God is the more worthy the faith. It takes issue with Pascalian wagers and Kierkegaardian leaps in this regard. It is much more attuned to the suggestion made by Basil Mitchell in his account of the sort of trust given to the member of the resistance. Trust has to be reasonable, and there has to be some evidence that it is justified. The trust will express itself in a total commitment on the part of the partisan, who does not allow his doubts to affect the level of support he gives. Uncertainty about whether there is a God need in no way lessen the degree of commitment shown to Christianity—after all, it is by their fruits that they shall be known. There may be a "certainty of commitment" even when the understanding is subject to moments of doubt, the point made in a different way by the liberation theologians whose faith is grounded in a particular understanding of Jesus and the society he lived in whose accuracy can never be guaranteed. Yet such uncertainty does nothing to undermine their commitment to the poor, which remains unwavering and demands so much of them, even their lives.

Chapter 4

The Limitations of Our Convictions

Part 1 of the book has argued strongly for something less than proof of God's existence and for an idea of faith as compatible with doubt and uncertainty. But it is important to attempt a little clarity on various terms because this may affect the credibility of the arguments used.

I have claimed that belief in God is compatible with not knowing whether there is one. By this I mean that nothing in the way of a person's religious commitment need be affected by the presence of doubts concerning the existence of what they believe in. The distinction between certainty of understanding and certainty of commitment makes this point. I see nothing contradictory in someone saying: "I don't know whether there's a God, but I'm going to live as if there was." The approach of Pascal's wager is relevant here. You make a bet—and though there might be a pundit saying, "Put your money on so-and-so; it's a racing certainty," we know that in practice all bets are based on probability.

Of course, we may say we are certain of something. That is a matter of our mental state. Not even proof is bound to give us certainty. There is no self-contradiction in saying, "It's true. Alvin Plantinga's proof of God is faultless. But I just can't believe it!" A demonstration of a mathematical proof is not logically bound to generate a state of complete conviction in those who encounter it and even those who accept it. Once again, this is a point that Newman was alive to. In his *Essay in Aid of a Grammar of Assent*, he explores the way in which we assent to what is certainly not demonstrable beyond question. He gives as an example Britain being an island, which while there may be overwhelming evidence that it is the case is not demonstrable in the way that a mathematical proof is demonstrable. On the other hand, we may refuse to assent to what is so demonstrable. As he puts it, "Prejudice hinders assent to the most incontrovertible proofs."[1] Newman's argument is that when we assent to what is likely or very likely or certain, the assent is in each case the same, unaffected by the strength of the evidence for whatever we assent to. Our mistake is to think that the stronger the evidence for what we assent to, the stronger will be the assent. It is this that leads us to mistakenly think that faith can exist only where there is absolute certainty of the truth of what we believe.

Knowledge and Certainty

The philosopher Ludwig Wittgenstein's *On Certainty* was at least partly prompted by G. E. Moore, and in particular by Moore's claim that there are certain things that he "knows." Like Descartes, Wittgenstein explores the idea that everything can be open to doubt. He asks whether certain doubts could not be had by a reasonable person, whether they could possibly doubt, for instance, that they had never been in the stratosphere, whether insanity might mean not doubting what I absolutely ought to doubt or doubting what I ought not to doubt. But one of the most important observations in his book concerns the relationship between knowing and being certain.

In *On Certainty*, Wittgenstein makes the following remark:

> The difference between the concept of "knowing" and the concept of "being certain" isn't of any great importance at all, except where "I know" is meant to mean: I can't be wrong.[2]

We can imagine, Wittgenstein suggests, someone saying, "I was certain that I had my keys in my pocket when I left the house, but it turned out that I'd left them on the kitchen table." This is the sort of thing we often say (some, admittedly, more than others!) and it represents an admission that things about which we are convinced may turn out to be wrong. There is an implicit acknowledgment that our subjective sense of being sure provides no guarantee that what we are sure about is in fact the case. So I can say, "I used to be certain God existed, but now I'm not so sure."

Suppose I said, "I knew that my keys were in my pocket, but it turned out that I'd left them on the kitchen table." It seems that saying "I know that" something is the case implies more than that I am sure about it. However, Wittgenstein adds a caveat:

---

1. Newman, *Essay*, 143; ch. 6, "Assent Considered as Unconditional," pt. 1, "Simple Assent."

2. Wittgenstein, *On Certainty*, para. 8.

For "I know" seems to describe a state of affairs which guarantees what is known, guarantees it as a fact. One always forgets the expression "I thought I knew."[3]

We do indeed say things like "I thought I knew what I was doing." What this means is that when something that I said I "knew" turns out to be wrong, that means that I never really knew it to be the case—"I thought I knew." I didn't really know it—for if I had really known it, it would have had to be true. Whereas when it comes to certainty, I can happily agree that I was certain of something, but all the same it turned out to be wrong.

One can say, "He believes it, but it isn't so," but not "He knows it, but it isn't so." Does this stem from the difference between the mental states of belief and knowledge? No. One may, for example, call "mental state" what is expressed by tone of voice in speaking, by gestures, etc. It would thus be possible to speak of a mental state of conviction, and that may be the same whether one is speaking about knowledge or false belief.

Hence, we may agree that knowing something to be the case, as opposed to believing it to be the case, rules out its not being the case. However, if I say that I "know" something is the case, as opposed to "believe" it to be the case, that does not mean that I am in a different mental state, as if the inside of my brain was buzzing with an implacable assurance. It is not as if I am transformed from a timid, nervous person who cannot make up his mind about what he thinks into a confident creature who lets no doubts come creeping in. For if that means anything, it means moving from a state of doubt to a state of certainty, and we have already seen that either is compatible with being wrong. "Knowing" something does mean that it must be the case, but, as Wittgenstein says, the fact that I can perfectly well say, "I thought I knew," shows that knowledge is not guaranteed by the confidence with which I affirm a proposition to be true.

The argument here is that, where God is concerned, in this life we cannot know. Even if we are certain we cannot know, we can say we know—and then discover that though we thought we knew, we didn't. The point is that we cannot get beyond doubt by relying on the strength of an inner conviction—inner convictions are often wrong. Even if I defend my conviction by saying, "I know," I may later say, "I thought I knew." Only after this life can we know as we are known (1 Cor 13:12).

The argument used in this chapter is not intended to undermine or belittle faith. It is intended to explain just why faith is important. Nor is it intended to belittle religious experience, or the sense of vocation that many people who enter the priesthood feel. We all too easily think that admitting

---

3. Wittgenstein, *On Certainty*, para. 12.

uncertainty means denying the importance of religious experience. It is presumed that a denial of certainty means underplaying the sort of tradition where people speak of being touched by God or experiencing faith as a kind of ecstasy. It is supposed that by arguing for uncertainty, we are behaving like dry intellectuals who treat everything as a subject for debate—and intellectual debate, it is assumed, leads only to dead ends and confusion, rarely to enlightenment. We feel convinced that no one would actually devote their life to God, for instance, by taking monastic vows or becoming a priest, unless they were absolutely certain that there must be one. They have a vocation—they have received a "calling"—and the existence of the caller must be somehow confirmed by the call they have received. They must be taking a bold step, which most of us would be incapable of taking, and we suppose that it is just because someone has tapped them on the shoulder during the night. We rarely reflect upon the fact that the devotion of the priest or the monk might be even greater and even more admirable precisely because they have no more assurance than we have but are simply throwing themselves into an adventure based on the understanding that they are making a commitment or a bet just like other believers and have no more assurance than anyone else has that theirs is the right one. Might it not be that they are able to glimpse what sort of a God might love us into the frightening uncertainty that attends all our waking days but makes an adventure of our lives? And why shouldn't such a glimpse be at the heart of an intense religious experience?

To put it crudely, you can stress all the emotional stuff and still not be transported into a world on the other side of doubt. You can be in love with God and wonder whether there is a God. You can feel transformed by hearing voices, but still be forced to accept that hearing voices does not guarantee the existence of a speaker at the other end of the line. One can be driven to make a choice, to take a certain decision—that is a "certainty of commitment"—without having any certainty that God exists. You can go to the outer edges of piety and claim that your heart is strangely warmed (John Wesley's famous observation) or that the ATM offers you money only when you say a prayer, and still feel that you are part of an adventure that may turn out to be delusion. You can have an experience on the road to Damascus and it may change your life, but it doesn't have to do so by removing those nagging doubts about the existence of God. Why should it? Why must we always associate religious experience with the removal of our doubts? We have Barth's strictures against intellectual idolatry drummed into us sufficiently to recognize that we cannot make an idol of our concepts, but we seem less protected from making an idol of our emotions.

Faith is not undermined by the constant, nagging fear that the whole enterprise of belief might be one of massive self-delusion. Knowing that one can be wrong is part of the excitement and certainly doesn't dampen the level of commitment. "Not everyone who says to me, 'Lord, Lord,' will enter the kingdom of heaven, but only the one who does the will of my Father who is in heaven" (Matt 7:21). A certainty of commitment means that "doing the will of my Father" is possible whatever one's doubts, even doubts about the Father's very existence. But one continues to be a follower, even as the partisan for all his doubts continues to support the stranger who claims to be part of the resistance.

In a fascinating sociological study of conventional religion entitled *The Need for Certainty*, Robert Towler had a concluding section entitled "The Lust for Certitude: A Partisan View."[4] He has two interesting quotations in this part of the book. One is something Lady Katharine Russell wrote of her father, Bertrand Russell:

> I believe myself that his whole life was a search for God, or, for those who prefer less personal terms, for absolute certainty. Indeed he had first taken up philosophy in the hope of finding proof of the existence of God, whose childish reality had vanished before the pressing questions of his adolescent mind.[5]

The second quotation offered by Towler comes from Father Morris of the Society of Jesus (Jesuits), quoted in M. D. Petre's *Autobiography and Life of George Tyrrell*:

> In all my life as a catholic, now fully 47 years, I cannot remember a single temptation against the faith that seem to me to have any force. The Church's teaching is before me, as a glorious series of splendid certainties. My mind is absolutely satisfied. Faith is an unmixed pleasure to me, without any pain, any difficulty, any drawback.... I have no private judgement to overcome, and no desire to exercise my private judgment. It is a greater pleasure to receive and possess truth with certainty, than to go in search of it and to be in uncertainty whether it has been found.[6]

We therefore return once again to Bertrand Russell and his debate with Copleston. Copleston insisted that the existence of God could be proved philosophically; Russell's position was "agnostic," he said, feeling that the existence of God was open to doubt. The two quotations above make a case

---

4. Towler, *Need for Certainty*, 99–109.
5. Towler, *Need for Certainty*, 100.
6. Towler, *Need for Certainty*, 100.

for that doubt as consistent with the existence of a God who wants us to grow and mature, even at the cost of some pain, difficulty, and drawback, to cite the very human feelings that the rather self-satisfied Father Morris celebrates having never encountered. The certainty that Russell sought and never found, according to his daughter's testimony, was a certainty that he would have done better never to have sought.

Conclusion

Part 1 began with the argument that nothing is certain, including the existence of God. Its central concern is to advocate the sort of God who, unlike Ozymandias, refuses to compel adherence. That means an acceptance of uncertainty, something that many atheists and many theists consider to be incompatible with true belief. It does not mean that we can claim that belief in God is not dependent upon the strength of the evidence before us—we are not in favor of Kierkegaardian leaps or even Pascalian wagers. But it does mean that the evidence we find will always fall short of the comfort of knowing. We believe, like Basil Mitchell's partisan, but there is much that will shake that belief, however passionately we are committed to the cause it represents.

Searching for the holy grail of certainty has endangered a recognition of the importance of historical studies into Christian origins. Inevitably, a lack of confidence in the benefits of historical research has undermined the social importance of Christian belief because that can be recognized only through probing the circumstances in which the religion emerged—working with historical evidence that is always open to question and doubt. In this respect a lot can be learned from the theology of liberation and its emphasis upon praxis, not in the sense that intellectual reflection is somehow not necessary or irrelevant, but in the sense that a strong and definite commitment is not undermined by intellectual misgivings.

The kenotic God, the God who is revealed when the Son "empties himself" in taking humanity, deliberately enters the ambiguities of human existence. That means we are forced to believe in God without knowing that God exists—without seeing that God has always been there. We are forced to choose something as an adventure without knowing that in the end we will be proved right. That doesn't matter. It's part of the rules—uncertainty, exploring, doubting—and it was deliberately made that way. Enchanting but elusive, God limits God so that we cannot know—we can only believe, though after death we may know as we are known, when the defensive shield that our hypocrisy puts up around us is peeled away in the purgatorial fire.

THE LIMITATIONS OF OUR CONVICTIONS

This section of the book can well end with a quotation from Newman's *Essay*, where Newman contrasts "notional" with "real" assent:

> Life is not long enough for a religion of inferences; we shall never have done beginning if we determine to begin with proof. We shall ever be laying our foundations; we shall turn theology into evidences, and divines into textuaries. We shall never get at our first principles. . . . I would rather be bound to defend the reasonableness of assuming that Christianity is true, than to demonstrate a moral governance from the physical world. Life is for action. If we insist on proofs for everything, we shall never come to action: to act you must assume, and that assumption is faith.[7]

---

7. Newman, *Essay*, 90–91; ch. 4, "Notional and Real Assent," sect. 3, "Notional and Real Assents Contrasted."

PART 2

Uncertainty in the Created Order

Chapter 5

The "Big Picture" People

Part 1 sought to establish the aspect of God's self-emptying that veils God's existence in order to strengthen our faith through imposing upon us conditions of uncertainty. Part 2, entitled "Uncertainty in the Created Order," asserts a connection between the way in which God has deliberately limited Godself in making us uncertain even about God's existence, and the nature of the universe God is creating. God limits God's powers in creating the universe, just as God limits God's powers in seeking to be loved by us.

Part 2 examines the natural order, which provides a necessary context for our existence. How does the act of creation connect to God's desire to be loved through the mist, the built-in state of uncertainty about God's existence that is the divinely willed condition of men and women here on earth? Part 2 will attempt to show how the kenotic imperative runs through the work of creation.

Ideas of examining the natural order or exploring the nature of the universe may sound beyond the scope of any reasonably well-defined book. It may seem to be an impossibly daunting and even pretentious task to attempt it. However, some have done so. The following extract comes from a *BBC Horizon* program broadcast in 2002:

> NARRATOR: At a conference in Cambridge pioneers of M Theory had been brought together to explore its implications. Burt was the star of the show. His vision of a violent eleventh dimension wowed the assembled physicists and caught the attention of the cosmologists.

PAUL STEINHARDT: We heard about a vast variety of ideas. The ideas that struck both Neil and myself most strongly were the ideas that Burt presented.

NARRATOR: On the last day of the conference Neil Turok, Paul Steinhardt and Burt decided to take time out. They went to see a play.

BURT OVRUT: We wanted to see the play *Copenhagen*, which was being performed in London at the time and the three of us took the train down to London one evening and we had whatever it was, an hour or so on the train to sit and talk about these ideas.

NARRATOR: On the journey they began to throw ideas around. Three physicists, one train, and the biggest secret about our Universe: what caused the Big Bang.

PAUL STEINHARDT: I think people get the wrong impression about scientists in that they think in an orderly, rigid way from step 1 to step 2 to step 3. What really happens that often you make some imaginative leap which at the time may seem nonsensical. When you capture the field at those stages it looks like poetry in which you are imagining without yet proving.

NEIL TUROK: Paul, Burt and me were sitting together on the train and just free associating.

PAUL STEINHARDT: One of us, maybe it was me, began by saying oh well why can't we make a universe out of collision and Neil sort of pitching in and saying well, if you did that then you could create all the matter and radiation of the Universe, so we had this conversation, one of us completing the sentences of the other in which we kind of just, just let our imaginations go.[1]

The three scientists in this dialogue were a professor of physics at Princeton University, a professor of mathematical physics at the University of Cambridge, and a professor of high energy physics at the University of Pennsylvania. They were, of course, determined to express their ideas in a way that might attract a typical audience for *BBC* science programs. Yet they were also highly renowned specialists in their fields and would be as determined as any serious professional to simplify without being simplistic.

All three were willing to draw upon ideas from right across the academic and even artistic spectrum. It is interesting that it is one of these three eminent scientists, Paul Steinhardt, who refers to a "wrong impression about scientists," who are presumed to move in an orderly, rigid way from

---

1. Barlow, "Parallel Universes," paras. 89–96.

step 1 to step 2 to step 3, supposedly in a "scientific manner," but who in reality are not unlike those who make imaginative leaps, look to literature as a source of inspiration, and even throw ideas around as if they were bouncy balls (like philosophers, like theologians?). If Steinhardt is right, we have to be very careful about too rigid a contrast between scientific and other approaches. These three scientists might, after all, have been three philosophers (or even three bishops) on a train, exploring ideas and looking for inspiration in unlikely quarters.

If scientists have a habit of reaching across the disciplines in trying to express their views, some of them also have a habit of reaching for religious terminology. Alexander von Humboldt was an extraordinary polymath of nineteenth-century Germany. He was a naturalist and explorer, who managed to secure access to what were then the South and Central American colonies of the Spanish empire. For five years he covered thousands of miles by foot, on horseback, and in canoes, suffering considerable hardship and danger (even though as a child he had been designated "sickly"), absorbing the rich natural diversity of the "New World" with the enthusiasm of a Columbus (indeed, enthusiasts for his work were to refer to Humboldt as the "second Columbus" or as the "scientific" discoverer of America). His journeys through the Orinoco River Basin were a great influence on Charles Darwin, who was prepared to describe Humboldt as the greatest scientific traveler who ever lived.

Yet Humboldt was more than this: he was also what would have been called in the eighteenth century a "natural philosopher," committed to a belief in the unity of nature, harboring the ambitious intention of explaining the interrelation of all the natural sciences. Toward the end of his life Humboldt set about writing what was to become his multivolume *Kosmos: Entwurf einer physischen Weltbeschreibung* (*Cosmos: A Sketch of a Physical Description of the Universe*), intended to be a complete survey of the material world.[2] It began as a lecture series and continued until his death, the last and incomplete volume being published in 1862, seventeen years after the first.

Humboldt was trying to view nature holistically and to point out the interrelation between the physical sciences. Opinions differ as to the success of his work (which was rapidly translated into English and read avidly in Britain and the USA), but the quest for unity that it represented persisted and influenced the German educational system. Eighteen months after his death in 1860, the *Alexander von Humboldt-Stiftung für Naturforschung und Reisen* (Alexander von Humboldt Foundation for Nature Research and

---

2. An English translation was published by the Johns Hopkins Press as part of its *Foundations of Natural History* series.

Travel) was established in Berlin, initially to support German scientists traveling abroad but now a foundation supporting several thousand scientists from other countries carrying out research in Germany in a wide range of disciplines.

In a letter written in 1834 Alexander von Humboldt himself declared:

> I have the crazy notion to depict in a single work the entire material universe, all that we know of the phenomena of heaven and earth, from the nebulae of stars to the geography of mosses and granite rocks—and in a vivid style that will stimulate and elicit feelings. Every great and important idea in my writing should here be registered side by side with facts. It should portray an epoch in the spiritual genesis of mankind—in knowledge of nature. But it is not to be taken as a physical description of the earth: it comprises heaven and earth, the whole of creation.[3]

The language of "spiritual genesis," "heaven and earth," and "whole of creation" can be interpreted in a variety of ways, but it does not seem unreasonable to say that Humboldt's appreciation of the fantastic complexity of the physical universe was expressed in terms of a religious sensibility.

The same is true of Charles Darwin's well-known closing words in *The Origin of Species* where he writes:

> There is grandeur in this view of life, with its several powers, having been originally breathed by the Creator into a few forms or into one; and that, whilst this planet has gone circling on according to the fixed law of gravity, from so simple a beginning endless forms most beautiful and most wonderful have been, and are being evolved.[4]

Given what is often written about him, it might seem strange that Darwin concludes *The Origin of Species* with language about powers "breathed by the Creator." It has itself become a source of controversy since "by the Creator" was not included in the first edition of *The Origin of Species*, published in 1859, but was included in subsequent editions, the first of which was published just a year later. It was an addition that Darwin later regretted,[5] so we should allow for the fact that he was under a degree of political pressure. Nevertheless, it is arguable that many scientific writers, whatever their

---

3. The letter describing his work *Cosmos* was to Karl Varnhagen. See Humboldt, *Letters*, 35–36.

4. Darwin, *Origin of Species*, 459–60.

5. According to a letter written to his friend Joseph Hooker on March 29, 1863. See Darwin, "Letter."

particular religious beliefs, feel impelled to express their awareness of nature as a whole in what can only be called religious terms. Take the most famous physicist of the modern day, Stephen Hawking. Though by no means a theist, he concluded *A Brief History of Time* by expressing his dissatisfaction with overspecialization in the following terms:

> In the eighteenth century, philosophers considered the whole of human knowledge, including science, to be their field and discussed questions such as: did the universe have a beginning? However, in the nineteenth and twentieth centuries, science became too technical and mathematical for the philosophers, or anyone else except a few specialists.[6]

Hawking's claims about philosophers are open to question, but the interesting suggestion in the quotation above is that *A Brief History of Time* might fill a gap vacated by philosophy. In the final paragraph of his book Hawking concludes:

> However, if we do discover a complete theory, it should in time be understandable in broad principle by everyone, not just a few scientists. Then we shall all, philosophers, scientists and just ordinary people, be able to take part in the discussion of the question of why it is that we and the universe exist. If we find the answer to that, it would be the ultimate triumph of human reason—for then we should know the mind of God.[7]

Whatever is meant by "a complete theory," it represents a desire for an overall explanation of the way things are, a desire that continues to be expressed—at least at times—in religious terminology ("we should know the mind of God").

Why is it that so many scientists appear to be at least tempted by religious terminology in describing their findings? Perhaps because many of them want to be "big picture" people like some of the theologians and philosophers who have themselves attempted a theory of everything in the past.

Hawking may be right in his description of science having become too technical and mathematical for all but a few specialists; yet these specialists are still expected to be able to provide a simple metaphor that can draw everything together and overcome the technical complexity that marks out their particular territory. Many of them are more than willing to do so. It is

---

6. Hawking, *Brief History of Time*, 193.
7. Hawking, *Brief History of Time*, 193.

surely no coincidence that *The Theory of Everything* was the title of a very successful film produced in 2014 about the life of Stephen Hawking himself.

Consider the following remark from Susan Watts, who was *BBC Newsnight* science editor, in September 2010:

> The physicists' ultimate dream is the search for a "theory of everything," a unifying explanation that can make sense of the infinitely tiny as well as the infinitely large.[8]

It is worth noting how this is described as the *physicists'* ultimate dream. The physicists have emerged as the *metaphysicists* or even as the new theologians, at least to the extent that, whether or not they use overtly religious language, they are the bearers now of an all-embracing explanation based on a single concept. Watts discusses various candidates for what she calls "that elusive theory of everything," before recalling the revealing title of what was then the physicist Hawking's latest book, *The Grand Design*,[9] and the author's conviction that "M-theory is the only (sic) candidate for a complete theory of the universe. . . . M-theory is the unified theory Einstein was hoping to find."[10]

Whatever the precise nature of "M-theory," what is noticeable is the confidence that such a theory can be developed at all. It is this confidence, despite the constraints of complexity and specialization, that suggests a degree of continuity between an older theological tradition and that of at least some contemporary scientists, the cosmologists and particle physicists who, according to Susan Watts, are now the ones seeking the right theory of everything.

When Marcus Chown chooses to subtitle his book *A Guide to the Universe*,[11] this is surely as ambitious an undertaking as any attempted in the past by theologians! If you're looking for popular "What's it all about?" studies in the 2020s, you'd probably do best to go to the popular science shelves of bookshops, the shelves to which the "secret of the universe" bestsellers have migrated from their original home in "theology and religion" (perhaps after a detour through "body, mind, and spirit").

8. Watts, "Are We Closer," para. 1.

9. Cowritten with Leonard Mlodinow, published in 2010.

10. See Watts, "Are We Closer," para. 7. See also Hawking and Mlodinow, *Grand Design*, ch. 1, "Mystery of Being," in which the authors explain that just as you need several different maps to represent the world, so you need several different theories to explain the universe. M-theory is therefore more a unified set of theories than a single theory. Hence Watts's surprise in her report at M-theory being the "only" theory has to be treated carefully.

11. Chown, *Quantum Theory*.

At times the way they write would seem to suggest that the physicists are at the top of the evolutionary scale. This is Nobel Prize–winning physicist Leon Lederman writing in *The God Particle*, the book that popularized the search for the Higgs boson, describing the arrival of humans on the planet:

> The human beings were different primarily because they were the only species intensely curious about their surroundings. In time, mutations occurred, and an odd subset of humans began roaming the land. They were arrogant. They were not content to enjoy the magnificence of the universe. They asked: "How?" How was the universe created? How can the "stuff" of the universe be responsible for the incredible variety in our world: stars, planets, sea otters, oceans, coral, sunlight, the human brain? The mutants had answered a question that could be answered—but only with the labour of millennia and with the dedication handed down from master to student for a hundred generations. The question also inspired a great number of wrong and embarrassing answers. Fortunately, these mutants were born without a sense of embarrassment. They were called physicists.[12]

Lederman doesn't seem to have much of a grasp of the way in which these questions were tackled by a far wider range of thinkers than the word "physicists" can possibly convey. In one way, however, quotes like this provide a clue as to why conflict is sometimes perceived between the claims of science and religion. The practitioners of both feel themselves to be competing for the big picture. These days scientists and theologians seem less like inhabitants of different universes than competitors in the same metaphysical marketplace, with the scientists making most of the running.

Closing Gaps and Receding Tides

It might be said that the theologians have no right to compete in the metaphysical marketplace at all, since all they do is hold back the advance of science. Some scientists and philosophers have seen theologians as Canutes desperately trying to prevent every scientific advance, from Galileo's conflicts with the papacy over astronomy to Darwin's debates with William Wilberforce over evolution. From such a perspective science is seen as an incoming tide sweeping away the sandcastles of the religious imagination one by one as it progresses toward a higher level of knowledge. This is the accusation of those who speak about the "God of the gaps" (though "God

12. Lederman and Teresi, *God Particle*, 2.

of the stopgaps" might be a better phrase). Every time there is a gap in a scientific explanation, the argument goes, in comes the theologian claiming that only belief in God can explain what is missing in the scientific analysis. Once it was believed that the planets moved because angels moved them; then Newton's law of inertia made the angels redundant. Later it was believed that new species appeared because of special acts of divine creation, but Darwin cleared the special acts away with the idea of natural selection. Eventually the scientist finds the explanation that eluded an earlier generation, and the theologian is forced to retreat to another mystery that supposedly only belief in God can explain. The upshot is that as science advances, God is driven into an ever-narrowing terrain of unexplained phenomena, until eventually there will be nothing left to explain. Belief in God will then have become redundant. It will be in a position like that of the astronomer Laplace who is purported to have said, when asked by Napoleon why the work on the universe he was being presented with contained no mention of its Creator: "I have no need of that hypothesis."[13] Professor C. A. Coulson pointed out the implications of this some seventy years ago in *Science and Christian Belief*:

> There is no "God of the gaps" to take over at those strategic places where science fails; and the reason is that gaps of this sort have the unpreventable habit of shrinking.[14]

The history of science is thereby seen as the gradual ousting of religion from one area after another in which the lack of a satisfactory scientific explanation has made it necessary—or at least acceptable—to claim that an "act of God" must have been at work.

Nor is this ousting of religion a mere matter of scientific progress. It also supposedly helps to drive away superstition. We can go back to the astronomer Laplace in order to examine this further. He wrote a short work entitled *Théorie analytique des probabilités* (*A Philosophical Essay on Probabilities*) in 1812. In this essay Laplace referred to a time when unusual phenomena in the sky—a comet with a long tail, the aurora borealis, or an eclipse—were regarded as so many signs of celestial wrath. These were

---

13. The words Laplace is supposed to have said during his famous encounter with Napoleon (*Je n'avais pas besoin de cette hypothèse-là* [I have no need of that hypothesis]) may have been apocryphal, but there is no doubt that Laplace did meet the emperor and his saying soon spread around. The Italian astronomer Lagrange declared of Laplace's own reply to Napoleon: "Ah, it is a fine hypothesis; it explains many things."

14. Coulson, *Science and Christian Belief*, 20.

events that seemed to oppose the order of nature, and hence the intervention of a wrathful heaven appeared to be a reasonable explanation of their occurrence:

> Thus, the long tail of the comet of 1456 spread terror throughout Europe, already thrown into consternation by the rapid successes of the Turks, who had just overthrown the Lower Empire.[15]

But such a resort to heavenly wrath was merely an interim measure before "the knowledge of the laws of the system of the world" managed to dissipate "the fears begotten by the ignorance of the true relationship of man to the universe."[16] Laplace pointed out that when the English astronomer Edmond Halley managed to identify this comet with that of the years 1532, 1607, and 1682, it became possible to foretell its next return for the end of the year 1758 or the beginning of the year 1759. Thus, in 1759 "the learnèd world" was able to await the return of what had come to be called Halley's comet, something that returned every seventy-six years whatever the political situation at the time, without fear of what it meant in terms of divine judgment, knowing that it was simply exemplifying a scientific law rather than representing a sudden display of divine anger. And Laplace concluded with these words:

> The day will come when, by study pursued through several ages, the things now concealed will appear with evidence; and posterity will be astonished that truths so clear had escaped us.[17]

This is a classic statement of the idea that science drives out superstition, steadily eroding the areas where religion can find temporary shelter behind strange events that elude a scientific explanation, until eventually reason drives them out.

However, this portrayal of an ever-receding tide of unexplained phenomena, which will eventually disappear when an all-embracing scientific explanation is achieved, is not the only view that can be taken. Three generations ago, reading Weizsäcker's *The World-View of Physics*, the famous theologian Dietrich Bonhoeffer wrote in one of his letters to Eberhard Bethge while awaiting execution (later published as *Letters and Papers from Prison*):

> If in fact the frontiers of knowledge are being pushed further and further back . . . then God is being pushed back with them and is therefore continually in retreat. We are to find God in

---

15. Laplace, *Philosophical Essay*, 5.
16. Laplace, *Philosophical Essay*, 5.
17. Laplace, *Philosophical Essay*, 6.

what we know, not in what we don't know; God wants us to realize his presence, not in unsolved problems but in those that are solved.[18]

This was written in 1944 and remains an inspiring approach to the relation between science and religion over three generations on.

The point is that this idea of an ever-receding tide of unexplained phenomena waiting for a scientific explanation is not itself scientific. Science solves mysteries, yes, but it also creates them. If one considers twenty-first-century arguments over relativity, quantum physics, and chaos theory, it is arguable that while these theories provided answers to questions that had hitherto remained unanswered, they also created difficulties that had never before existed. They answered questions, yes, but they also questioned answers. For though it is true that scientific explanations can drive out superstition, and that comets can become phenomena explicable by science rather than expressions of divine displeasure at Turkish military success, it is also the case that new scientific discoveries can upend the very all-conquering systems that previous generations of scientists were firmly committed to. And this is precisely what has happened over the last hundred and fifty years.

The most important scientific development during the last century and a half is relativity. It transformed our understanding of the universe from one established model, based on the ideas of Newton, to another that was completely different. But it hardly sent the theologians scurrying behind another bush. It is noticeable that for a number of theologians this was a discovery that seemed rather to deepen than to threaten their theological convictions. Visiting probably the twentieth century's greatest and most well-known theologian, Karl Barth, a few days before the latter's death, the Scottish theologian Tom Torrance (who had also been a professional scientist) suggested a parallel between Barth's understanding of revelation and the insights of relativity theory. Excited and modest at the same time, Torrance writes, Barth declared that "I must have been a blind hen not to see that parallel before."[19] The thinking behind this remark will be examined later. For now, it is enough to note the warm embrace of contemporary science on the part of the twentieth century's most renowned theologian.

There is a further point that is often missed. Few would now argue that heliocentrism was a dangerous belief or even that evolution undermined belief in God. However, it is true that even the religious establishment can

---

18. "Letter to Eberhard Bethge on 29 May 1944," in Bonhoeffer, *Letters and Papers*, 310–12.

19. Torrance, *Space, Time and Resurrection*, x.

at times welcome scientific innovation and even prove more supportive of it than the scientific establishment. This is a point that needs to be emphasized and does not concern only more recent discussions of quantum physics or relativity. It is also true of past scientific controversies, concerning which there is something of a consensus that the role of religion was an entirely negative one. The famous debate between Thomas Henry Huxley and Bishop Wilberforce in 1860 over evolution, for instance, has acquired a status comparable to the papal denunciations of Galileo centuries earlier—scientific progress struggling in the teeth of religious reaction. In reality, the position is much more complicated. As Midgley points out, Darwin's most serious opponents by far were the official scientific establishment of his day, and among his supporters could be counted Christians such as Charles Kingsley and H. G. Baden-Powell. Indeed, Midgley produces a telling remark from Thomas H. Huxley himself as an epigraph to this chapter of her book:

> If a general council of the Church Scientific had been held at that time, we should have been condemned by an overwhelming majority.[20]

Nor was the Oxford debate between Huxley and Wilberforce exactly as it has often been presented to posterity. Wilberforce was a scientist as well as a bishop, had corresponded with Darwin as an ornithologist (and Darwin had responded to his criticisms), and was firmly committed to Darwin's scientific approach. It may be, as Midgley suggests, that Huxley found Wilberforce's typically Victorian dabbling in various areas of knowledge irritating; but then again Huxley was a dabbler, too, his opinions ranging far beyond the question of natural science. This was not a confrontation between science and religion but between a range of scientific views, and the confrontation often became nastiest when it was confined to the scientists.

It is all too easy to assume that the religious establishment even today must find the concept of evolution threatening and desire to reject it altogether. Undeniably there are some, the so-called "creationists," who do reject it, but ignoring for the moment the views of other faiths, it is clear that the majority of Christians and their leaders have no difficulty with it. It would be a mistake to presume that just as Bishop Wilberforce, representing the church, took on Thomas Huxley, representing science, in a debate in Oxford in 1860, so Pope Francis, the archbishop of Canterbury, the Orthodox patriarchs, and anyone else holding high ecclesiastical office must be prepared to challenge the theory of evolution as put forward by the heirs of Huxley today.

---

20. Midgley, *Evolution as a Religion*, 10–12.

Conclusion: A Shared Entitlement

There is no need to hunt for gaps in our knowledge that can provide theologians with temporary cover until they are duly filled by the onward march of science. As science develops it provides both solutions to existing problems and new problems requiring to be solved. Perhaps the failure to recognize this reflects that false search for certainty described earlier in this book, the delusion that if one more intellectual hurdle is jumped the runners will finally reach the end of the race. Doubt is not a temporary obstacle to progress but a permanent accompaniment to life and a condition of progress.

Resistance to new scientific discoveries has not been the general approach of theologians in the face of scientific advance, even when that advance has proved and continues (at least on the fringe) to prove controversial, as is the case with evolution. Indeed, theologians are sometimes criticized for jumping upon each fresh scientific discovery, usually before they fully or even partly understand it, and then trying to make it serve their own purposes. Whether or not such criticism is justified (and in some cases it certainly is), it shows that the approach of theology to new scientific advances is not one of blanket opposition.

As for the scientific view of theologians, there may well be some scientists in 2020 who, like Richard Dawkins, think of religion as intellectually wrong and morally dangerous. Dawkins certainly makes some bitter and hostile comments about religious belief, but then many theists have made bitter and hostile comments about unbelievers too. Yet when confronted by the challenge of a Dawkins, theists can recognize that there is still a real debate going on. Even where theologians face hostility, there is not the instant dismissal that they received three generations ago from the logical positivists. For the positivists, metaphysical speculation was an example of insufficient training in the proper use of language, and sometimes one feels that they viewed theistic statements with the sort of irritation that the rigid grammarian feels in the face of "less biscuits." For them, any suggestion that religion might be dangerous—which Dawkins certainly feels it can be—was already giving it more significance than it deserved, like imagining an international conspiracy of dianetics enthusiasts.

There is more of a sense in the 2020s that the debate between theist and atheist can be a real one in which each side accepts that the other is making meaningful statements, even if it disagrees with them. In terms of the argument in part 1, we at least have "meaning" theists talking to "meaning" atheists. The scientists have welcomed the opportunity to act as metaphysicians themselves, laying out their theory of everything, while the theologians have not just sought to reconcile their ideas with science but have found that science actually contributes to the way in which they explain their own beliefs.

In this century it is often the scientists who dare to wonder and explore, even at the risk of moving away from the safe area of their specializations, and they have attracted the interest of millions in doing so. At the same time, scientific developments over the last century, like relativity, quantum mechanics, and chaos theory, have often proved to be an inspiration to those writing theology. This chapter has mentioned the effect of relativity theory upon the Scottish theologian Tom Torrance. One could equally mention the effect of quantum theory on John Polkinghorne or chaos theory on the writings of Paul Davies.[21] One may not agree with the way in which these writers appropriate scientific theories, but it is undeniable that they are inspired by new forms of scientific thinking and that science helps them to present their own theories of everything.

However, it is one thing to argue for a shared entitlement between scientists and theologians to search like Hawking for a theory of everything. It is quite another to know what such a theory might be. And since the theme of this book is one of rescuing God (or the plausibility of belief in God) through a recognition of the divinely willed disorder that characterizes the created universe, what exactly is meant by "divinely willed disorder"? The book of Genesis emphasizes the order brought by God when chaos was "upon the face of the deep" (Gen 1:2). So what sort of order did this God who apparently wills or at least accepts disorder bring?

---

21. See Polkinghorne, *Quantum Physics*; Davies, *Demon in the Machine*.

Chapter 6

God and the Nature of Chance

It is time to try to present in more detail God's "disordered" universe. Given the attempts of Bultmann and others to keep God from inserting a finger-wagging divine finger into the ordered universe where light comes at the flick of a switch and another switch fills a room with sound from a wireless (as Bultmann put it some seventy-five years ago, when such things marked the height of technological progress[1]), it might seem odd for some to insist that one of the strongest arguments against the existence of God is that the universe is a product of blind chance and clearly cannot be the work of any Creator. Carefully designed, cog by cog, by a benevolent watchmaker it most certainly is not, they would say. A look at how the universe has come to be what it is supposedly demonstrates that it is essentially out of control.

Such a view is interesting because it contrasts with another tendency we have pointed to, namely the search for some kind of overall formula or "theory of everything" or even an image—string, membrane, Higgs boson—that can once and for all identify the fundamental structure of all that is. On the one hand, the scientists are presented as about to get to the bottom of it all; on the other hand, they are warning that it's all out of control. These are not necessarily contradictory ideas, but they make it clear that we need to be as precise as possible about definitions.

Why has the theory of evolution, for instance, prompted ideas of our being ruled by blind chance? What sort of chaos is involved in "chaos theory"? What exactly is the nature of the gaps in our knowledge presupposed

---

1. See "Jesus Christ and Mythology," the famous essay written in 1941 with which Bultmann sparked off a huge reaction (Bartsch, *Kerygma and Myth*, 5). Bartsch includes the original "manifesto" as he describes Bultmann's essay and a number of responses to it in his collection.

by quantum theory? I believe that if we go through each of these questions carefully, we can accept a degree of randomness and yet still allow for a Creator—a God who lies behind and within, rather than being disproved by the "divine disorder" of things.

The World as Playground and as Battleground

Two arguments are put forward to defend the view that theologians have difficulty with the theory of evolution. In the first place, it is presumed that they dislike the idea that something previously unexplained, and therefore attributable to a form of divine intervention in the form of "special acts of creation," now has a perfectly natural explanation. A gap has been closed, a gap that could previously be filled by a special act of God.

We have dealt with this idea already, pointing out that science has a habit not only of closing old gaps but also of opening up new ones. The theologians are not running out of places to hide, even if they wanted to.

Moreover, if the theory of evolution had done no more than close a gap—or even all gaps—it might still be possible to claim that the overall design can be attributed to God, a view that was arguably present in Charles Darwin's own mind.

This is where a second difficulty theologians are supposed to have with evolution comes in. According to this second difficulty, even those who accept that a gap has been closed dislike the *way* it has been closed. They say that there has been a terrible cost in terms of physical suffering—something Darwin himself pointed out in his *Origin of Species*:

> Thus, from the war of nature, from famine and death, the most exalted object which we are capable of conceiving, namely, the production of the higher animals, directly follows.[2]

It is easy to see how Darwin's theory might appear to play havoc with more sentimental assessments of the natural universe. By way of comparison to Darwin, consider the following quotation taken from William Paley's *Natural Theology*, which was subtitled *Evidences of the Existence and Attributes of the Deity, Collected from the Appearances of Nature*:

> It is a happy world after all. The air, the earth, the water teem with delighted existence. In a spring noon, or a summer evening, on whichever side I turn my eyes, myriads of happy beings crowd

---

2. See Darwin, *Origin of Species*, 459. Almost the concluding words of *The Origin of Species*, but immediately followed by the sentence beginning, "There is grandeur in this view of life."

upon my view. "The insect youth are on the wing." Swarms of new-born flies are trying their pinions in the air. Their sportive motions, their wanton mazes, their gratuitous activity, their continual change of place without use or purpose, testify their joy, and the exultation which they feel in their lately discovered faculties. A bee amongst the flowers in spring, is one of the most cheerful objects that can be looked upon. Its life appears to be all enjoyment; so busy, and so pleased: yet it is only a specimen of insect life.[3]

Paley's *Natural Theology* was originally written in 1802, half a century before Darwin. It is a book associated mainly with the so-called "watchmaker thesis," which was discussed in part 1, when questioning Flew's idea that theological statements were meaningless as opposed to merely contentious. If one stumbled across a watch—as opposed to a stone—when out walking, it would immediately be recognized as something designed, so the intricacy and complexity of the universe must suggest to us that it, too, has a designer. Paley's thesis has been criticized in numerous ways, but in the quotation above his conviction about design is reflected in what his critics would call another form of naivety, that which sees in the natural world a happy playground for delighted existence on the part of myriads of happy beings. Paley talks of "continual change of place without use or purpose," but one might feel that this is more like constant flight as predators are avoided and the victims necessary for survival are sought out. It is easy to see Paley's world "teeming with delighted existence" as reflecting the sort of naivety that a less self-confident Victorian age was to undermine (although it had already been challenged by Hume in the eighteenth century when similar views were expressed before Paley wrote his *Natural Theology*). Nature was more battleground than playground for later writers who wanted to stress the way in which it was "red in tooth and claw," the famous quotation from Tennyson's poem *In Memoriam* written in 1849. Tennyson's poem continues:

> Are God and Nature then at strife,
> That Nature lends such evil dreams?
> So careful of the type she seems,
> So careless of the single life.[4]

It is hardly the kind of overwhelming concern about each individual expressed by the famous parable of the lost sheep (Matt 18:10–14; Luke 15:1–7). The most Tennyson can do is "faintly trust the larger hope."[5]

---

3. Paley, *Natural Theology*, 238–39.
4. Tennyson, *In Memoriam*, canto 55.
5. Tennyson, *In Memoriam*, canto 55.

The conviction of design has become faint trust in the larger hope. What challenges Tennyson's confidence in design is a sense of nature's wastefulness, finding that of fifty seeds she often brings but one to bear, and her willingness to sacrifice the individual to the interests of the collective ("So careful of the type she seems, / So careless of the single life"). It appears that nature is on the side of Caiaphas in thinking it expedient that one man should die for the sake of the people (or at least the species) as a whole (John 11:50).

It is certainly arguable that Tennyson's poem, written just a decade before the *Origin of Species* was published, provided a necessary corrective to Paley's naïve enjoyment of playful insects on a summer's day. But the idea of perpetual struggle, of lives dedicated relentlessly to a constant battle for survival, is a limited vision of nature too. It is the vision that provides good media copy almost in the manner of bad news: the tiny turtles hatching from their eggs and beginning the run to the water's edge while being picked off by birds as they go; the prowling lion selecting its victim from a group of terrified antelopes; and so on. Easy to proceed from that to a kind of imprimatur from nature for humans putting all their energy into the accumulation of riches while their neighbors are picked off through weakness or misfortune, and eventually the lucky few acquire an ocean of wealth. But though, of course, these things happen, and it is naïve to deny that they do, this is only part of the story.

In a very important passage, the philosopher Mary Midgley wrote:

> The particular mistake of treating all animal life as a matter of individual cut-throat competition was one which it was out of the question for Darwin to make, because he was a serious, full-time naturalist. He knew a great deal about the life of (for instance) birds, about parental care, warning cries and loyalty to the family and flock. The "social instincts" were a central interest of his. In his mind, they were always present in proper balance against the waste and cruelty of natural life.[6]

Midgley's own study of this subject is contained in a book called *Beast and Man*, originally published in 1978 but revised and republished with a useful new introduction in 1995. This book, a classic of moral philosophy, is a general study of the qualities that supposedly make us different from other species and provides a profound and caustic undermining of any view built on the obvious superiority of what is "human" (which we generally consider a positive word, where "inhuman" is not) to the "beastly" (generally seen as a negative word). Many of its arguments are not directly relevant to the discussion here, but an important implication of the book is. Midgley

---

6. Midgley, *Evolution as a Religion*, 139.

suggests that animals have a more sophisticated environment and behavior pattern than we commonly assume when we assure ourselves that wolves are "savage," and more generally when we assume that they are engaged in an endless competitive struggle for survival.

As a moral philosopher, she is keen to make the additional point that we too easily understand animal life to be one of savage warfare because that is precisely how our own lives have often turned out. A Martian dispassionately observing earthly species might well conclude that among the most savage animals are human beings. Though the Martian might well observe lions leaping to devour their prey, he or she (if such terms are appropriate on Mars) would note that humans (who have a choice that lions don't have) generally choose to be meat eaters, though they prefer stun guns in sheds to public displays of ferocity on the plains (again, having a choice that lions don't have). This is not to argue a case for vegetarianism: it is to argue a case against human beings considering themselves morally superior to "wild beasts" (a favorite term of judges to refer to the worst forms of human behavior). If wolves are "savage," what are we? As Midgley puts it:

> We have thought of the wolf always as he appears to the shepherd at the moment of seizing a lamb from the fold. But this is like judging the shepherd by the impression he makes on the lamb at the time when he finally decides to turn it into lamb chops.[7]

The conclusion is that nature may well be red in tooth and claw, but so are human beings. The truth is that we are not uniquely virtuous beings who find ourselves plunged into an alien world of savagery and violence. Like other animals, we have our moments of cooperation and our moments of savage destruction. That is an important consideration to make when we encounter presentations of human beings as hapless innocents lost in a world of brutality. Though Midgley might be seen (unfairly) as following Paley in underestimating the savagery of the animal kingdom, she might well be said to have a much less naïve view than many others concerning the savagery of human beings.

A World in Which We Are Strangers or a World That Suits Us?

In 1969 Jacques Monod published a book that emphasized what he believed to be a lack of design in the emergence of life within the universe. He offered a rather romanticized portrayal of humanity "that, like a gypsy . . . lives on

---

7. Midgley, *Beast and Man*, 24.

the boundary of an alien world."[8] In fact, human beings live in a world that is more appropriate to their nature than alien to it. Tenderness and self-sacrifice are mixed with violence and destruction, both in their own case and in the case of the other life-forms around them.

Monod's human being, conceived as living in isolation in a hostile universe, appeals to those who think that the evolutionary process, like a chance throw of the dice that scores a double six, has somehow thrown up a superior being who looks down on the savage conditions in which he/she arrived on the world scene with sensitive abhorrence. To Midgley that is not us at all, except when we are deceiving ourselves. Yet, as she points out, it is often very important to us to deceive ourselves, or to try to, especially concerning the nobility of our own motives. Nature red in tooth and claw becomes a convenient contrast to humanity meek and mild. Nature's savagery becomes a foil to humanity's supposed goodness. The truth of the matter is that we are capable of savagery as well as goodness, just as animals are capable of behavior that is far from a constant struggle for survival. We are like the animal, which is unsurprising in view of the fact that it would be more accurate to say that we *are* animals, one of the more troublesome primates.

Monod set a picture of a universe ruled (or at least affected) by "chance" (*le hasard*) against the sort of universe he associated with the classical physicists of the Enlightenment, whose confidence in the argument from design was expressed through such images as that of the perfectly formed clock. His idea that random mutations effectively reduce the cosmos to a chaos and take order out of the universe survives in the twenty-first-century debate. Richard Dawkins, for instance, wrote of God as a "blind watchmaker," the title of a book he first published in 1986 and which is subtitled: *Why the Evidence of Evolution Reveals a Universe without Design*.

But does it? The first thing to say is that even supposing one accepts the idea (as some scientists wouldn't) of entirely random mutations appearing in the course of evolution, there is a further process outlined by Darwin that is far from being ruled by chance, namely that by which the mutations that offer the most favorable opportunities for survival come to predominate. Evolution, in other words, is a theory that combines elements of chance and elements of clear predictability. There may be random mutations, but then there is a process of natural selection between them.

It is very important to consider what "chance" (as the English translation of Monod's *Le hasard et la necessité*, originally written in French, puts it) means in this context. We use the word in two senses. On the one hand, we talk about a "chance encounter," in which case we are pointing to

---

8. Monod, *Chance and Necessity*, 172–73.

something entirely unforeseen and coincidental. In this sense, what happens by chance happens at random. On the other hand, we say: "There's a good chance you'll get the job," in which case "chance" means something more like level of probability (compare the way we say: "The chances are that she will turn up").

This is important, because a belief in random mutations may introduce an element of "chance" in the first sense into evolution, while the way in which natural selection acts upon these random mutations and determines which will survive is more like "chance" in the second sense. The one that is most suitable for survival is the one that is likely to become dominant. It has the best "chance" of superseding the others.

The point may be put differently: How much apparent disorder is compatible with a belief in the universe as a product of design? What Monod (and later Dawkins) does is claim that randomness can in no way be an element in an overall arrangement that can be termed designed. But is this right? Why can't God allow for the emergence of unpredictable events (random mutations), knowing that they will then be subject to a selection process that will retain only those that are most suitable? This point was made by Arthur Peacocke when he wrote that God cannot see behind indeterministic events any more than we can. But this does not worry him when it comes to believing in God as Creator because he is convinced that:

> instead of being daunted by the role of chance in genetic mutations as being the manifestation of irrationality in the universe, it would be more consistent with the observations to assert that the full gamut of potentialities of living matter could be explored only through the agency of the rapid and frequent randomization which is possible at the molecular level of DNA.[9]

This is the theologian Arthur Peacocke in the 1990s, but the same point was made by Aquinas centuries before in the *Summa contra Gentiles*:

> It would be contrary to the character of divine providence if nothing were to be fortuitous and a matter of chance in things.[10]

There is an interesting parallel, which is looked at in more detail in part 3, to the way in which God allows human beings free will and some of the problems that raises for ideas such as divine "foreknowledge" and divine "omniscience." There is a similarity between Monod's reluctance to accept a degree of randomness as compatible with God's overall design and the reluctance of some theologians to accept that God so limits Godself in

---

9. Peacocke, *Creation*, 94.
10. Aquinas, *Summa contra Gentiles*, 3.74, 2; quoted in McCall, *Modern Relation*, 115.

order to give us free will that God chooses not to know what our choices will be. God gives human beings freedom and in doing so brings into being a set of events where even God does not know what they will lead to. God's omniscience expresses itself through God's choice not to know. God's omnipotence expresses itself through God's choice not to compel the outcome God wants.

Is God, then, still the Creator and designer of the universe in any meaningful sense? I would argue that God is—but we have to recognize the painful outcome of God's desire to wait upon the actions of those God created on the sixth day. God chooses to let human beings determine the nature of the world they live in, and the divine initiative toward them has in part the character of a response. God faces disobedience and coldheartedness. God reacts with anger and, as the Hebrew Bible tells us, almost brings God's creative endeavors to an end. God even repents. God is like any parent who gets angry with a child. There is never a smooth determining of outcomes, knowing in advance every move humanity will make. The makeup of the natural order reflects this in the random variations that then are subject to the laws of natural selection, ensuring that some of them survive. In this sense one could say that nature, like we ourselves, learns from her mistakes.

The Escalator

Midgley is deeply suspicious of those who are inclined to think in terms of a glorious ascent from the first stirrings of life to its pinnacle in human beings. Evolution, when conceived in terms of escalators or trees (who does not want to be top of the tree?), uses the imagery of height to suggest inevitable improvement as nature makes its way upwards. But is this an accurate portrayal? In its own way, is it any better than Monod's gypsy on the boundary of an alien world? Midgley prefers the imagery of a bush, a development radiating outward, upwards, and downwards in a complex manner, with an emphasis upon complicated interconnections rather than upon getting to the top of the bush, a position that hardly seems to be of particular advantage.

The danger of the escalator and the tree is that they are likely to focus too much on reaching the top: what led to the top can all too easily remove the ladder, deciding to throw it away once the summit is reached. Midgley's lifelong concern to avoid a dismissive and all too often cruelly unthinking attitude to the animal kingdom recognizes the danger of such imagery. Responding to an essay by the economist Kenneth Boulding in which the author suggested that there was no need to study animal behavior because we have its "raison d'être," man himself, "the finished product," already before us, she commented:

> This sort of thing leaves me speechless. A device can put another out of date only so far as they are means to the same end. Does Boulding think it just obvious what the aim of all human life actually is? And, having solved that question, does he think it clear how all other existing species—elephants and albatrosses, whales and tortoises and caribou—are just bungling and inadequate shots at the same target? Is there nothing to a giraffe except being a person manqué?[11]

Darwin, we have already said, was a full-time naturalist, as many of those who sought to adapt his views to theories of "social evolution" (like Herbert Spencer) were not. It is all too easy to interpret him as someone who, rather than studying the richness of life, was determined to see some clearly identifiable route out of its lower reaches into the sunlit uplands of human rationality, providing a blueprint for some of his interpreters to follow as they pointed to the sort of ruthlessly competitive behavior that alone could guarantee their necessary ascent. Midgley recognizes a clear sense in which seeing human beings as the top of the tree, or even seeing some potential successor as the top, goes hand in hand with a failure to appreciate the animal kingdom and our place as one of the animals within it. It leads to an instrumentalist view of every other living being, which becomes ours to manipulate to our own "higher" ends. Other creatures are merely the means by which we manage to haul ourselves up and free ourselves of unwanted entanglements.

It is the opponents of evolution, such as the creationists, who are often seen as the ones who cannot accept humanity's supposedly less-than-glorious ancestry. They are identified with those who recoiled—as in the famous moment during the Oxford debate over evolution where Huxley was asked to consider the "monstrous" thought that his grandmother might have been an ape—from the idea of having an animal as an ancestor. Their belief in separate acts of creation is seen as a way of putting clear blue water between ourselves and those created on earlier days.

In reality, some of evolution's supporters are even more prone to look down on all that preceded this new arrival at the top. Because they think of climbing out of the tree, they can't enjoy living in the bush. And they are always dreaming of the "next stage" of evolution rather than concentrating on how to live comfortably with the world around them, despite the urgent need, intensified by climate change, for us to learn how to live in a sustainable manner with all the other creatures on the planet. The escalator

---

11. Midgley, *Beast and Man*, 345.

is always moving upwards for them. We saw it a generation ago, when many scientists were excited by genetic engineering, and the same thing can be discerned now in some of the claims made for artificial intelligence or for some kind of cyborg supremo, an all-conquering man-machine mix. It is always a question of going to the next level rather than recognizing the multilayered universe with which we have not yet learned to live in harmony.

In a strange manner the idea of evolution has inspired both the tragic pessimism of a Monod and the (perhaps more dangerous) radical optimism of those who put their confidence in the next stage of evolutionary development. One minute human beings are lost in a hostile universe, the unintended consequences of randomly occurring mutations. The next minute they are a key stage in a carefully structured advance up the escalator from pre-nature to supernature, an advance that tempts some scientists into a kind of *folie de grandeur* as they envisage ways of promoting it. What seems to be excluded is the idea that God created us as one of the animals, behaving in many ways just like the others, though, of course, with abilities all our own. We are in a universe that rather suits us, just as it suits antelopes and whales—unless, of course, as currently appears more than possible, we manage to destroy it.

The Irreducibility of the Gaps

This section touches on other scientific developments that have affected our big picture of a universe designed by God. Through looking at chaos theory and quantum mechanics, it will suggest that some twentieth-century scientific developments appear to make gaps in our knowledge a permanent feature of the landscape rather than a dwindling characteristic of the unfinished business of science. This has a considerable impact on presumptions behind the so-called "God of the gaps" argument.

Consider another famous passage from the *Philosophical Essay on Probabilities* by Laplace. It refers to what has come to be known as "Laplace's predictive demon" (though "demon" was never a word he used). Laplace wrote:

> An intelligence knowing all the forces acting in nature at a given instant, as well as the momentary positions of all things in the universe, would be able to comprehend in one single formula the motions of the largest bodies as well as the lightest atoms in the world, provided that its intellect were sufficiently powerful

to subject all data to analysis; to it nothing would be uncertain, the future as well as the past would be present to its eyes.[12]

This was later adopted as a classic statement of causal determinism, or the view that it is only the limitations of our knowledge (limitations we are overcoming at an exponentially increasing rate) that prevent us from determining the future with as much assurance as we recall the past. Once again, we encounter the confidence that all remaining problems will be solved and the final picture of what the universe is like will be laid down before our eyes.

Let us leave aside for the moment the issue of free will versus determinism as it is often perceived. In other words, let us ignore the nature of the human input and whether that, too, is determined or whether room must be made for the irreducible impact of free will. Instead, let us consider an important scientific development of the late twentieth century (it really dates from the early years of computing), which became known as "chaos theory." The theory was popularized in terms of the so-called butterfly effect, a term invented by the meteorologist and mathematician Edward Norton Lorenz (1917–2008), who claimed, in a paper given in 1972, that the movement of an insect's wings in one part of the world might eventually cause a hurricane in another.[13]

The term "chaos theory" reflects the idea that certain systems may be at once deterministic and unpredictable, and that the sort of confidence expressed by Laplace some two centuries ago in our capacity to overcome the limitations of our knowledge was misplaced. The ideas of Laplace were associated with the movements of planets, but the principle could equally be applied to the weather movements that concerned Lorenz as a meteorologist. The intelligence referred to by Laplace as knowing "all the forces acting in nature at a given instance"[14] might now be a weather forecaster equipped with a mass of information from data-gathering equipment and a bank of computers programmed to analyze it in ways that Laplace could barely have imagined. Yet no weather forecaster has achieved the position of Laplace's intelligence, for which "nothing would be uncertain, the future as well as the past would be present to its eyes."[15] Though the forecasters have been able to amass more and more information, using more and more powerful computers, in order to attempt to move from present conditions to future outcomes on a short-term or long-term basis, they constantly discover themselves to be in error.

12. Laplace, *Philosophical Essay*, 4.
13. Lorenz, "Predictability."
14. Laplace, *Philosophical Essay*, 4.
15. Laplace, *Philosophical Essay*, 4.

The forecasters began with the Laplacian presumption that were they to set out from a clear understanding of the initial conditions from which these systems developed, then it follows that they would discover how these systems will behave in future. They would therefore be able to make precise determinations of weather outcomes. But the forecasters soon found the task beyond them. Precisely because the slightest variation in initial conditions may produce a profoundly different outcome (the butterfly's wings that produce a storm), it appears to be impossible to arrive at such knowledge. What the huge potential of computers has revealed is not a way of unravelling a complexity that was previously impenetrable, but more a way of appreciating a complexity that was previously under-acknowledged. Even when it is agreed that every event has a cause, the sequence of events is so complex that endless possibilities remain in nature's womb.

As a by-product of the computer age, chaos theory reveals how intricate this world is. Appreciating that intricacy means understanding the subtle ways in which different systems are interrelated and affect one another. Indeed, it seems fair to say that chaos theory represents "chaos" only in the sense that the patterns of deterministic interconnection are too complex to unravel, not in the sense that there are no patterns to discern. It supports a contemporary ecologist's vision of a world at once complex and very finely balanced, an easily disturbed equilibrium that human activity has begun seriously to threaten (as the increasingly obvious effects of climate change make clear).

Earlier in this chapter, when discussing evolution, I questioned whether the form of evolution based on random mutations specified by Darwin is really incompatible with the notion of God's design. I argued that God could perfectly well allow for the emergence of unpredictable events (random mutations), knowing that they would then be subject to a selection process that will retain only those who are most suitable. A similar argument might be made concerning chaos theory, namely that it is more a statement about the irreducible complexity of the world than about its being in what we would normally think of as a chaotic state. Chaos theory tells us less that the world has been left in the chaos that was on the face of the deep before God's creative impulses got to work (Gen 1:2), than that those creative impulses express themselves by building into the created universe an innate flexibility.

Chaos theory, then, has not so much enabled science to plug another gap in our knowledge as uncovered just how many gaps there continue to be. The whole "God of the gaps" argument is undermined by the fact that new scientific discoveries do not simply fill in gaps in our knowledge but create new problems for future generations to solve. Arguably science is only beginning to uncover some of the complexities of our existence, and it would be a strange sort of overconfidence that would presume to say there wasn't much left to discover. But the more important point is that, as with the discussion of the theory of evolution, we are in danger of adopting too narrow a view of what order means in the context of God's creation. There is a built-in unpredictability to the whole process, whether it is the linkage between butterfly wings and hurricanes or the outcome of a random mutation. This is the form of looser divine management that tempts some to say the universe is out of control but leads others to recognize that the guiding hand of the Creator is at work in a more subtle way than they imagined.

A further undermining of the view that science is in the business of closing gaps, and in the process driving the theologians out of them, comes from quantum mechanics. In 2007 John Polkinghorne, in a book with the interesting title *Quantum Physics and Theology: An Unexpected Kinship*, wrote in the following terms of the "dawn of quantum theory." Quantum theory implied, he wrote,

> the consequent abandonment of belief in the total adequacy of the classical Newtonian paradigm. A physical world previously considered to be clear and deterministic was found to be cloudy and fitful at its subatomic roots.[16]

The fundamental claim of quantum mechanics (namely that laws at the micro-level were irreducibly statistical) meant that it was simply impossible, however much information about prior conditions had been gathered, to say whether a particular photon, for instance, would act in a certain way. This appeared to be an even more significant undermining of Laplace's conviction that if we knew enough about initial conditions we would be able to set out clearly the future course of events. It was suggesting not only that there was a level of complexity about the way events interacted in the physical universe that had been severely underestimated, but that there was an element of randomness built into the system so that it was simply impossible to determine the future, even if one could somehow obtain all the data required in order to do so.

Conclusion

Whether it is the random mutations highlighted at the beginning of the chapter, the astounding complexity of the delicately interwoven networks highlighted by chaos theory, or the indeterminacy highlighted by quantum mechanics, this remains the "divine disorder" that is compatible with the

16. Polkinghorne, *Quantum Physics*, 48.

idea of a universe designed by God. Although the universe is developing in an unpredictable manner, this does not mean an absence of design. Just as the moral order requires a divine willingness to allow for the chaotic consequences of letting humans loose upon the world, so the natural order evolves through random mutations and unavoidable complexities.

The theory of evolution does not destroy our sense of being at home in the universe. Certainly, it presents a struggle for survival and a picture of nature red in tooth and claw, but this is not all that nature is, besides which it is undoubtedly part of what we ourselves are! We both underestimate the other animals on this planet and overestimate ourselves if we think we are a lonely mutation of purity in a hostile universe. We are not. We are animals living in a world well suited to animal life.

We may have emerged from other animals, but this doesn't mean that we don't have abilities they lack, while they have abilities we lack. Midgley's philosophy asserts differences between humans and other animals while denying superiority. Hence her dislike of seeing evolution in terms of an escalator or a tree where everyone wants to climb to the top. She prefers the image of a bush, where we are all different and yet interconnected.

Before it is assumed that the universe is somehow out of control, we have to be clear about the nature of that control. Concern over whether the natural world is "out of control" bears an interesting parallel to concern that our life on earth is out of control, given that God's self-chosen limitation of God's powers means that even God does not know whether God's creation will destroy itself.

Part 1 suggested certainty delivered through the perfect piece of philosophical reasoning or through the overwhelming experience of a heart strangely warmed (Wesley's rather coy version of the ecstasy of St. Theresa) is not on offer. Part 2 suggests a life driven by faith rather than certainty is appropriate to the innate complexity and resistance to precise determination of the universe uncovered by chaos theory and quantum mechanics. God takes an enormous risk in creating us—enough to drive (so legend has it) one-third of the heavenly host into becoming fallen angels. God is accepting for Godself the possibility of failure, accepting uncertainty about the outcome of God's own actions.

This is the willed self-limitation of a God of love,[17] but that has not stopped people searching for ways of releasing God from the self-limitation God alone willed for Godself. Part 2 ends by examining this tendency further.

---

17. See Oord, *Uncontrolling Love of God*.

Chapter 7

Quantum Mechanics and Divine Tampering

The last chapter tried to develop the argument that although the universe is developing in an unpredictable manner, this does not mean an absence of design. It also suggested that the random mutations, the butterfly effect, and the nature of events at the quantum level bear some parallel to the way the powers acquired or stolen by men and women at the time of the fall have turned history into a process with an uncertain outcome, even for God.

Implicit in this analysis is the idea of a universe created and sustained by God—but without any interference. If the kenotic approach is correct, then surely God does not act in what modern parlance might decry as an invasive manner. If God created a world that has a degree of independence (so much of the kenotic approach seems to rest on this idea of God standing back in some way in order to give us our freedom), then can it ever make sense for God to come "meddling" in order to put right things that are going wrong? This is a very powerful argument, though as we shall see later it is arguably a flawed one. However, what I want to do in the rest of this chapter is to challenge a certain approach by some theists, who use the insights of quantum mechanics in order to suggest that irreducible gaps provide the perfect cover for God's actions in the world—for instance, through miracles.

Making Room for God to Act in the World?

In *Divine Action and Modern Science*, Nicholas Saunders considers whether there is any truth in the argument "that science is such an accurate predictive tool that there is no flexibility within nature for the actions of God."[1] In the rest of the book he focuses upon quantum theory and chaos theory. "The importance of these two sciences," he explains, "is that they are widely claimed to be intrinsically indeterminate, or to contain enough inherent flexibility to accommodate the actions of God."[2]

The idea that God acts at certain specific times and in certain specific places has been an essential element in the Christian understanding of God (and that of many other religions). Saunders's book begins by quoting a passage from *The Acts of the Apostles*, where the disciples are choosing who will replace Judas. They cast lots to determine whether it will be Joseph or Matthias. The lot falls on Matthias, but as Saunders says, "it is clear from the Greek text that it was God himself who chose the appropriate lot" (Acts 1:24–6).[3]

Of course, what Saunders calls SDAs (special divine actions) may take many different forms. There may be the sort of intervention that appears to break the laws of nature (naturally this description begs a lot of questions), such as the parting of the Red Sea or Jesus walking on water. Or there may be the sort of intervention that doesn't break any law but shows God making use of the laws that exist. The way the dice fall for Matthias might be seen as an example of this. This is the way in which quantum mechanics and chaos theory are understood as allowing for divine intervention. It is not as though God usurps any laws; it is more that there's a gap in the queue and God can muscle in unnoticed, becoming one agent among others having an effect. It is in this sense that they reveal what Saunders calls "a flexibility inherent in the natural processes of creation."[4]

In the last chapter I discussed indeterminacy in the context of its being an element in God's overall plan. In the rest of this chapter, I shall discuss indeterminacy in another context, as somehow providing an entry ticket for God to carry out specific divine actions in the world. Sometimes the distinction is expressed in terms of general divine action (GDA) and special divine action (SDA). GDA represents the idea of a universe governed by universal laws, and the point of the last chapter would be to claim that these universal laws reflect an overall design on the part of God, even though God doesn't micromanage all the details. SDA represents what we might describe as tampering from outside, essentially sticking a divine finger into the works. The question raised by the study of quantum theory, at least for some theologians, is whether it allows God to stick a finger in without in the process being forced

---

1. Saunders, *Divine Action*, 3.
2. Saunders, *Divine Action*, 4.
3. Saunders, *Divine Action*, 3.
4. Saunders, *Divine Action*, 12.

to push some other cause to one side. Of course, even if God could stick a finger in without in the process elbowing another cause out of the way, there would still be a question about whether God actually did so and what sort of God we are imagining as wanting to act in this manner.

One point to be borne in mind is that scientists have different opinions just as theologians do: it also has to be remembered that they may have an inkling that a theory does not quite work without a clear idea of how it can be wrong. They struggle in the half-light, if not the dark—just like the theologians. It is sometimes suggested that Einstein, at the forefront of modern physics with his work on relativity, later became less pioneering and even somewhat reactionary with his "God does not play dice" view of quantum mechanics. However, what he actually said is interesting. He declared, "I cannot bear the thought that an electron exposed to a ray should on the basis of a free decision *(aus freiem Entschluss)* choose the moment and the direction in which it wants to jump away."[5] It is understandable that he had reservations about the idea of electrons as decision-making bodies. However, it is clear that for some writers who are enthusiastic about the theological implications of quantum theory, the point is rather that the decision is made not by the electrons themselves but by God.

One of the earliest discussions of the relationship between quantum mechanics and free will came from Arthur Compton, who offered a thought experiment involving a "demon" who controls the shutter over a slit through which certain photons pass. The photons may either trigger or not trigger a stick of dynamite. The demon uses the shutter to determine which photons will pass through and thereby whether or not the stick of dynamite will explode. Compton's point is that since nothing can be said about what a particular photon will do, but only about what will happen overall, there is room for the demon to slip in and determine the outcome of a particular photon without any physical law being violated.

From a God *of* the Gaps to a God *in* the Gaps

Compton's "demon" can easily become Polkinghorne's God, a being who takes advantage of the indeterminate nature of quantum mechanics in order to act positively in the world without in so doing violating any physical laws. Saunders points to the work of Karl Heim, who quoted from Matt 10:29–30, where Jesus says that "the very hairs of your head are all numbered," in order

---

5. Letter of Albert Einstein to Hedi Born, April 29, 1924. Her husband Max Born was one of the pioneers of quantum mechanics, alongside Heisenberg and Schrödinger. See Jammer, *Philosophy of Quantum Mechanics*, 124.

to suggest that the smallest parts of our bodies are under divine management because it is down at the quantum level that God can slip in some favorable interventions! One can almost imagine a guardian angel at the micro-level, steering invading microbes or bacteria away to less harmful locations.

According to quantum theory, laws at the micro-level are irreducibly statistical. It is impossible to say whether a particular photon will trigger an explosion or not, only that this will happen in a certain proportion of cases. An analogy is drawn to the exercise of free will; one may say that a certain proportion of the population will marry, or vote in a particular way, or commit a crime: what one *cannot* do is know what a particular person will do, precisely because human beings are free to choose their partners, vote as they wish, or obey the law (of course, this is clearer in the case of some individuals than others, and there are a huge number of important social and cultural factors at work in these cases, but that does not affect the general argument). There is clearly room here, the argument goes, for a particular divine intervention to pass under the radar. Moreover, the intervention, rather like the touch on the tiller, might have far-reaching implications (especially if we bring in ideas from chaos theory and Lorenz's flap of butterfly wings that creates hurricanes elsewhere).

Advocates of this approach like William Pollard end up with an interesting perspective.[6] God does not break any laws, but through God's understanding of the whole complex and interactive process of creation, something we can never have ourselves, those divine tweaks can have enormous significance in the long term. Divine intervention becomes scientifically respectable because it is never usurping natural law, just using it in a way that from our limited, finite perspective we could never hope to recognize. The micromanagement is overwhelming but law abiding. It is reminiscent of those strange defenders of miracles who point out that Jesus walking on water happened upon a submerged sandbank, as if the literal truth of the nature miracle could be defended in terms of coincidence without recourse to any violation of natural law.

From a philosophical point of view, the argument seems more than a little confusing. It is certainly possible to claim that we can make general statistical observations about human beings, without being able to say precisely what a particular human being will choose. But surely when we say that human beings "choose" what actions to take, we are saying something more than that we cannot predict what their actions will be. We are saying something about our belief in a certain power they have that is not shared

---

6. See Pollard, *Chance and Providence*.

by electrons or worms. Otherwise, as Einstein said in the quote above, we will have decisions being made by electrons.

This makes for a degree of suspicion about the fact that for some writers who are enthusiastic about the theological implications of quantum theory, the decision is not made by the electron but by God. The limitation of our knowledge in relation to particular quantum events becomes an opportunity for God to step in without in the process sweeping any other causes aside—or without being noticed. There is divine action without divine intervention. As Saunders puts it when summarizing Pollard:

> The indeterminacies of quantum theory are shown to be a nexus for the purposeful interaction of God and his creation.[7]

In other words, quantum mechanics makes possible a revised form of the God of the gaps, because it proclaims some gaps in principle unfillable.

In one way, it is clear how attractive this approach seems. We can go back three generations to Rudolf Bultmann's famous essay of 1941, "Jesus Christ and Mythology," described as a "manifesto" by Hans-Werner Bartsch, the editor of a collection of writings about it published in German in 1948. According to Bultmann, all our thinking today is shaped irrevocably by modern science. Bultmann felt that the scientific developments of his day required a positive response from theologians, and indeed that such a response was a condition of theologians being regarded as having anything significant to say. The right approach, he believed, was not to deny those developments but to reinterpret religious beliefs in order to make them compatible with contemporary scientific thinking. In a famous if now obviously dated comment, Bultmann remarked:

> It is impossible to use electric light and the wireless and to avail ourselves of modern medical and surgical discoveries, and at the same time to believe in the New Testament world of spirits and miracles.[8]

Science and technology had brought human beings to mastery of the world. This was a view perhaps more easily entertained in the mid-twentieth century than in decades to come when awareness of the environmental costs of this technological revolution, in particular through climate change, became more apparent. Nevertheless, it is easy to see how confidence in the practical applications of scientific technology made it impossible to hold that we are not in control of our own lives but are constantly being

---

7. Saunders, *Divine Action*, 105.
8. Bartsch, *Kerygma and Myth*, 5.

manipulated against our will by supernatural powers. As John Robinson put it in his bestselling work *Honest to God*, when referring to Bultmann's essay:

> If he is right, the entire conception of a supernatural order which invades and "perforates" this one must be abandoned.[9]

Invades and perforates. It is the language of oppression, the language one might almost say of military conquest and sexual violation. At all costs, Robinson believed, it had to be avoided. The self-respect of a mature technological environment demanded that there be no invasions from above.

The point of Bultmann's veneration of wirelesses and washing machines was that scientific laws could not be broken—even by God. But now there appeared to be a possibility of seeing things differently. Belief in divine intervention need not represent a primitive and prescientific worldview according to which the regularities of nature were swept aside by God. If we were to have a proper understanding of quantum mechanics, we would find that irregularities are in fact perfectly scientific—at least at the micro-level. This seems to be Polkinghorne's point. God can intervene without any offence to scientific law.

Not Even God Can Fill an Unfillable Gap

However, we have to be very careful of what is being claimed about the effect of quantum mechanics. If the argument is that there are gaps that need to be filled, certain effects for which we have not yet been able to find a cause, then there might be room for God acting directly at the micro-level to push things in a certain direction. God makes the dice fall for Matthias. But that is not what quantum mechanics says. It says that at a certain level it is logically impossible to consider a cause *of any sort* for a specific effect, because of the irreducibly statistical character of what takes place. But if this is so, then it is as impossible to identify God as a specific cause of a certain effect as it is to identify any other course. As McCall puts it, referring to Peacocke's *Paths from Science towards God*, it raises the question of whether or not even God knows the outcome of situations/systems that are unpredictable to humans.[10] In part 3 this is discussed in terms of not even God knowing what people will do in the future. But it applies as much to the way electrons jump inside an atomic orbit as to the decisions, however fateful, that human beings might make to alter the course of their lives or the lives of others.

---

9. Robinson, *Honest to God*, 24.
10. McCall, *Modern Relation*, 91.

It is the conundrum of whether God can tie a knot that God cannot untie. It appears to challenge God's omnipotence either way. Either there's a limit to the knots God can tie or a limit to the knots God can *untie*. The point is that God cannot do what is logically impossible, not because there are limits to God's power but because it is meaningless to assert that God is capable of something that is logically impossible.

This is the point made by John Wren-Lewis when he says that "they (theologians) have mostly been content to argue that even if we don't know exactly how an electron is going to jump from one atomic orbit to another, God does."[11] But this, he continues, begs the question:

> For the whole point of the "laws of chance" governing collections of random events is that they presuppose that there is no order whatsoever in the individual events; that being so, just what does the statement that they are under God's control mean?[12]

However, the price of this is that quantum mechanics doesn't necessarily open up the possibility of divine intervention. It opens up gaps, but it doesn't let God fill them any more than it lets someone else fill them. God cannot act inside the interstices of the quantum world any more than God can see what the universe will look like tomorrow.

Part of the attraction of the interpretation Polkinghorne tries to give to quantum mechanics is that it makes a virtue of what has often seemed to be (from a theological point of view) a vice in understanding the world as created and maintained by a deity. It is the idea we encountered in the second chapter of part 2, namely a world ruled by "blind chance." As mentioned above, some fifty years ago, Jacques Monod caused a considerable stir with his book *Chance and Necessity*, which sought to suggest that evolution was based on pure chance and therefore that it was purely accidental that the products of evolution should have led to the development of human beings. Monod's point was that we just happened to have emerged at the end of (or at this stage of) the evolutionary process. But as I suggested, we have to be very careful to distinguish between chance as pure coincidence ("we just bumped into each other by chance") and chance as probability ("he has a good chance of winning the race").

Pollard would say that this talk of chance suggests not a universe that is clearly unmanaged, like a vehicle without a driver rocketing out of control, but a universe whose manager uses the elements of indeterminacy in order to weave a divine design into the fabric of the universe, without in the

---

11. John Wren-Lewis, as quoted in Saunders, *Divine Action*, 91.
12. John Wren-Lewis, as quoted in Saunders, *Divine Action*, 91.

process overriding any other natural cause. Monod's universe is not out of control after all but is open to a kind of soft control by a God who doesn't in the process elbow other causes out of the way. As Polkinghorne puts it, "Part of a notion of *creatio continua* must surely be that an evolving universe is one which is theologically understood as being allowed, within divine providence, to 'make itself.'"[13]

As a general approach I think this is correct, but Pollard wants to take it further. Pollard's view is that quantum mechanics allows God to tinker under the radar, because at the micro-level specific causes cannot be assigned to specific effects. We can therefore allow the guiding hand of the Creator to be involved without being able to identify specifically where it is at work.

Do we need a guiding hand in this sense at all? Isn't the point about indeterminacies being part of the divine design that we can accept that there is no divine tinkering, that there is an irreducible element of uncertainty in the way things develop? Quantum mechanics should not become a way of bringing the clockmaker God back to put the clock right at awkward moments, veiled by the invisible cloak of unpredictable micro-happenings.

Robert Russell suggests that God acts by "realizing one of several potentials in the quantum system, not of manipulating subatomic particles as a quasi-physical force."[14] The title of his article shows how keen Russell is to rescue the God who acts from what he sees as the enforced *in*activity of God in a contemporary scientific environment. But manipulating subatomic particles as a quasi-physical force is surely precisely how people do imagine God acting when they seek to rescue divine intervention at the quantum level. The fact that it is impossible for specific causes and effects to be attributed at the micro-level allows God to fly in under the radar and drop the divine load, sneaking in like a dam buster, just like Compton's demon controlling the shutter unnoticed. Russell insists that he means something else, namely a God who acts by "realizing one of several potentials in the quantum system,"[15] but surely this means the same thing. How else can these potentials be realized, except through a surreptitious divine touch on the tiller that is too circumspect to be registered by anyone else? Russell insists that they can indeed be realized by God, who acts without intervening. It is a case of "noninterventionist special divine action."[16] But what exactly can this mean? Thomas F. Tracy makes one ask a similar question when

13. Polkinghorne, *Serious Talk*, 84.
14. R. Russell, "Does 'the God Who Acts,'" 64.
15. R. Russell, "Does 'the God Who Acts,'" 64.
16. R. Russell, "Does 'the God Who Acts,'" 51.

he talks about God's activity at the quantum level as something other than acting as a "quasi-physical force," but instead by acting to "realize one of the several potentials in the quantum system (the 'wave packet')."[17] I would be the first to admit my ignorance of quantum mechanics and have to rely perhaps overmuch on the logic of language! But it seems to me that if God is "realizing a potential," that means prodding the donkey with a divine stick. God is acting.

The same problem arises with Nancey Murphy and her ideas of divine action. God's will is "assumed to be exercised by means of the macro-effects of subatomic manipulations," she writes.[18] But what can these subatomic manipulations be except divine interventions under the radar? All sorts of images come into play here, all designed to say that something other than intervention takes place, something other than God's bursting in on the scene and sweeping other forms of causality aside. Murphy makes use of the image of Buridan's ass, for instance. This is a donkey that can't decide between two piles of hay. Quantum entities are like miniature donkeys that can't choose between the piles of hay. But for the analogy to work they must still come in for some divine prodding. Somewhere there is still a divine stick quietly whacking a recalcitrant mulish backside.

What seems to be happening is that a constant attempt is being made to square the circle. On the one hand, God doesn't intervene, so no natural processes must be swept aside. It is still the ass that finally goes for the hay. On the other hand, God acts, and so it must be God who is finally responsible for what happens. Hence the adoption of complicated mechanisms that involve the ass doing the eating but God doing the prodding—at the micro-level, where the prodding can go unnoticed. The idea seems to be (as Saunders puts it, discussing ideas of Thomas F. Tracy) that God can exploit loopholes, gaps in the natural order that allow for divine action without disruption. But when we try to pin down what this nondisruptive action means, it seems to me that it is not a denial of divine intervention at all, but a claim that God can intervene without in the process being seen to push any other actor out of the way. So long as God doesn't start disturbing any laws of nature, God can intervene as often as God likes. It is also necessary for God to act unrecognized. Hence Tracy's talk of the veil of ignorance revealed by chaos theory with regard to the determining conditions of many events in this world.

In *A Brief History of Time*, Stephen Hawking made the following comment on the idea of special divine actions at the quantum level:

---

17. Saunders, *Divine Action*, 122.
18. R. Russell et al., *Chaos and Complexity*, 327.

With the advent of quantum mechanics, we have come to recognize that events cannot be predicted with complete accuracy, but there is always a degree of uncertainty. If one likes, one could ascribe this randomness to the intervention of God, but it would be a very strange kind of intervention: there is no evidence that it is directed toward any purpose. Indeed, if it were, it would by definition not be random.[19]

The only way to avoid this conclusion is to imagine some all-knowing deity who, with the full knowledge that the weather forecasters struggle but fail to achieve, knows what a tweak now will do in the distant future. But although these deft little tweaks on the tiller might make sense in terms of long-term planning (David Jones estimates that if God wanted to steer an asteroid into the earth in order to get rid of the dinosaurs, God would have to have started God's strategy some one hundred million years previously in order to be able to operate "under the radar"[20]), they don't explain the sudden production of good wine out of water or the emergence of Lazarus from the tomb. There is even some uncertainty over whether deft tweaks can achieve much of a result. Koperski suggests that:

> Chaotic Quantum determination (CQD) describes a causal pathway in which God could alter the arrangement of bubbles in the crest of a tsunami but not redirect its course.[21]

Going "under the radar," even if scientifically respectable in the sense that it doesn't involve breaking any laws, may not enable God to achieve very much.

Conclusion

There is an irreducible element of uncertainty in the way things develop. This is a point that it is sometimes difficult to concede, as if it would render God somehow no longer in charge or would present a universe supposedly careening out of control. But the lack of control has been exaggerated in one sense. This chapter has rejected the suggestion of human beings as isolated discrepancies in a hostile universe. Such ideas, like many interpretations of Darwin, play on the idea of a cruel universe engaged in constant warfare between species struggling for survival. They both overstate the inhumanity, so to speak, of mankind's fellow creatures and understate the inhumanity of humans.

---

19. Hawking, *Brief History of Time*, 201–2.
20. David Jones, as quoted in Saunders, *Divine Action*, 171.
21. Jeffrey Koperski, as quoted in Saunders, *Divine Action*, 206.

We need a broader understanding of what God's being in charge might mean. The recognition that the created order contains its own innate and divinely willed elements of randomness and indeterminacy does not make it impossible that it is proceeding to develop (to use an ancient metaphor) under its own steam according to God's will. That randomness in its design and development is arguably the homage that the created order pays to the kenotic purpose of a God who deliberately limits Godself. Hence Bradford McCall's remark that "the resurgence of kenotic theology has thus been helpful in reformulating divine action in an evolutionary world."[22] It is why the collection of essays by a group of theologians called *The Work of Love* is subtitled *Creation as Kenosis*.[23]

The problem with so-called SDAs (special divine actions) for theologians like Bultmann was based on a belief that in an age of technology one must defer to a scientific understanding of the world. This belief was also characteristic of some theologians who tried to use quantum mechanics and chaos theory to suggest that a form of divine intervention is possible that apparently doesn't break any scientific law. This chapter has been dubious about their approach. In the first place, it suggests that where quantum mechanics is concerned, the point is that at the quantum level no cause can be identified, including that of God. If it is possible to fly in under the radar and cause something to happen, there is no way of knowing that it is God who has done so. And in the case of chaos theory, a special divine action would have to be put into effect perhaps millions of years before the desired outcome took place.

In any case, there is something strange about trying to use a system that makes clear how God has accepted a degree of uncertainty in the way things develop precisely in order to try to find ways of allowing God to interfere in order to put things right. But we must face the implications of this. Much of the debate about miracles, for instance, has been along the lines of "Are they possible?" and some enthusiasts for quantum mechanics feel they have found a way of answering yes to that question. But some would say the question ought to be "Would God carry them out anyway?" The real question, in other words, is whether it is consistent with God's purpose for any generation to be given "a sign" (Matt 12:39).

If it is morally dubious to think of divine interference in a world set up to have its own autonomy, are we forced to deny that special divine actions ever take place? Do we have to reject them as thoroughly as Bultmann does, but from a perspective that questions their ethical rather than scientific

---

22. McCall, *Modern Relation*, 51.
23. Polkinghorne, *Work of Love*.

validity? Is the effect of kenoticism to arrive at the same conclusions as Bultmann by a different route?

This question, important though it is, must be held over until we turn, in parts 4 and 5, to the nature of God, but it is worth saying here that such a conclusion would be a mistake. It has to be borne in mind that all these questions about "acts of God" and whether or not divine intervention takes place operate against the background of certain presumptions about how God is related to the world. They presuppose a God above and humanity below and then ask whether God has the right to interfere. That is arguably a misleading image of how God is related to human beings. A final conclusion concerning the plausibility of special divine actions, including miracles, must therefore wait until part 4 has attempted to redefine the context within which the discussion of "acts of God" takes place.

PART 3

Uncertainty in the Moral Order

According to most philosophers, God in making the world enslaved it. According to Christianity, in making it, He set it free. God had written, not so much a poem, but rather a play; a play he had planned as perfect, but which had necessarily been left to human actors and stage-managers, who had since made a great mess of it.

G. K. CHESTERTON, ORTHODOXY

Chapter 8

The Omnipotence of Divine Love

Part 2 described the irreducible complexity of the created order and tried to suggest how an inherent instability and unpredictability might be compatible with the notion of divine design. Exactly the same issue arises in relation to the moral order, whose instability lies in the possibility of a tragic outcome to the whole process of creation. By giving human beings freedom, God opens up the possibility of failure, including God's own, if God's creatures choose to blow up or burn up the planet.

We can begin by returning to the argument used by John Wren-Lewis in part 2 in relation to quantum mechanics. He said that "they (theologians) have mostly been content to argue that even if we don't know exactly how an electron is going to jump from one atomic orbit to another, God does."[1] He went on to say that this begs the question. "For the whole point of the 'laws of chance' governing collections of random events is that they presuppose that there is no order whatsoever in the individual events; that being so, just what does the statement that they are under God's control mean?"[2]

I suggested that this was why quantum mechanics doesn't open up the possibility of divine intervention. It opens up gaps but doesn't let God fill them any more than it lets someone else fill them. As I pointed out then, God cannot act in the interstices of the quantum world any more than God can see what the universe will look like tomorrow.

It is an argument that can be compared to the one about God's omniscience, when it is said that if God doesn't know the future then God's powers are obviously limited, because there is something that is impossible

---

1. John Wren-Lewis, as quoted in Saunders, *Divine Action*, 91.
2. John Wren-Lewis, as quoted in Saunders, *Divine Action*, 91.

for God; and yet if God does know the future, what possible meaning can be given to the idea that I am free to decide, for instance, whether to stay working at home or go out and sit in a café reading the newspaper? Attempts are sometimes made to square the circle, for instance, by introducing a spatial metaphor that suggests God is like someone on the top of a hill looking down at two cars approaching each other on either side of a bend down below. God can see the future from God's vantage point; we, from down below, cannot foresee (in this case) the crash to come. It could be said that from God's vantage point outside space and time, the past, present, and future are immediately present.

The analogy is based on Boethius's interesting idea that for God, the past, present, and future are gathered together into an eternal present. "Thus, if you will think about the foreknowledge by which God distinguishes all things, you will rightly consider it to be not a foreknowledge of future events, but knowledge of a never-changing present."[3] If sense could be made of this, then the point would be that what we call God's "foreknowledge" is wrongly conceived, since it implies that God, like us, is in time. We should think simply in terms of God's "knowledge," the knowledge of one for whom past, present, and future are gathered together in the timeless moment of God's eternal understanding. From the deity's timeless vantage point, God is simply acting as an observer of all that was, is, and will be, laid out before God like a diagram in space-time. As Hebblethwaite puts it:

> The appeal of such a view to the more mathematically minded physicist or philosopher is obvious. Abstracting from experienced reality, he can treat any object as a function of four variables, representing the four-dimensional whole—the three spatial dimensions and the temporal one.[4]

However, "spatializing" time in this way in order to treat reality as a four-dimensional whole arguably treats time as unreal. Moreover, it is one thing to say (correctly) that God is outside time and space. It is another to say that from God's vantage point outside time and space God can somehow see into and grasp the whole space-time order at one glance, as if it was a map spread out on God's heavenly table. That is surely to force God back into space.

However, we do not need to find a way of visualizing how God can know the future. The whole point of a kenotic approach is to suggest that in creating space and time God creates an order of being within which it is

---

3. Boethius, *Consolation of Philosophy*, 106.
4. Hebblethwaite, "Some Reflections," 435.

impossible—even for God—to read the future. If that is so, then God need not be lifted out of a temporally structured world in order to see what is to come. Indeed, the question is whether, if human beings are free, the future can possibly yet exist. Hebblethwaite argues that "if the future is genuinely open, then the future does not only not yet exist; it has yet to be decided."[5]

Hebblethwaite supports the view of Nelson Pike that if one takes the view that an omniscient being "would hold beliefs about the outcome of human actions in advance of their performance," then "one is committed to the view that no human action is voluntary."[6] The term "open theism" was introduced in the following year with Richard Rice's book *The Openness of God: The Relationship of Divine Foreknowledge and Human Free Will* (Rice was an Adventist, and the book proved controversial with the community he belonged to). The point of the "open theist" is that God *doesn't* know what you or I will do and that this is part of God's purpose in creating. If such a position sounds like a limitation, then it is a freely willed one, expressing what God has chosen to be (or eternally is). Not knowing outcomes is part of the divine disorder willed by God for Godself—and it is part of the rescue of God insofar as it makes sense of what might otherwise appear to be an unacceptable limit upon God's omniscience, something to be ruled out if God is to be God. But it is not a limit to God's power, beyond the fact that God has chosen, in creating a world full of free beings, to create a universe whose development God cannot know in advance. That is God's will. As Hebblethwaite puts it:

> If the eternal God creates a temporally structured open world, then he must—logically must—relate himself to it, in knowledge as in action, in a manner appropriate to its given nature.[7]

Many will balk at what appears to be telling God what God must do. But the logic of this "must" is simply that certain consequences logically follow from what God has already chosen to do:

> If he creates a world whose future is open, then what will be is not yet there to be known, nor is it decided yet what it will be.[8]

To say, as Hebblethwaite does, that "the future cannot be known by omniscience any more than by finite minds"[9] is not to make an insupport-

---

5. Hebblethwaite, "Some Reflections," 438.
6. Pike, "Divine Omniscience," 46.
7. Hebblethwaite, "Some Reflections," 439.
8. Hebblethwaite, "Some Reflections," 439.
9. Hebblethwaite, "Some Reflections," 439.

able claim to be able to outline what God can or cannot know. It is to outline what must be the case, on the basis of God's choice to be related to the world and its creatures in a certain way. It is to set out the innate conditions of a created order, so that to say that God cannot know the future as part of that created order is to do no more than to say that we are able to sin and to refuse to receive God's grace. That is the nature of the world that God has chosen as a means of being freely united to human beings by grace rather than compulsion, and it imposes certain constraints upon what God can do just as it imposes constraints upon what we can do. But these are constraints that God has freely chosen. Hebblethwaite once again:

> Creation is an act of God's omnipotence, but in order to relate himself to the creatures he has made, he must limit himself in a manner appropriate to the nature of what he has made, in the case we are considering, free finite persons. Similarly, the creation does not escape the purview of God's omniscience. He knows every past and present fact and every future possibility. Nothing takes him by surprise. But he has so made the world, with its temporal structure and open future, that the task of constructing a specific future has been given to the creature. God's omniscience, like his omnipotence, is self-limited by the nature of what he has made.[10]

As we argued in part 2, if a quantum event is by definition random, then not even God can sneak in and tweak a particular result. In the same way, if our actions are the product of our free will in choosing them, they cannot in any sense already exist, to be glimpsed through God's all-seeing eyes somewhere outside time or to be predetermined through God's knowledge in the present. There is a parallel between the two, another point that Hebblethwaite brings out:

> Human beings being the product of physical and biological evolution in nature, can hardly be thought of as the only points of non-determined development in the universe.... We may well expect to find elements of openness in nature at every level of created being ... indeterminacy randomness and spontaneity are discovered to characterize the behavior of the fundamental quanta of material substance. Just when we think we have established a tidy, determined macroscopic universe openness—like cheerfulness—keeps breaking in.[11]

---

10. Hebblethwaite, "Some Reflections," 440–41.
11. Hebblethwaite, "Some Reflections," 445.

One must beware of identifying randomness in matter with freedom in human beings, but it can be seen as another example of the way in which creation entails an act of divine self-limitation. It is an illustration of the manner in which an element of indeterminacy, like the denial of God's omniscience, can be so provoking to those who have too narrow a view of an ordered universe. Monod believed that any notion of divine design was undermined by the random mutations he rightly observed in the process of evolution. In a similar way, the idea that God does not know the future is seen by some as evidence that God cannot really be in control, and the idea that "he's got the whole world in his hands" becomes an absurd description of a globe that is manifestly slipping through God's fingers. But Hebblethwaite insists:

> It is only because the texture of our physical nature includes an element of indeterminacy that it can produce free creatures like ourselves. The wonder of God's Providence in and through the creative process is precisely that he gives it that openness and lets free creatures evolve relating himself to them appropriately as they emerge.[12]

The point was made by Karl Popper in his *Unended Quest: An Intellectual Biography*,[13] words that became an epigraph at the start of the philosopher Charles Hartshorne's *Omnipotence and Other Theological Mistakes*:

> Appealing to his [Einstein's] way of expressing himself in theological terms, I said: If God had wanted to put everything into the universe from the beginning, He would have created a universe without change, without organisms and evolution, and without man and man's experience of change. But he seems to have thought that a live universe with events unexpected even by Himself would be more interesting than a dead one.[14]

Conclusion

This book supports Hebblethwaite's view that God's omniscience, like his omnipotence, is self-limited by the nature of what God has made. But one should not take too much comfort from this self-limitation. Ironically, we

---

12. Hebblethwaite, "Some Reflections," 446.
13. Popper, *Unended Quest*, 150.
14. Hartshorne, *Omnipotence*, epigraph. Hartshorne's point is that "omnipotence" is a mistake because it suggests that God must be able to bring about every detail of world history. But to describe God in that way allows no room for creaturely freedom.

have a tendency to draw satisfaction from assuring ourselves that, after all, God is all-powerful and God's omnipotence will therefore, sooner or later, come to our rescue. However, such is the nature of God's voluntary self-renunciation of power that God may no more be able to save us from the consequences of our own actions than know in advance what they will be. There is a hard side to the divinely willed self-limitation that lies at the heart of a kenotic approach. The next chapter will attempt to make this point in more detail.

Chapter 9

Hell and Divine Failure: The Hard Side of Kenoticism

One of the perhaps less recognized implications of a kenotic approach is that it strengthens the moral seriousness of the New Testament message by making the most plausible case for hell, not in the sense of a perpetual battle against pitchforks and fire but as the complete absence of God's saving grace.

The "Problem" of Hell

It would be useful to begin by rehearsing some of the arguments used in an earlier book, *Death Be Not Proud*.[1] The problem of hell is easily stated. On the one hand, it seems clear that a God of love would not condemn people, however bad they have been, to everlasting torment of some kind. After all, we don't do that ourselves. In most "civilized" countries even the worst crimes are met with fixed jail sentences. Even when life means life, it is couched in terms of tens or hundreds of years—the rest of a person's life but not forever. And even those countries that apply capital punishment are doing something less than imposing everlasting torment. The torment, though intense, is short lived. Why should God be more barbaric even than we are?

On the other hand, denying the existence of hell is seen as a way of taking human wickedness too lightly. The world we live in, for good or ill, is one in which human beings are permitted to inflict the most terrible suffering

---

1. See Corner, *Death Be Not Proud*.

on each other. Cruelty, sadism, and torture are daily events, causing levels of misery and pain in this life that most of us can barely imagine and would run from if it came anywhere near us. Are the perpetrators of such crimes to be let off with no more than an expression of divine disappointment?

Either God inflicts everlasting pain on the wicked, in which case God is worse than the most sadistic and vengeful of human authorities, or else God forgives them, in which case why allow them so much power to inflict pain on others in the first place? For if there is a reason why we feel drawn to allow for a doctrine of hell, it is that nothing else will do justice to the seriousness of the choices we have to make in this life.

It could be argued that even a God who condemns a Hitler to hell has an unlimited appetite for revenge. In the camps one could be sent to die or commit suicide—no such opportunity for making an end to one's suffering exists in hell. On the other hand, a God who forgives a Hitler belittles the sufferings of those whom God left, without once raising a hand in their defense, to suffer the consequences of human evil.

Hume's Case against Hell

"Punishment, without any proper end or purpose, is inconsistent with our ideas of goodness and justice," wrote Hume in his essay "On the Immortality of the Soul."[2] We can see the point of this. Despite the fact that they have to deal with people who have committed great crimes, most countries nowadays outlaw torture, reject capital punishment, and very rarely imprison indefinitely. Of course, one of the strongest arguments against the death penalty on earth is that there can be mistakes, whereas this will not be a danger in the case of God's judgment. Nevertheless, the view of a substantial number of countries—for instance, all twenty-seven members of the European Union—is that there shall be no capital punishment in any circumstances and that almost all criminals, even some of the worst, should be given a release date. Moreover, while they suffer from the loss of liberty in prison, they do not suffer the sort of agonies traditionally associated with those in hell or even purgatory.

Hume further points out that when human courts do exact severe punishments like permanent incarceration or execution, they do so because they perceive the individuals concerned to be dangerous to the well-being of society. Contemporary measures against terrorists might be justified in such a way. But this hardly applies to souls in the afterlife. An unpunished sinner is not likely to harm the interests of those in heaven. Therefore, God

---

2. Wollheim, *Hume On Religion*, 266.

lacks the justification for treating sinners harshly that human beings have, namely that of preventing them from causing further damage to society.

Hume adds:

> Heaven and hell suppose two distinct species of men, the good and the bad; but the greatest part of mankind float betwixt vice and virtue. Were one to go round the world with an intention of giving a good supper to the righteous and a sound drubbing to the wicked, he would frequently be embarrassed in his choice, and would find the merits and demerits of most men and women scarcely amount to the value of either.[3]

Hume's conclusion is expressed in the strongest possible manner:

> The damnation of one man is an infinitely greater evil in the universe than the subversion of a thousand millions of kingdoms.[4]

Hume's argument as it stands is incontrovertible, but it is so because we allow the image of the courtroom drama followed by a final sentence to determine our views of what the last judgment is. Understood in these terms, Hume is quite right. Were it a matter of God pronouncing sentence upon individuals in the dock, it would certainly make no sense of heaven (presumably a somewhat more positive verdict than "not guilty," more like a pronouncement of infinite compensation) and hell. The idea of purgatory might be thrown in as a way of dealing with Hume's argument about the different shades of grey in human character that make a "heaven" or "hell" judgment seem so crude, but not even this can rescue the approach. If the notions of punishment or suffering in the afterlife (assuming that these are more morally questionable than that of reward) are to make sense, we have to find a completely different way of making sense of them.

God's Justice as a Quality of God's Love

The dilemma outlined in the previous section is often presented as a problem of reconciling God's justice with God's love. Distinguishing between these two things is characteristic of discussions of heaven and hell. We are given the impression that we are first to be offered God's love, which God would like us all to receive with gratitude. However, if the hard of heart refuse this love—and God has given us the power to refuse God's love, precisely because it is in the nature of love to invite but not to compel—then

---

3. Wollheim, *Hume on Religion*, 266–67.
4. Wollheim, *Hume on Religion*, 267.

we encounter God's justice instead, an altogether more ruthless character. Rather in the manner of the nice and nasty policeman, those who refuse the carrot are faced with the stick. Unwilling to be drawn by God's love, sinners are made to bow to God's justice instead. In practical terms, God's love may will that all be saved, but God's justice demands that some be damned.

However, it is possible to take issue with the notion that God's love and God's justice can be separated from one another in the manner just described. To do so arguably undermines the love of God and the justice of God equally. Divorced from God's love, God's justice becomes unrelenting and even vengeful; divorced from God's justice, God's love becomes sentimental and weak.

John Robinson made the point in the following way:

> His is a love of cauterizing holiness and of a righteousness whose only response to evil is the purity of a perfect hate. Wrath and justice are but ways in which such love must show itself to be love in the face of its denial. . . . The impression is often given that God has reserves of power upon which God could fall back if the power of love were to fail; that souls that cannot be won to a free response fall under a judgment condemning them to an involuntary destruction. But God has no power but the power of love, since God has no purpose but the purpose of love and no nature but the nature of love. If that fails, God fails. Justice is no second line of defense: it has no power of its own. For it is no other than love being itself, love in the face of evil, continuing to exercise its own peculiar power.[5]

It is vital to maintain both parts of the argument, lest this talk of God as "nothing but love" be seen to issue in too comfortable an expectation of sins swept aside in some kind of all-embracing "warts and all" divine acceptance of any and every human being. Robinson's point is not to deny God's justice, but to integrate it into our conception of God's love. Hence his description of that love as "cauterizing holiness." The point is not that there is nothing in the biblical or ecclesiastical injunction that we should fear God's wrath or stand to be condemned by God's justice; the point is that this is all a part of being loved by God.

---

5. Robinson, *In the End, God*, 104–5.

Cauterizing Holiness—God's Justice in the Pain of Self-Discovery

Given that the justice and the love of God are seen as inseparable, more both sides of the same coin than different approaches to the last judgment, what are we to make of this "cauterizing holiness" of which Robinson speaks?

Miroslav Volf argues that in the afterlife there is "no other suffering than the pain of self-discovery."[6] This might seem to be a lenient version of what has traditionally been seen as punishment for the wicked. But one should beware of this presupposition. There is no reason to suppose that such suffering will be light.

At least part of the impetus to measure the seriousness of human conduct on earth by proposing real physical tortures or deprivation in the afterlife comes from a tendency to see the alternative as an airy dismissal of the past, a universal welcoming mat for everyone, whatever their background, to drown their sorrows in the pleasures of paradise. We think of everyone being received into the arms of a loving God and interpret that welcome in saccharine terms, on the lines of the prodigal son turning up for his fatted calf. This is a misconception. The self-discovery that is entailed by moving closer to God is not painless. The book of Revelation talks of the return of Christ in judgment in the following terms:

> Behold, he is coming with the clouds! Every eye shall see him, and among them those who pierced him; and all the peoples of the world shall lament in remorse. (Rev 1:7)

Such "lamentation in remorse" will be a form of suffering; as Balthasar points out, there is another piercing to add to that mentioned here, the piercing of our own souls by the realization of the magnitude of our sin.[7] Jüngel supports this when he emphasizes that "there is no more severe judgment possible than that which is effected by grace and measures everything against grace."[8]

It is not necessary to believe in an ever-burning and yet never-consuming fire in order to make sense of hell—nor is it clear that many of those who described it in such terms meant it to be understood in this literal sense. The argument that we used to believe in a literal hell but have since grown out of the notion is unjust to Christian tradition. The early church itself contained many who recognized that the condemnation we receive for our sins will take the form of a self-condemnation, the work of an unbearable conscience when we are forced to confront ourselves as we really are. Basil of Caesarea

---

6. Volf, "Final Reconciliation," 95.
7. Balthasar, *Dare We Hope*. See esp. ch. 9, "The Self-Consumption of Evil?," 105–11.
8. Jüngel, "Last Judgment," 397.

argues that at the judgment our only accusers will be our own sins, which will rise up before us in our memory. Gregory of Nazianzus argues that we shall be arraigned by our own past thoughts and deeds and hauled away condemned by our own selves. Augustine develops a similar idea. The book that will be opened at the last judgment, he argues, will be the conscience of each individual, whose sins will come flooding in on his or her recollection.

The harrowing descriptions of literary tradition retain their force even when not taken literally. Dante describes a sinner in hell in "The Inferno" of his *Divine Comedy*:

> And suddenly, at one of the sinners at our side,
> A serpent leapt up, and transfixed him there
> At the point where the neck is fastened to the shoulders.
>
> Never was "o" or "i" written so quickly
> As he caught fire and burnt, and turned to ashes
> Which fell together and showered to the ground;
>
> And when he was in this manner destroyed,
> The dust collected itself without assistance
> And suddenly returned to the same shape.
>
> So it is, according to the experts,
> That the phoenix dies and then is born again
> When it approaches its five hundredth year.[9]

The idea appears to be of a person being burned to ashes, which then, like the phoenix resurrecting itself, reassemble themselves in order that the torture may be endlessly repeated. The fate of the sinner is like that of Prometheus, tied to a rock while his liver renews itself so that it can be endlessly picked to bits by an eagle. But no one, even those on the lookout for weak appeals to the poetic imagination, is going to take Dante's description to be a journalistic report on his experiences of the underworld under the guidance of Virgil. Dante's imagery describes the way in which a sinner in hell must live with his or her own misdeeds forever. Every time they try to come to terms with what they have done and accept it or put it behind them, awareness of it rises up and strikes them again. They live in an agony of eternal regret.

Such an idea was perhaps in the mind of one of the leaders of the nineteenth-century Oxford Movement, Edward Pusey, when he is quoted by John Hick, talking of how those he was preaching to "know the fierce, intense, burning heat of a furnace, how it consumes in a moment anything

---

9. Dante, *Divine Comedy*, "Inferno," canto 24, lines 97–108.

cast into it," and then adds, "Its misery to the damned shall be that they feel it, but cannot be consumed by it."[10] Hick accuses Pusey of "moral perversity" and concludes:

> Between the moral outlook of that sermon and the general ethical outlook of today, both inside and outside the Christian church, there is a great gulf fixed.[11]

In a similar manner, Antony Flew thinks that the theist is committed to the belief "that omniscient Omnipotence will on that Judgment Day infallibly ensure that the unending torments and the eternal ecstasies are allocated to the right people: that is, in the one case, to the same people as had incurred His disapproval and, in the other case, to those who had won His favor." The quotation comes from his introduction to the philosophical issues involved in belief in an afterlife.[12] Flew thinks of God as the mafia boss rewarding his henchmen with a good time and his opponents with a short (or rather an infinitely long) river journey in concrete boots.

But there's another way of looking at this. Pusey's sermon, like Dante's poetry, may have been trying to convey the pain of remorse. After all, when we say that the memory of something "tears our guts out" it isn't meant literally.

Moreover, what would Hick say to passages of the New Testament like:

> If your hand or your foot is your undoing, cut it off and fling it away; it is better for you to enter into life maimed or lame, than to keep two hands or two feet and be thrown into the eternal fire. If it is your eye that is your undoing, tear it out and fling it away; it is better to enter into life with one eye than to keep both eyes and be thrown into the fires of hell. (Matt 18:8–9)

Are we to say that this is an example of thinking on the other side of Hick's "gulf," a first-century rant in favor of self-mutilation that has given rise to the abuses of flagellants? Doubtless there are those who have read the text in this way, just as there are those who have interpreted the verse (Matt 19:12) about making oneself a eunuch for the kingdom of heaven as a ground for self-castration (the church father Origen was accused of having done this, probably unfairly). But a more plausible reading would be that it is intended to make a point about the seriousness of the choices we make. Again, in the previous passage (Matt 18:1–7) Jesus tells his disciples that they must become like children in order to enter the kingdom of heaven. He says that

10. Hick, *Death and Eternal Life*, 200.
11. Hick, *Death and Eternal Life*, 200.
12. Flew, *Body, Mind and Death*, 7.

"if a man is a cause of stumbling to one of these little ones who have faith in me, it would be better for him to have a millstone hung round his neck and be drowned in the depths of the sea" (Matt 18:6). At one level this could be read as a "drown the bastards" headline worthy of a *Daily Mail* editorial on pedophiles. If we follow the literalism of Hick, then we associate Jesus (or at least the author of the Gospel) with those who talk of ever-burning but never-consuming (and therefore never releasing their victims) fires. But there is no need to do this. Jesus is not saying they should be drowned; he is saying that it would be better for them if they had been. He is pointing to the consequences of sin—to the agony of conscience that will be theirs when their own actions are finally opened up to them.

To dismiss hell on the grounds that there is a great gulf of enlightenment between Pusey's day and Hick's enables Hick to throw the baby out with the bathwater. Condemning a doctrine of hell as morally perverse because it supposedly supports a view of unceasing physical torture enables him to suggest that in an enlightened age we have simply grown out of any belief in hell whatsoever. But was unceasing physical torture ever really the point of it, even in the unenlightened past? Surely the doctrine was there for a reason—to point to an aspect of human accountability. The agony of hell, as we have already seen in the quotations from Basil, Gregory of Nazianzus, and Augustine, is a self-imposed agony, one that follows from the unveiling of everything that allows us to mask from ourselves what we are really like. It may, of course, be that for all of us the "perfect memory of our evil actions," as Murphy describes a possible way of understanding the experience of hell,[13] will be transformed into acceptance and forgiveness. But this cannot be presumed, and at the very least the process of transformation will be a painful one.

Purgatory and the End of Hypocrisy

In a telling phrase, Hans Küng talks of purgatory as "God himself in the wrath of his grace."[14] The notion of being "purged" has a sense of cleansing through a powerful act of intervention, but is often conceived negatively, as in "political purges." The German word *Fegfeuer* conveys the sense better; this is the winnowing fire that consumes the chaff and purifies—more purgative than purge.

The notion of purgatory is seen by Küng as "an element of the encounter with God: that is, the encounter of the unfinished person, still immature

13. Murphy, *Bodies and Souls*, 140.
14. Küng, *Eternal Life*, 139.

in his love, with the holy, infinite, loving God; an encounter which is profoundly humiliating, painful and therefore purifying."[15] It is a view shared by Cardinal Newman's famous poem *The Dream of Gerontius*, where the angel explains to the soul what it will be like for him to encounter the Judge of all people:

> There is a pleading in His pensive eyes
> Will pierce thee to the quick, and trouble thee.
> And thou wilt hate and loathe thyself; for, though
> Now sinless, thou wilt feel that thou hast sinn'd,
> As never thou didst feel; and wilt desire
> To slink away, and hide thee from His sight:
> And yet wilt have a longing aye to dwell
> Within the beauty of His countenance.
> And these two pains, so counter and so keen,—
> The longing for Him, when thou seest Him not;
> The shame of self at thought of seeing Him,—
> Will be thy veriest, sharpest purgatory.[16]

This is not an answer to the question of whether "the wrath of God's grace" might be a wholly destructive process in the case of some individuals. The question of universalism is not an easy one and is made more difficult by the kind of Aunt Sally that suggests, as Antony Flew does in the quotation cited above, that any believer in the reality of hell must be committed to endless physical tortures with forks and whips. It may be more a question of the "irreducibly tragic" character of aspects of human life, as Donald MacKinnon observed.[17] There is an interesting discussion of this in John McDowell's *Hope in Barth's Eschatology*. It is worth remembering that McDowell edited an excellent collection of MacKinnon's writings, where Barth's universalism is subjected to careful scrutiny.[18]

There is every reason to suppose that being welcomed into the arms of God will be a heartrending and humiliating experience, something we may find almost unbearable. For all our defenses will have gone. We shall be stripped of all the hypocrisies and rationalizations that enable us to deceive ourselves and maintain our self-esteem during life.

We are told that in the afterlife the pure in heart shall "see God" (Matt 5:8). But this encounter will be a searing one. When Moses asks to see the glory of God, the Lord shows his back but not his face. "My face you cannot

---

15. Küng, *Eternal Life*, 139.
16. Newman, *Dream of Gerontius*, 39.
17. McDowell, *Hope in Barth's Eschatology*, 226–32.
18. See McDowell, *Philosophy and the Burden*.

see, for no mortal man may see me and live" (Exod 33:20). To see the face of God is to have your soul pierced by the purity of God. It is to be bitterly, unbearably aware of the mistakes, omissions, and destructive passions that have colored so much of one's life. To quote Newman's *Dream of Gerontius* once more:

> Learn that the flame of the Everlasting Love
> Doth burn ere it transform.[19]

In canto 5 of the "Purgatorio" in *The Divine Comedy*, Dante refers to the souls who repented late in life:

> We all are people who met a violent death,
> And were all sinners up to the last hour:
> But then the light of heaven made us wary,
>
> So that, repenting and forgiving, we
> Came out of life having made our peace with God
> Who stabs us with desire of seeing him.[20]

To be "stabbed with desire" describes the souls in purgatory who have repented and will ultimately be able to accept themselves and be accepted by God. But such acceptance will be painful. The desire for God "stabs"—it is not simply a warm glow of anticipation. Augustine, Aquinas, and Dante all agree upon one thing—that the pain of purgatory is greater than any that might be suffered in this life.

Paul in his First Letter to the Corinthians talks of the "glass darkly" through which we see now, as opposed to the seeing "face-to-face," which shall be our final experience after death. This verse (1 Cor 13:12) comes at the conclusion of his famous hymn to love (1 Cor 13), the love for which there is nothing it "cannot face" (1 Cor 13:7). Yet this seeing face-to-face with God will be a harrowing encounter to the extent that we are pierced by God's purity. It is an encounter that, as Paul reminds us, will entail complete self-knowledge, the agony of knowing the truth about ourselves. "My knowledge now is partial; then it will be whole, like God's knowledge of me" (1 Cor 13:12). We will know as we are known.

If such an unravelling of what we really are after death is recognized as entailing this winnowing fire of self-recognition, then at least we shall not suppose that meeting God is simply the fulfillment of the sybarite's dream of endless luxury. The dilemma of deciding between the sadistic God who inflicts everlasting torture, and the indulgent God who overlooks the heinous

---

19. Newman, *Dream of Gerontius*, 34.
20. Dante, *Divine Comedy*, "Purgatorio," canto 5, lines 52–57.

crimes of a Hitler on this earth, may perhaps be resolved in these terms. We must suppose the Hitlers of this world not in a lake of boiling fire but exposed to a regret so intense that the boiling fire seems attractive by comparison, facing the unbearable awareness of having destroyed everything that they now see they loved. It may be that even this is too explicit an attempt to describe what cannot be anticipated on earth; the point to stress is that the encounter with God after death must be harrowing for any sinner (and therefore for all of us). The notion of purgatory expresses this; it is a description not of an interim state before seeing God face-to-face, but of the intensity of that experience itself, to cite Küng once again, "the wrath of his grace."[21]

A similar notion is developed by C. S. Lewis in *A Grief Observed*, a book written shortly after the death of his wife. Lewis wrote this, one of his most interesting books, in what he calls "the torture of grief." He insists that, "If there is a good God, then these tortures are necessary. For no even moderately good being could possibly inflict or permit them if they weren't."[22] The effect of this realization is to make it clear to him that belief in God's love does nothing to remove the need to fear God. Lewis is caustic about many of the clichés that accompany death, including the idea that the dead are at rest or even that they are in God's hands. He points out that his wife was "in God's hands all the time, and I have seen what they did to her."[23] Lewis goes on:

> Do they (God's hands) suddenly become gentler to us the moment we are out of the body? And if so, why? If God's goodness is inconsistent with hurting us, then either God is not good or there is no God; for in the only life we know He hurts us beyond our worst fears and beyond all we can imagine. If it is consistent with hurting us, then He may hurt us after death as unendurably as before it.[24]

If God is to "hurt us" after death, to use Lewis's words, this should not be thought of in literal terms of devils with pitchforks but in terms of the unendurable self-knowledge that comes when pretense is shaved away. That is why hypocrisy and the need to tear it down are such a crucial part of Christian teaching.

---

21. Küng, *Eternal Life*, 139.
22. Lewis, *Grief Observed*, 38.
23. Lewis, *Grief Observed*, 25.
24. Lewis, *Grief Observed*, 25.

Self-Deception and Wickedness

Any reading of the New Testament is likely to come to the conclusion that Jesus campaigns relentlessly against hypocrisy. So many of the images that we have taken from the story of his life and death have entered into the cultural and literary traditions of Christian civilization. Though one can never make sense of the New Testament simply as a record of moral teaching, it is the moral teaching that remains embedded even in our modern secular culture.

It is embedded not as a list of rules or precepts so much as in the literary characterizations of the New Testament itself, read as a powerful piece of drama. On the one hand there are the minor characters referred to in passing, as in the story of the publican and the Pharisee. Both go to the synagogue to pray; the Pharisee declares himself glad that he is not a sinner like the publican; the publican confesses his sins. Jesus asks: Who goes away forgiven? (Luke 18:9–14). This short parable suggests that self-deception lies at the heart of our sin. We do not want to admit what we are.

But the theme of self-deception is also played out with the main characters. The Pharisees and the lawyers taken as a group are condemned time and again for their hypocrisy. "Alas for you, lawyers and Pharisees, hypocrites" is the leitmotif of Matt 23 (see vv. 13, 15, 23, 25, 27, and 29). It is the imagery that has lived on in our tradition—such as the painted sepulcher ("You are like tombs covered with whitewash; they look well from outside, but inside they are full of dead men's bones and all kinds of filth. So it is with you: outside you look like honest men, but inside you are brim-full of hypocrisy and crime" [Matt 23:27–8]).

Self-deception marks the climax to the Christian story also. Judas denies that he will betray Christ, as one by one each of the Twelve dips into the same bowl—"and one by one they said to him, 'Not I, surely?'"(Mark 14:19); Pilate denies that the matter involves him ("My hands are clean of this man's blood" [Matt 27:25]); Peter denies that he was a disciple following Jesus's arrest (Matt 24:73–75); even those who crucify him deceive themselves— "Father, forgive them, for they know not what they do" (Luke 23:34). This is the pattern for wickedness throughout history, where those who cause harm do not on the whole consciously commit to evil in the manner of Milton's Satan—"Evil, be thou my Good"[25]—but convince themselves that the evil they are doing *is* in fact good. They fall into hypocrisy, the so-called tribute vice pays to virtue. Only when their true nature can no longer be hidden from them do they change—and suffer. Peter breaks down in tears; Judas, he of whom "it would be better had he not been born," cannot face the reality

---

25. Milton, *Paradise Lost*, 4:110.

of his sin. He hangs himself (Matt 27:5). In hell, of course, there would be no opportunity for suicide. The burden of past sin, without the possibility of self-deception that everybody takes advantage of in this life, would be inescapable.

In her book *Wickedness* the philosopher Mary Midgley quotes Erich Fromm, explaining part of his motivation for writing *The Anatomy of Destructiveness*. Fromm wanted to show, he said, that "as long as one believes that the evil man wears horns, one will not discover an evil man."[26] People fail to recognize potential Hitlers because they expect them to "look the part." In reality they come in a disguise that is as much keeping the truth from themselves as from others. They do not have the relative honesty of an Ernst Röhm, saying that "since I am an immature and bad man, war appeals to me more than peace."[27] They proclaim their innocence and good intent—to themselves and to the world. Midgley agrees in general (clearly it is not always the case) with Aristotle that "vice is unconscious of itself; weakness is not."[28]

The notion of a last judgment implies some kind of assessment of a human being's behavior after their death. The closest parallel to such a general assessment in human history is probably a war crimes trial. Ordinary trials do attempt to assess human responsibility and determine guilt or innocence where a particular crime is concerned, but the wider setting of crimes against humanity allows for a more general examination of an individual's responsibility for a slice of history. Where such earthly tribunals take place, as at Nuremberg, there is evidence neither of defiance nor of repentance. What struck writers like Hannah Arendt was that those arraigned at Nuremberg neither tried to declare that their ideology was right and that of their captors wrong, nor admitted their crimes and apologized. They betrayed and blamed each other, or they tried to insist that they'd always been against what was happening, or, as in the case of Eichmann, they claimed that they never realized what they were doing. This last is Arendt's description, where she claims that Eichmann is one of those who willfully neglects to think through the consequences of their own actions. She concludes that in Eichmann's case "it was sheer thoughtlessness—something by no means identical with stupidity—that predisposed him to become one of the greatest criminals of that period."[29] As Midgley points out, modern technology makes this form of evil easier, since it enables people—politicians

---

26. Midgley, *Wickedness*, 5.
27. Heiden, *Fuehrer*, 30.
28. Midgley, *Wickedness*, 65.
29. Arendt, *Eichmann in Jerusalem*, 289.

in particular—to distract themselves from what they are actually doing, as in the idea that by using "smart bombs" or pilotless drones one can avoid civilian casualties.[30]

The evidence of such trials would seem to suggest that they do not lead many people to come to terms with what they have done, though they might allow others, most notably the victims or those that are left of them, to come to terms with what happened. Such a process would require human beings to stop deceiving themselves—and this is very hard for them to do. Midgley returns to this theme later in her book, when she quotes Bishop Butler wishing that people who would be wicked showed the "common vicious passions" rather than a "deep and calm source of delusion, which undermines the whole principle of good."[31] The experience of human trials (whatever the problems and even injustices of "victor's justice") would seem to be that they do little to bring people to enter into themselves and acknowledge what they have done.

Midgley examines various examples of "evil" in literature, such as Milton's Satan, Shakespeare's Iago, and Stevenson's Hyde. Of all the failings she identifies—pride, vanity, selfishness—it is vanity, she suggests, that most obscures from us the true nature of ourselves—the vanity of the Pharisee in the synagogue with the publican, of the politician seeking to dictate his legacy, or the churchman eyeing his sainthood to come. Though the miserable creatures who ended up at Nuremberg might seem to have had very little room for vanity, it was still there in the way that they continued to obscure from themselves, at whatever cost, the truth of what they had been doing.

In this life we can convince ourselves that our evil deeds are, in fact, good. We can become unaware, whether by design or neglect, that what we are doing is wrong—indeed, we can persuade ourselves that it is right. The bad guys very rarely admit to being bad—indeed, we tend to have a sneaking respect, perhaps rightly so, for the ones who are self-confessed villains. In the life to come there is no pretense, for this is when we know as we are known. If that were an easy thing for us we would not bother with hypocrisy. But it is not easy. Right up to the last moment of our lives, we go on making of ourselves what we are not and deceiving ourselves concerning what we are. If we put so much effort into doing so, it is clear that any direct unravelling of what we truly are will feel unbearably harsh. This is surely—if no more—a clue as to the nature of hell.

---

30. Midgley discusses Eichmann as seen by Arendt in a section of her book called "The Paradox of Responsible Negligence." See Midgley, *Wickedness*, 64–66.

31. Butler, *Fifteen Sermons*, 113; quoted in Midgley, *Wickedness*, 118.

Kenoticism and the Limitation of Divine Power

Kenoticism is centered around the idea of a divine self-emptying in the act of creating and becoming reconciled to the world. What is not always made clear is that this self-emptying, as a self-imposed limitation on God's powers, may apply not only to God's knowledge of the future or ability to change it but also to God's ability to guarantee the salvation of all of us. In other words, the self-limitation of divine power entailed by kenoticism may extend to a voluntary renunciation of the very universalism that some theologians see as somehow demanded by the nature of God as both all-powerful and all-forgiving. This is the often misunderstood hard side of the kenotic imperative. It is as if God is not only giving up the power to know the earthly future of God's creation or the people that are part of it but is also giving up the power to sweep them into eternal bliss after their earthly lives are over.

The argument against universalism is sometimes expressed by saying that hell is a mark of the respect God has for God's creatures, refusing to force any of them into heaven against their will. This is not quite right, because it might suggest that human beings are confronted by an attractive prospect that out of masochistic perversity they refuse to embrace. It is more subtle than that. What human beings are confronted with is themselves and what they have made of themselves. The question is whether they can bear to acknowledge what they plainly see before them. The kenotic imperative that expresses God's voluntary self-renunciation includes the fact that God gives us a power of self-determination that may mean we are unable to survive God's love.

In *The Person and Place of Jesus Christ*, P. T. Forsyth wrote of how "the lay mind becomes only too ready to interpret sin in a softer light than God's and to see it only under the pity of a Lord to whom judgement is quite a strange work and who forgives all because he knows all."[32] One can put aside the reference to the "lay mind," perhaps, and concentrate upon the "softer light." It is not that God proves a harsh judge where one might prefer a softer one. It is rather that we like to be assured, unconsciously if not overtly, that because God is merciful only an exercise of pity is really conceivable. But the point is not that God would not want to forgive. It is that God may be *unable* to forgive, that the same voluntary renunciation of power that applied to creating us also applies to our redemption. Recourse to the idea that God forgives all because God knows all will not do and is another illustration of the false comfort that comes from assuring ourselves that, after all, God is

---

32. Forsyth, *Person and Place*, 13.

all-powerful and God's omnipotence will therefore, sooner or later, come to our rescue. Chapter 8 suggested that we are dealing with a God who has chosen not to know, but this may apply to more than the self-limitation implicit in being unable to know the future. There may be a self-limitation that goes beyond God's not knowing what choices people will make tomorrow. The hard side of kenoticism reveals itself not in what God is unable to know but in what God is unable to do. As Jesus puts it at the end of the Sermon on the Mount, the irreconcilable sinner faces not the sentence pronounced by a judge but a simple statement of unavoidable fact that God has voluntarily declared Godself unable to alter: "I never knew you" (Matt 7:23).

Conclusion

The conclusion is that there is no need to be complacent about the fact that all we will encounter in the afterlife is God's love.

This chapter tried to examine the apparent paradox that affirming hell associates God with a barbarism not even most human societies would inflict on those they disapprove of, while denying hell seems to belittle the reality of human wickedness. God lacks either mercy or seriousness.

Such dilemmas require us to consider precisely what hell is meant to be and what the pain of hell consists of. Despite the powerful nature of his arguments, Hume does not think this through. Nor does the bland dismissal by Hick of what he takes to be Victorian beliefs about endless physical agony do any better. This is not the point of hell. The point of judgment in the afterlife is to confront us inescapably with ourselves—and this will be painful for everybody. We will experience the wrath of God as a part of experiencing God's searing love for us—it is this that the doctrine of purgatory brings out, rather than offering a "grey alternative" to heaven and hell.

Purgatory is not an antechamber to heaven that we pass through during an interval of earthly time between death and bodily resurrection. It is a description of the searing nature of the encounter of meeting God. It is the other side of the beatific vision, where it is said that we will have the supreme enjoyment of seeing God and be absorbed in the love that, in Dante's words, moves the sun and the other stars. The emphasis is upon an opening up of our understanding to God's presence in all that is around us, a lifting of the veil. However, this experience is one that also removes all our defenses. It is a closeness to God that may prove unbearable. When the soul tells the angel in *The Dream of Gerontius* that he would like "one sight" of God to strengthen him in purgatory, the angel responds:

> One moment; but thou knowest not, my child,

What thou dost ask: that sight of the Most Fair
Will gladden thee, but it will pierce thee too.[33]

Confronted with so much love, we may be torn to pieces. The poet T. S. Eliot's idea that "humankind cannot bear very much reality" is as applicable to its relation with God as to its relation with the world.[34]

Erich Fromm is famous for his argument in *The Fear of Freedom* that (among other things) we have to learn to accept responsibility and autonomy, rather than relish the comfort of submitting ourselves to dictators. It may be that the dictator God is the last dictator that we will be willing to give up. The dictator God takes no notice of what we want. This God knows we are sinners, knows we have no good in us, so stuffs us full of grace and hauls us up to heaven where we will serve God's needs forever. The God of love, on the other hand, invites and does not compel, and no invitation makes sense without a possibility of refusal. As David Brown puts it, discussing Vanstone's *Love's Endeavour, Love's Expense*, "There will be no avoidance of the hurts that inevitably come in love's train when the other's flourishing fails to be realised."[35]

What a hard God to live with this truly is! We prefer to bend our knees before a patriarchal God who can do anything; we find ourselves with a God who has voluntarily limited God's power. And that is a much, much more dangerous option, not the God who chooses to say no but the God who cannot say yes. Is this one reason why some theologians fail to take a kenotic theology seriously?

---

33. Newman, *Dream of Gerontius*, 34.
34. See quartet 1, "Burnt Norton," in Eliot, *Four Quartets*.
35. D. Brown, *Divine Humanity*, 166.

Chapter 10

The Strange Doctrine of the Fall

The first chapter in this part of the book argued that though God is traditionally described as omnipotent, an omnipotence of love may choose weakness for itself. Similarly, the omniscient God may choose not to know, accepting that this is an inevitable part of creating human beings. God cannot give us freedom without limiting God's own power, even to the extent of being unable to predict the outcome of what God did on the sixth day of creation.

In the last chapter I suggested that the self-imposed divine weakness asserted by a kenotic theology opened up the possibility that God would be unable rather than unwilling to save everyone. The possibility of a tragic outcome to human lives cannot be ruled out—even by the presumption of an all-powerful God. A kenotic approach introduces the possibility of ultimate failure into human life as it does into the life of God. I believe that this was a central theme of MacKinnon's writings.[1]

The doctrine of the fall takes this possibility of failure further and understands it in terms of the impossibility of empowering human beings without risking disaster. It is perhaps the burden of this risk that helps us to understand what is in some ways a strange doctrine, which has puzzled theologians, but which might be looked at differently in the light of what has been said about a kenotic approach.

---

1. See, for example, the chapters "The Transcendence of the Tragic" and "Ethics and Tragedy," in MacKinnon, *Problem of Metaphysics*.

Back to the Fall—A Reinterpretation

The doctrine of the fall traditionally suggests an ejection of human beings from the divine world (the garden in which God once walked [Gen 3:8]) as a punishment, sending them to a world of sin and death in which they live out their banishment. But that interpretation is not the only one that has been given. Instead, this always-difficult doctrine has been reworked by some theologians. For them the world has become not a place of punishment but a testing ground for human beings, effectively their space, while any banishment becomes effectively our banishment of God rather than God's banishment of us.

The banishment of Adam and Eve becomes less a punishment (for the sin of eating the apple) than something akin to the expulsion from the parental home of adolescents who need to take responsibility and get a life on their own. This interpretation was written up at the end of the 1960s by a theologian called John Hick in a book called *Evil and the God of Love*.

Hick identified two different traditions in Christianity in relation to the doctrine of the fall, which he labelled "Augustinian" and "Irenaean," since he saw the two approaches as reflecting the differing opinions of two early church writers, Irenaeus and Augustine.[2] Augustine, he suggested, presented what is undoubtedly the more familiar tradition, one in which the first human beings lose the perfection of paradise as a punishment for their disobedience, and later generations are forced to participate in that loss. Irenaeus, on the other hand, is seen by Hick as presenting a less well-known tradition, one according to which God is the reformer or educator of humanity rather than its punisher. In his *Against Heresies* Irenaeus points out that without the knowledge of good and evil (which Adam and Eve acquire precisely by eating the fruit of the tree they are forbidden to taste), we could never really have a proper understanding of the good. The section entitled "Why Man Was Not Made Perfect from the Beginning" has a very clear answer to the question of why human beings could not be made flawless from the start:

> For as it certainly is in the power of a mother to give strong food to her infant [but she does not do so], as the child is not yet able to receive more substantial nourishment; so also it was possible for God Himself to have made man perfect from the first, but man could not receive this [perfection], being as yet an infant.[3]

---

2. See Hick, *Evil and the God*. First published in 1966, Hick's work has been republished many times (recently by Palgrave Macmillan in 2010). Part 2 examined what he calls the "Augustinian" type of theodicy, and part 3, the "Irenaean" type.

3. Irenaeus, *Against Heresies* 4.38, 521.

Once it is understood that perfection is something that must be learned rather than given in one fell swoop, it becomes possible to argue that the whole process of fall and redemption is really an educative one. Human beings are expelled from paradise in order to learn the perfection that cannot simply be imposed upon them. In a phrase Hick was to use often, there has to be an "epistemic distance" between God and human beings if the latter are truly to understand the difference between good and evil.

Hick's approach had been anticipated a decade earlier in the writings of Paul Tillich, the second volume of whose *Systematic Theology* (first published in 1957) dealt with the interpretation of the fall. Adam before the fall, wrote Tillich, represented the "dreaming innocence of undecided potentialities." This state is lost when human beings actualize their "finite freedom," becoming aware of their finitude and knowing the fear that it produces (anxiety in the face of death). "Human beings decide for self-actualisation, thus producing the end of dreaming innocence," writes Tillich.[4] Expulsion from Eden becomes effectively a wake-up call to life.

The Paradox of the Fall

The Bible begins with the book of Genesis, in which God declares that God will make men and women "in God's image and likeness" (Gen 1:26). When the serpent tempts Eve to eat the apple from the forbidden tree in Gen 3:5, it tells her, "Your eyes will be opened and you will become like God, knowing good and evil." It is an assessment that God agrees with when banishing Adam and Eve from the garden of Eden, declaring that if they were not expelled, they might also eat from the tree of life and live forever:

> See, the man has become like one of us, knowing good and evil; and now, he might reach out his hand and take also from the tree of life, and eat, and live forever. (Gen 3:22)

Of course, the story is one with a hundred different interpretations. Genesis has been put together not as a single narrative but as a number of different texts going through endless redactions. However, many readings of the biblical text have broadly followed Hick's position. One might cite Lynn Bechtel, whose reading of the text is expressed in the following way:

> Adolescent maturation (3:1–19). The serpent acts as catalyst for the next stage of maturation. . . . The serpent becomes, then, a symbol of material adult potential for discernment, for "street wisdom" required for survival. It is "wiser" than all the other

---

4. Tillich, *Systematic Theology*, 2:34.

creatures. Thus, the snake of discernment is associated with the tree of discernment.[5]

It is clear that this reading of the garden of Eden story rescues Eve's status from one of temptress to the mature half of the first human pair:

> The woman is the one who interacts with the snake perhaps because physiologically women mature earlier than men or perhaps because both the snake and women are associated with life renewal and wisdom. . . . The serpent invites her to eat knowing the potential for adult awareness. From her childish point of view, she can see only the potential (3:6o) not the limitation, which will be the "death" of childhood not immediate physical death. Like an adolescent she sees only the good.[6]

The wise serpent therefore contacts Eve as the one with a better understanding of what maturity means, even though she is as much an adolescent as Adam is and both need to move toward maturity:

> In eating the fruit, the man and woman become self-conscious for the first time (their eyes were opened: 3:7). The world does not change, only their perspective. They begin to see the world as it truly is.[7]

When they've eaten from the tree, they feel shame and try to hide. But Bechtel refers to this shame as "a positive and necessary value in group-oriented cultures."[8] Rather than representing a breakdown of their original relationship with God and with each other in a state of innocence, it shows that "they are becoming mature members of the community."[9] Their "shamed hiding" alerts God to the fact that something has changed because it is not the act of a child but of someone beginning to grow up. God therefore registers that they are ready for the next step in their education:

> The act of disobedience does not destroy their relationship to God; it is only now that they begin to engage in full conversation with God. Not yet fully mature, they prove unable to accept responsibility for what they have done and seek to blame each other and the serpent. They have only begun the process, and God takes the lead in the next step by orienting them to the realities of human life. What the "sin and fall" model calls "curses"

5. Kille, *Psychological Biblical Criticism*, 116. Bechtel's article, "Rethinking the Interpretation," was originally published in Brenner-Idan, *Feminist Companion to Genesis*.

6. Kille, *Psychological Biblical Criticism*, 117–18.

7. Kille, *Psychological Biblical Criticism*, 118.

8. Kille, *Psychological Biblical Criticism*, 118. See also Bechtel, "Genesis 2:4b—3:24."

9. Kille, *Psychological Biblical Criticism*, 118.

> or "punishments," Bechtel contends, are simply descriptions of the tensions of potential and limitation inherent in real life. Previously sheltered from the oppositions of the outside world in the safety of the garden, the man and woman now must learn about conflict and ambiguity.[10]

In a very different context to that in which Hick wrote, this interpretation comes to a strikingly similar conclusion. The fall becomes the condition of the progress toward which men and women are now able to make their way. The woman ceases to be a temptress and becomes the more mature of the original pair, able to discern that eating the apple is the only way in which human beings can move forward.

The result is a broad theological position according to which human beings learn to be in control of their lives while God applauds from a distance. We are being encouraged to reach the maturity that God has always intended for us, rather than receiving the punishment God reluctantly has to administer.

It is a powerful idea—one that could reinforce the idea of a God who ruled out any intervention in the affairs of humanity. How far could this approach be tied in with the kenotic theology that this book is intended to advocate? Could one argue that God's love meant giving us room to breathe and develop, while ideas of a fall or of original sin were really variations on this theme of enabling us to progress and develop in our understanding of God through an "epistemic distance" (that favorite phrase of John Hick's) between ourselves and our maker, whose voluntary self-limitation was the other side of our own power as human beings? Is this not the perfect example of that self-emptying that is at the heart of a kenotic approach? God ceases to be the sort of intrusive father who constantly tries to meddle in the lives of his offspring. Or (as some feminist theology argued) God is an enabling mother rather than a compelling father.

And yet, simply taken as a story, a story that most people, whatever their religious leanings, are still fairly familiar with, it is interesting how the narrative appears to have a very different message. It chooses to present the knowledge of good and evil not as God's final gift to the crown of God's creation, made on the last day before God rested, but as something seized hold of under the unfortunate influence of others (the serpent is described as "cunning" in many English translations, but the original Hebrew has a more positive or at least neutral meaning that could be translated as "clever"—though perhaps this serpent was too clever by half). When God's creatures have this knowledge, God can no longer stay with them—after all, God discovers what has happened while walking in the garden (where they cower before God in shame) and proceeds to expel them from it, barring the

---

10. Kille, *Psychological Biblical Criticism*, 118.

gate by means of the angel with the flaming sword. Autonomy—that great prize of the Enlightenment, which is so often prized above all else—comes at the price of separation, setting creature and Creator apart. And death arrives to mark that separation, fixing clear limits upon humanity's newfound autonomy. Autonomy, however desirable, is a partial and temporary characteristic of human beings, each of them destined to see it disappear when they die.

Human beings have got what they wanted, or what they thought they wanted, but its immediate consequence, paradoxically enough, is an end to the autonomy they might have had through never dying. Immortality is taken away from them in order to let them have their freedom. *Leben zum Tod* (a phrase of Heidegger's that might be rendered "living under the shadow of death") is the condition under which they must exist with what they have grabbed for themselves.

Thus, we get our autonomy only under conditions where we are bound to lose it. Existentialist writers as different from each other as Sartre and Heidegger have recognized this. Though we might live as beings who are uniquely aware of the fact that every day brings us closer to death, the anxiety or *angst* that awareness of our mortality produces is the only context within which we can hope to realize our freedom and assert ourselves. God has made our finitude the condition under which we exercise the power we have taken upon ourselves in knowing good and evil. Whoever and wherever we are, we know that there's no way out of this world alive.

In this sense, we might feel that the biblical narrative is close to the story of the *tikkun*. This story, told by Luria, the Jewish rabbi who developed the school of Kabbalah in the sixteenth century, is known as *Tikkun ha-Olam*, meaning "repair of the world." It refers to a process by which God contracted the divine self to create space for creation. In the process, divine light became contained in special vessels, some of which were unable to sustain the pressure and shattered. As a result, the light was scattered, and though most of it returned to its divine source some light remained attached to broken shards of the vessels and became the basis for the material world.[11]

What both the biblical narrative and the story of the *tikkun* share is a warning against easy assumptions that God moved to the crowning achievement that was God's purpose all along—the formation of that destructive little biped known as a human being. Both of them suggest instead that creating humans did damage to the divine unity, whether conceived of in terms of the unsustainable self-contraction in the *tikkun* or the rebellion by one-third of the heavenly host in Milton's dramatic representation in

---

11. Brouwer compares the Lord's "holy humility" to "the Jewish kabbalistic conviction of divine limitation, in which YHWH makes room for his creatures to be and to act of their own accord." See Nimmo and Johnson, *Kenosis*, 68.

Paradise Lost of a fall from heaven that preceded that on earth. God did not come into being in order to be able to make humans. Humans appeared if anything as a troublesome by-product of other conflicts.

Christianity has been willing to accept this by risking the illogicality of saying that God punished human beings for doing what one might reasonably have supposed to have been God's purpose all along. The result is that the knowledge of good and evil in human hands is not presented as part of their opportunity to move up the Hickian ladder to the secondary level of their education and understand something of what it means for God to be God. Instead, it is presented as something stolen, something dangerous and destructive. If it is somehow to be turned into something good, that must be only through a painful process that cannot be seen as part of God's original plan. Even human beings themselves recognize that it may be more than they can bear. Franz Rosenzweig points out in *The Star of Redemption* that both Jews and Christians pray: "Lead us not into temptation" (for Christians it is part of the Lord's Prayer). It recalls the temptation in the garden of Eden, and Rosenzweig remarks:

> He himself is now supposed to be the one whom one believes capable of permitting himself the "outrageous" game of tempting his child and creature.[12]

Rosenzweig suggests that "lead us not into temptation" implies that the temptation comes from God. But since God is determined not to redeem human beings "without them," it is necessary that they should have the freedom that enables them to be victims of temptation. God did not will that human beings took the powers they stole in the garden. But once they have those powers, God will not redeem them without their being able to continue with those powers, even if they lead to destruction. In this sense God must continue to tempt human beings:

> Not only must he hide his sway from man: he must deceive him about it. He must make it difficult, nay impossible for man to see it, so that the latter have the possibility of believing him and trusting him in truth, that is to say in freedom.[13]

The essence of a kenotic theology is that through a freely chosen weakness ("self-emptying") God makes room for human beings to develop their potential. But the interpretation of this made by Hick was hardly convincing. The image of the divine parent who gives her children freedom and does not interfere with them contains problems of its own. What parent

---

12. Rosenzweig, *Star of Redemption*, 265.
13. Rosenzweig, *Star of Redemption*, 266.

would fail to interfere if their child was in danger? And yet, to recall Flew's powerful imagery in part 1, God apparently allows many of her children to die gruesome deaths, some at the hands of other people and some a result of disease or misfortune. It's all very well to advance this idea of God the noninvasive parent, but there are times when noninvasive parents are rightly taken to task for neglect. Once we get carried away by the idea of God looking on but respecting us too much to interfere, we find ourselves thinking of instances when God is more likely to be accused of callous indifference than respectful behavior.

In Rosenzweig's presentation, God hides from human beings in order to provide them with the space in which to respond freely. This is not the positive journey to the schoolroom imagined by Hick. It is bound to have tragic and painful consequences—so painful that it isn't even possible to say that God willed them. All one can say is that God wills that the dangerous power that human beings have stolen cannot now be relinquished if humans wish to return to the garden. There is no happy departure of two adolescents to the adventure of their first day in school. There is an angel with a flaming sword who sends the disobedient couple away into exile.

The paradox implicit in the story of the fall provides a revealing, if to some degree curious, commentary upon how we might understand our origins in ethical terms. On the one hand we cannot really say that the knowledge of good and evil is not something we want. We may try to argue that if ignorance is bliss it is folly to be wise, and certainly there would be the bliss of immortality without such wisdom, but still we tend to welcome the fact that we have the degree of autonomy that we do have through such knowledge. Yet on the other hand, driven out of paradise against our will, we are supposed to regret what we also desire, and the book of Genesis suggests that we are made to know the cost of it (the serpent on its belly, the woman in the pains of childbirth, the endless toil of hard labor). We want it and yet we are made to pay so much for it that we believe we have been punished for having it. And we might even suggest a division internal to God in the very act of accepting the process of development marked by creation and fall. When Milton's *Paradise Lost* suggests that Lucifer, a fallen angel, takes a third of the angelic host to be Lucifer's followers, it is not difficult to imagine a defeated minority who opposed the dangerous self-abnegation implicit in the assertion of divine love, allowing a potentially destructive freedom to prevail through human knowledge of good and evil. And given the parlous state of the world today, it is easy to sympathize with the defeated minority who recognized that the experience of human freedom might never provide a stepping stone toward an eschatological resolution of an "all's well that ends well" kind.

Milton and Nietzsche—
Humans Are Not the Center of the Universe

The story of the fall undermines the idea that, with humanity as the crowning point of creation, God's real point in creating was to make us. This assumption envisages a universe made for human beings, a school to educate them and make them upstanding citizens of heaven. The traditional idea of a universe made not for our sake but for God's, in which human beings emerged and stole what was not intended for them, is a further reminder not to assume that the whole created order was made simply in order to please us or to enable us to improve ourselves.

As pointed out earlier, Christian tradition has often represented a war in heaven preceding creation, as if the divine plan was subject to intense debate before it was finally carried into being against the will of those angels who dissented and became themselves fallen. Having taken *Evil and the God of Love* as an example of what Hick interpreted as the "Irenaean" tradition of the fall, we can look at John Milton's *Paradise Lost* as an example of the "Augustinian" approach. In *Paradise Lost*, Satan "the false dissembler" asserts (book 3) that humans are the result of an earlier act of rebellion (one which he led) by part of the heavenly host. Satan now determines to engineer another act of rebellion, this time a rebellion by human beings:

> One fatal tree there stands, of Knowledge called,
> Forbidden them to taste. Knowledge forbidden?
> Suspicious, reasonless. Why should their Lord
> Envy them that? Can it be sin to know?
> Can it be death? And do they only stand
> By ignorance? Is that their happy state,
> The proof of their obedience and their faith?[14]

Satan's argument is a powerful one. The great Enlightenment injunction *sapere aude*—dare to know—the motto enshrined in Immanuel Kant's famous essay of 1784, "What Is Enlightenment?," would seem to be at one with Satan's observations in the garden of Eden. Satan declares that he "will excite their minds with more desire to know," and one might well sympathize with him, feeling that the Enlightenment (though only the first stirrings were apparent when Milton wrote, and Kant's famous essay was still more than a century away) lifted us free of a blind obedience to tradition. Did not God intend us to become mature and exercise free will? Or did God perhaps, as Satan suggests, view human beings as dangerous rivals and deliberately keep from them the powers that would enable them to become divine themselves? By tempting Adam and Eve in the garden, Satan was

14. Milton, *Paradise Lost*, 4:514–20.

simply encouraging them to "reject envious commands, invented with design to keep them low, whom knowledge might exalt equal with gods."[15] The same argument comes to Eve in a dream, and she confesses to Adam that it has an effect on her:

> O fruit divine,
> Sweet of thyself, but much more sweet thus cropped,
> Forbidden here, it seems, as only fit
> For gods, yet able to make gods of men!
> And why not gods of men, since good, the more
> Communicated, more abundant grows,
> The author not impaired, but honoured more?[16]

The more power that human beings acquire, the dream seems to say, the more honor they will be able to give their Creator. The same argument is repeated later by Adam as he seeks to know from Raphael the secrets of God's "eternal empire," daring to ask because it will enable him and his partner in Eden "the more to magnify his works the more we know."[17]

A win-win situation. Everyone benefits. It is a powerful argument, which presents Satan as the one who has come to release human beings from an infantilism that surely cannot really be divinely willed since it can only be a means by which God receives even more acknowledgment than God has already received. Can we really be persuaded by Raphael's argument to Adam that the divine Architect's secrets should not "be scanned by them who ought rather admire"?[18] Adam's submission to Raphael is beautifully expressed but unlikely to be very persuasive:

> How fully hast thou satisfied me, pure
> Intelligence of Heaven, Angel serene,
> And, freed from intricacies, taught to live
> The easiest way, nor with perplexing thoughts
> To interrupt the sweet of life, from which
> God hath bid dwell far off all anxious cares,
> And not molest us, unless we ourselves
> Seek them with wandering thoughts and notions vain![19]

It sounds like a recipe for intellectual repression. When Satan having entered the serpent comes to tempt Eve, he explains how eating from the

---

15. Milton, *Paradise Lost*, 4:522–24.
16. Milton, *Paradise Lost*, 5:67–73.
17. Milton, *Paradise Lost*, 7:97.
18. Milton, *Paradise Lost*, 8:74–75.
19. Milton, *Paradise Lost*, 8:180–87.

tree gave him powers he'd never had before, a "strange alteration"[20] that provided him with powers of reason and speech:

> Thenceforth to speculations high or deep
> I turned my thoughts, and with capacious mind
> Considered all things visible in Heaven.[21]

Surely "capacious minds" is precisely what those who enroll in Hick's training program in the School of Banishment are encouraged to develop! The knowledge of good and evil is simply a part of their moral training. What people are capable of understanding, they are capable of resisting, if it is something bad. "If what is evil be real, why not known, since easier shunned?"[22]

But in Milton's epic poem the outcome of eating from the tree of knowledge is a disaster. It is a losing rather than a gaining. New powers flood through the first humans, taking them over and destroying their judgment:

> As with new wine intoxicated both,
> They swim in mirth, and fancy that they feel
> Divinity within them breeding wings
> Wherewith to scorn the Earth.[23]

They have wrested hold of something they cannot manage. By acquiring divine powers, they use them not to honor their Creator more fully but in order to "scorn the Earth," as fair a description of the twenty-first century as it prepares to burn us up with uncontrolled emissions as of the seventeenth. Rather than moving closer to God with their new powers, Milton describes Adam and Eve as moving further away. Adam declares:

> How shall I behold the face
> Henceforth of God or Angel, erst with joy
> And rapture so oft beheld? Those heavenly shapes
> Will dazzle now this earthly with their blaze
> Insufferably bright.[24]

It is not just that Adam and Eve hide from each other, wearing clothes; they have to hide themselves from God. It is not that they have been punished for trying to achieve a higher degree of knowledge; they have acquired powers that they are unable to deal with. They cover themselves in shame, their shortcomings exposed before each other and before God.

20. Milton, *Paradise Lost*, 9:599.
21. Milton, *Paradise Lost*, 9:602–4.
22. Milton, *Paradise Lost*, 9:699.
23. Milton, *Paradise Lost*, 9:1008–11.
24. Milton, *Paradise Lost*, 9:1080–84.

Milton's presentation of the fall is far subtler than a kind of prototypical illustration of the consequences of not listening to one's superiors. It should not be taken as an example of what happens when human beings do not show blind obedience. The myth suggests more that human beings have bitten off more than they can chew than that they have dared to take a bite when forbidden to do so. The traditional understanding of the fall in terms of punishment rather than education is true to the extent that this is a punishment that human beings feel in the humiliation of acquiring powers that they cannot handle. Adam declares himself "unable to perform thy terms too hard."[25]

I would argue that this interpretation makes more sense when we bear in mind that we are not the reason for the existence of the universe. If we were, then Satan's argument might make sense. You are right to grasp something that will elevate you even higher and enable you to worship your Creator even more effectively. But God was not in need of human company in the way that Adam was in need of company in the garden of Eden. Adam himself makes this point to Eve in *Paradise Lost*:

> Nor think, though men were none,
> That Heaven would want spectators, God want praise.
> Millions of spiritual creatures walk the Earth
> Unseen, both when we wake and when we sleep;
> All these with ceaseless praise his works behold
> Both day and night.[26]

God has angels to sing God's praise. There is no need to insist that only human beings can satisfy God's needs. God did not make the universe in order to raise human beings and bring them to the divine status where God could enjoy an end to the divine solitude. The introduction of angels, whatever the theological difficulties in such an idea (and it is a good rule in doing theology to assume that the most apparently implausible doctrines are the most revealing), at least helps to overcome the view that this universe has no other purpose than to serve our own needs and that there are no other beings of significance apart from ourselves.

Human beings are not necessary to the self-realization of God as God. It is easier from this perspective to understand the idea of their being overwhelmed by things they cannot manage rather than guided toward ever greater mastery. But this is an interpretation that they are unwilling to subscribe to—one that depreciates their role and suggests the humiliation of their ancestors in the garden.

25. Milton, *Paradise Lost*, 10:750–51.
26. Milton, *Paradise Lost*, 4:675–80.

Nietzsche saw how unwilling human beings were to come to terms with the idea that God had not made the universe simply for their sake. From the time of Copernicus, it had been recognized that the planets did not orbit around the Earth like courtiers paying homage. Instead, the Earth was one of the courtiers paying homage to the sun, itself a monarch in only one kingdom, while spread out across the galaxy were hundreds or thousands of other kingdoms (a figure that has since been revised incessantly upward). The Earth became one of several satellites orbiting a sun that was located in a remote outpost of the universe. As Nietzsche put it in *The Will to Power*, "Since Copernicus man has been rolling from the center into x."[27] And at somewhat greater length Nietzsche comments in the third essay in *Toward a Genealogy of Morals*:

> Since Copernicus man seems to have got himself on an inclined plane—now he is slipping faster and faster away from the centre into what? Into nothingness? Into a penetrating sense of his nothingness . . . all science, natural as well as unnatural—which is what I call the self-critique of knowledge—has at present the object of dissuading man from his former respect for himself, as if this had been but a piece of bizarre conceit.[28]

Rather than being placed deliberately at the center, human beings feel themselves to be in the middle of nowhere, uprooted and homeless. There was this sense with Monod, too, but in his case it was as if human beings had found themselves in a world that didn't suit them. In Nietzsche's case it is not as if human beings are in an environment so alien to them that it is as if they landed there by mistake, the outcome of some bungling by what Dawkins calls "the blind watchmaker." It is rather that the environment is entirely appropriate to them, as an insignificant drop in the ocean. They are victims of cosmic indifference rather than the result of a divine error. In Monod there is a sense of the duchess throwing open the penthouse suite in the five-star hotel and exclaiming as she sees a room no bigger than a cupboard: "There must be some mistake." For Nietzsche it is more the "penetrating sense of [their] nothingness" that people have never learned to live with.

Nietzsche's point was that people could not accept the idea that, wherever they were placed in the physical universe, they were not the point of its creation, the be-all and end-all of its making. Even if people could understand that they were not at the center of the universe (if it made any sense to talk of a physical center), they wanted to see themselves as the *point* of the universe. They still liked to see themselves as the top of the evolutionary

---

27. Nietzsche, *Will to Power*, 8.
28. Nietzsche, *Genealogy of Morals*, 155.

tree. They were the crowning glory of a development seen in terms of trees and escalators, as if evolution was nothing but a movement upward. Certain bipeds—human beings—become the obvious point at which the escalator completes its ascent. All they need to do is admire the view from the top. They would accept their place in the universe so long as they could be assured that it was made for them. But it was not.

Conclusion

Hick's "Irenaean" interpretation of the fall has its obvious attraction, namely that it avoids having to face the difficult question of how we can make sense of ourselves (let alone Adam and Eve) being punished for some original act of disobedience. The idea of an educative rather than punitive purpose behind the banishment from Eden appears to offer a way around that problem. Similarly, the feminist interpretation outlined in this chapter has the attraction of exonerating Eve, replacing the stereotypical female temptress leading man into bad ways with the mature part of the first couple who had a better understanding of what was needed in order for humanity to grow.

However, the traditional understanding of the fall is crucial in one respect. The story can certainly be read as a suggestion of humanity's need to grow wise like the serpent (one thinks of Jesus's interesting suggestion that his disciples should be wise as serpents as well as innocent as doves [Matt 10:16]), but it also presents the power human beings acquire as something grasped rather than given, something that comes at a cost, that overwhelms and humiliates those who receive it, driving them into hiding from themselves and from their maker, a benefit—if it is a benefit—with an irrevocably tragic side to it.

The problem with the "Irenaean" interpretation is its implicit anthropocentrism. It thinks in terms of the benefit the fall can bring to the human race, as if human beings were somehow the raison d'être of the creative process. The traditional understanding avoids this. This chapter illustrated such an understanding from Milton's *Paradise Lost*, where it is suggested that human beings arise more as a by-product of disturbances in heaven than as the crowning achievement of God's design. Nietzsche undermined the anthropocentric viewpoint in a different way, using the fact that the Earth was not, after all, the center of the universe to suggest that its inhabitants were not as important as they liked to think they were. The disobedience of the first pair, like a fly buzzing around God's head while walking in the garden, leads to a banishment, a swatting, that should not be glorified as admission to the school prepared all along for the realization of the divine purpose.

This is a book intended to support a kenotic theology, and a teaching of God's creatures to live without God (to use a famous saying from Bonhoeffer) is implicit in a kenotic approach of freely willed divine self-limitation. But it is a process attended by much more danger, suffering, and needless pain than the imagery of a school could ever manage to convey. The traditional understanding of the fall conveys the potentially tragic consequences of giving human beings the knowledge of good and evil, the danger of empowering humans and the risk of tragic consequences from doing so, a risk that the biblical text presents in terms of these powers as being stolen rather than adopted by God's command.

We need to match our understanding of human development to the sense of calamity implicit in the story of the fall. It is not just a question of how we might underestimate our capacity to destroy rather than educate ourselves. It is a question of seeing that we were not in any case the fundamental reason for God's creating. God was not doing it all for us. In a well-known image (which we will return to in later chapters) offered by Gerard Manley Hopkins in his retreat notes of 1880 and often quoted by Professor Donald MacKinnon, the poet presents the creation of the universe, in a powerful piece of almost sexual imagery, as follows:

> It is as if the blissful agony or stress of selving in God had forced out drops of sweat or blood, which drops were the world.[29]

The image has the merit of firmly rejecting any idea that God's time has been eternally devoted to finding a way of creating human beings. The kenotic approach, with its stress upon the self-emptying of God and the voluntary divine embrace of weakness, must not be taken to mean that God could find fulfillment only in the creation of a universe in which human beings might prosper and return God's love. Here, too, as in the second chapter, we conclude by stressing a hard side of kenoticism. The voluntary self-renunciation of God may mean an inability to save all of those God has made, while the possibility that human beings may use their powers in order to destroy themselves and their environment is not ruled out by the possibility that such an outcome would unacceptably frustrate God's plans. Kenoticism is a powerful statement of divine self-giving, but it must not be a means of encouraging a false sense of self-importance among those for whom God has admittedly sacrificed so much.

---

29. See also MacKinnon, *Themes in Theology*, 146. MacKinnon quotes from Hopkins, *Sermons and Devotional Writings*, 197. It is from one of Hopkins's spiritual writings titled "Creation and Redemption: The Great Sacrifice," dated November 8, 1881.

PART 4

The Nature of God

Introduction

It might seem from the first three parts that this book is working toward the idea of a God who essentially stands off and apart from the world, a God who beyond creating never interferes, a God who, much as the deists conceived God, allows the created order a free hand to develop in its own way below, a God who would never force a way into human lives by miraculous intrusion. The fourth and fifth parts of this book intend to show this to be far from what I am suggesting, but a recap of the arguments in the first three parts may help to provide some useful context for what is to come.

Part 1, "Understanding Uncertainty," examined what has been underrated by Christian theology on account of a false demand for certainty (for instance, a serious study of history where Christian origins are concerned) and what has been falsely assumed to make such certainty available by another route (religious experience). It suggested that we have to live in a state of uncertainty even about God's existence.

The theme of part 2, "Uncertainty in the Created Order," examined the nature of the autonomy implicit in God's act of creation. It explored an understanding of kenosis in terms of God's willingness to give a degree of independence to the created order, and challenged the idea that evolution suggested a universe out of control. The book of Genesis emphasizes the order brought by God when chaos was "upon the face of the deep" (Gen 1:2). But it is an order whose very nature (and not just its complexity) makes its development unpredictable. Part 2 suggested that there was nothing in the theory of evolution, the nature of chaos, or quantum theory to make it impossible to talk about design or to present the watchmaker as blind (Dawkins). It also questioned the idea of human beings as if they were a lost mutation inhabiting a world completely alien to their nature (Monod).

Part 3, "Uncertainty in the Moral Order," suggested that alongside the inherent instability of the created order, even one that is a product of God's design, is the instability of the moral order. Unlike the God whose power knows no limits, even self-imposed ones, human beings face the much more challenging prospect of a God who by God's own choice is unable to save them from the consequences of their own actions, whether this is understood in terms of their own individual destinies or the future of the created universe they have been allowed to blow up or burn up. By giving human beings freedom, God opens up the possibility of failure, including God's own. Such are the dangerous consequences of giving human beings the knowledge of good and evil, their acquisition of such power presented in the tradition of the fall as stolen rather than freely received.

Now it might seem from all this emphasis upon God's self-limitation and God's determination to give a degree of independence to the created order, while being unable to predetermine or foresee what decisions human beings will make, that the book is clearly moving toward the sort of position outlined by Maurice Wiles in his Bampton Lectures of 1986, entitled *God's Action in the World* and attacked by critics as God's inaction in the world. In other words, it is surely bound to rule out what are often referred to as acts of divine "intervention" or "interference," as miracles are often described by those who feel that they have no place in the thinking of Christian theologians.

However, that is not the position supported by this book. The fact that, as was suggested in the discussion of quantum mechanics in part 2, this book sees the moral constraints upon miracles, for instance, as a much more powerful argument against them than their supposed incompatibility with modern science, does not mean, as later chapters will attempt to show, that they never occur. The nature of divine action, already mentioned in a cursory way in the discussion of SDA (special divine action) and GDA (general divine action) above, certainly needs to be very closely examined. It was the subject of a great deal of philosophical exploration following the publication of Wiles's book, which if questionable in its conclusions was always clear, and was taken up particularly by theologians deeply affected by the writings of Austin Farrer. Shortly after Wiles's Bampton Lectures, a group of them published (in 1990) a book entitled *Divine Action*, which examined the problems in detail.[1] There is a great deal that might still usefully be said thirty years on in the light of that discussion, but this book will proceed rather differently. The first three parts having provided some suggestions concerning the nature of God's self-limitation in relation to humanity and the physical universe, part 4 will try to answer the question: What, then, is the nature of this self-limiting God? What can we know about God? How is God related to the world God has made? In what sense is God present in it? This God described by Hopkins as creating the world almost

---

1. See Hebblethwaite and Henderson, *Divine Action*.

in a moment of madness, as a drop of sweat falling from the process of God's eternal divine selving; what exactly can we say—if anything—of this God's nature? It seems to me that by doing this we can approach the question of divine action from the other end, as it were, from the side of the divine initiator rather than the human receiver. Of course, it may be said that such an approach is impossible, compromising the divine transcendence. Certainly, it is necessary always to be clear about what we cannot possibly say or know without effectively reducing the object of our knowledge. But the main thing to say when challenged by the question of whether it can really be the case that God intervenes in order to put things right in the world is that the question betrays a failure to understand the way in which God and the world are connected, turning God into a tinkering outsider or perhaps a reluctant observer, but in either case failing to appreciate just how the Creator and God's creation are related to one another.

In the first chapter, part 4 explores the notion that God is Creator. The second chapter seeks to make sense of God as both immanent and transcendent, and the third chapter considers the doctrine of the Trinity. This discussion of the doctrine of God will hopefully clarify some of what has been said in the first three parts of the book about God's actions in the world. But it also intends to provide the metaphysical scaffolding for the consideration of the doctrine of Christ in part 5. The doctrine of creation must not present the universe as an eternal backdrop to the events of salvation history, including the life, death, and resurrection of Jesus of Nazareth. The incarnation does not represent God the Son dropping in to see us from some distant abode above and then popping off again. The doctrine of God's immanence and transcendence is related to Christology too. It confirms that when in the world as a frail human being, God the Son does not set aside or conceal but expresses his transcendence. Third, Christology compels that any doctrine of God must be Trinitarian, in order to make sense of the idea that the life of Jesus is part of the eternal life of God and in order to avoid separating off the life of Christ from the life of the Father and the Spirit, who must not be presented as if they are minding the shop while the Son is off conducting a dangerous mission "below." These three different (but closely interconnected) aspects of the doctrine of God are the setting for the doctrine of Christ in part 5.

Chapter 11

Creation and Kenosis

God as Creator I: Avoiding Deism

We have already mentioned one of the most famous and controversial arguments for the existence of God given by William Paley in his *Natural Theology*, where he compared tripping over a stone when out walking on the heath with tripping over a watch. Tripping over a stone, one would simply assume that it had always been there, but tripping over a watch, one would immediately recognize it as an artifice and would presume that someone had made it. The world in which we live, Paley argues, is just such a watch that we trip over in our daily lives and are led to suppose has some maker.

Such imagery presupposes that the world is a finished and self-sufficient object, which once fashioned is able to survive on its own (with perhaps some occasional tinkering, for instance, in order to rewind the watch, though doubtless the sort of perfect timepiece constructed by God would be self-winding) without any further intervention. The approach is often traced back to Matthew Tindal's *Christianity as Old as the Creation*, first published in 1730 and known as the "Deist's Bible." It posited a deity necessary to begin the world but thereafter not intervening, whether through special acts of revelation or through miracles. By ruling out any divine interventions (assuming that God's perfect timepiece is indeed self-winding) such an approach is assumed to be acceptable to modern science. Science can sit comfortably with this deist God who sets the whole thing going and then lets us get on with managing it for ourselves.

CREATION AND KENOSIS

What is often seen as an example of a passing wave of thought associated with aspects of the Enlightenment can easily be dismissed as a theological Aunt Sally. But if so, it is a persistent Aunt Sally. A perfect example of such thinking can be found in one of the world's most brilliant modern physicists, Stephen Hawking. At the end of the last century, he produced *A Brief History of Time*, a book that had colossal sales (ten million copies) and ensured that in future no bookshop would be without its popular science section.

In the book he recalls an instance when he met John Paul II in 1981:

> At the end of the conference the participants were granted an audience with the Pope. He told us that it was all right to study the evolution of the universe after the big bang, but we should not enquire into the big bang itself because that was the moment of Creation and therefore the work of God.[1]

The remark made Hawking recall an earlier conflict between Pope Urban VIII and Galileo concerning the question of whether the sun orbited the earth. John Paul II seemed to be enthusiastic about the theory of the big bang (seen as consistent with the idea of a Creator God who effectively lights the blue touch paper that sets off the universe), but this caused Hawking some concern, because it was precisely the big bang theory that he was beginning to question at the time. The physicist commented (in a way that must be considered a little self-dramatizing given the limited powers of a late twentieth-century pontiff):

> I had no desire to share the fate of Galileo, with whom I feel a strong sense of identity, partly because of the coincidence of having been born exactly 300 years after his death![2]

Whether or not this is an accurate account of what the pope said, it assumes a particular understanding of the concept of "creation." Did Hawking think that this is what theologians mean when talking of God as "Creator"? Later in *A Brief History of Time*, he wrote as follows:

> With the success of scientific theories in describing events, most people believe that God allows the universe to evolve according to a set of laws and does not intervene in the universe to break these laws. However, the laws do not tell us what the universe should have looked like when it started—it would still be up to God to wind up the clockwork and choose how to start it off. So

---

1. Hawking, *Brief History of Time*, 128.
2. Hawking, *Brief History of Time*, 128.

long as the universe had a beginning, we could suppose it had a creator.[3]

When Hawking was writing *A Brief History of Time*, he was beginning to have doubts about the views he had previously held concerning the big bang. He wrote a paper in 1970 with the British mathematician and physicist Roger Penrose, proving there *was* a big bang singularity when most physicists had serious doubts about the idea. Ironically, having been the champion of such a singularity in the teeth of opposition in the 1960s, he found himself at the end of the 1980s changing his mind.

> I am now trying to convince other physicists that there was in fact no singularity at the beginning of the universe . . . it can disappear once quantum effects are taken into account.[4]

Hawking was convinced that the undermining of the big bang singularity entailed an undermining of the belief in God as Creator. By the time of his later book published jointly with Leonard Mlodinow entitled *The Grand Design*, he believed that no initial "putting together" was needed, and so for him religion's area of authority had effectively been undermined. On September 2, 2010, the *BBC* duly carried a bizarre news release bearing the headline "Stephen Hawking: God Did Not Create Universe."

One can question whether Hawking's interpretation of creation could ever be described as orthodox Christianity, whatever the pope might have said to the physicist behind closed Vatican doors! However, it seemed to provide a simple way of reconciling human progress toward autonomy and self-management with continued belief in God. This is the attraction of the "two realms" idea, where it is made clear that God above (in the heavenly realm) does not intervene or tamper with creation (in the earthly realm below). Humanity takes control down here, but God remains up there and has an essential role in starting the whole process off.

The change in Hawking's view between *A Brief History of Time* and *The Grand Design* illustrates the dangers implicit in an essentially deist understanding of God's relation to the universe. Once humanity is said to be in charge down here and God remains up there, the danger is that God's role will become marginalized and eventually nonexistent. Hawking adopted the view that so long as the universe had a beginning, we could suppose it had a Creator. Therefore, once he had determined that the universe did not have a beginning after all, the Creator's days (as it were) are numbered.

---

3. Hawking, *Brief History of Time*, 57.
4. Hawking, *Brief History of Time*, 156–57.

God as Creator II: Clocks, Pots, and Continuous Creation

Hawking's suggestion is open to challenge. The challenge, it need hardly be said, is not to his insights into a beginningless universe, but to his view of what creation means in orthodox Christian thinking and to the whole "two realms" thinking that lies behind it. Indeed, what is so striking about the whole debate is the way in which perhaps the most brilliant physicist of our day had such an old-fashioned Enlightenment view of God's relation to the world, one which sits much more comfortably with the outlook of Isaac Newton than with the scientific discoveries of the last century. It seems to be the deist God (one that is external and non-interfering) that is still taken out of the toolbox when people consider what "God" means. Hawking's discussion in *A Brief History of Time* shows that even twenty-first-century scientists think that they can make the pope happy if God has a role in igniting the big bang, much as earlier generations thought it was enough that God had wound up the clock that then ticked away merrily of its own accord. Whether or not they believe in God, they seem to be willing to define the God who may or may not exist in fundamentally deist terms.

Ideas of a craftsman fashioning a complex timepiece or of a potter making a pot—or even someone setting off a big bang—provide comprehensible and recognizable images. Hawking—and perhaps John Paul II—was simply reflecting what many people would probably regard as the traditional understanding of creation, as represented by the famous beginning to the book of Genesis. They would know that the six days of creation or the seventh day of rest should not be taken as being a literal twenty-four-hour period. They might be aware of questions about the relation of Gen 1 to the rest of the Pentateuch (the first five books of the Bible) and the fact that it was not necessarily the earliest biblical account of creation. Nevertheless, not least because of its place in tradition and in the history of our culture, they would register the idea of a God who gradually brings order out of chaos, realizing a design and allotting functions to the various parts of it. This is what they would understand by "creation," by the opening salvo of the Judeo-Christian corpus—"In the beginning God created the heavens and the earth"—the earth being "without form and void" before the divine spirit begins to work on it. Creation happens in the beginning, God brings cosmic order out of chaos, after which the cosmic order develops under its own steam, much as the finished watch continues to tick or the finished pot sits on the shelf.

However, the idea that there comes a point where the universe, having been started in some way, continues under its own steam is misleading. Take the well-known biblical image used to describe God as Creator mentioned above, that of the potter. At first sight this seems rather like the image of the watchmaker, though with more of a sense of the fragility of humankind than is discerned in the watchmaker image. "O Lord, you are our Father, we are the clay, and you are our potter; we are all the work of your hand" (Isa 64:8). In modern idiom, we are putty in God's hands. Isaiah 45:9 asks, "Does the clay say to him who fashions it: 'What are you making?,'" once again stressing the subordination of the pot to the potter. Nevertheless, once the pot is finished it stands in the same relationship to the potter as the finished watch does to the watchmaker—it is self-sufficient. This remains the case even if each may need repairs from time to time. The watch might break, and the pot might develop cracks.

Yet the biblical image of the potter is not the same as that of the watchmaker. In the book of Jeremiah, the prophet is sent to prophesy before some of the elders and senior priests by taking a potter's earthen flask and breaking it in their presence. This is a reminder both of the people's disobedience and of their complete dependence upon God. "Thus says the LORD of hosts: So will I break this people and this city, as one breaks a potter's vessel, so that it can never be mended" (Jer 19:11). God can at any time destroy what God has made. It is a regular theme in the biblical text that God repents of having made the world because of the behavior of God's people, seeking out a faithful remnant that will remain true (as in the story of Noah's ark and the flood).

The God of Israel watches over the pot in a way that the clockmaker does not watch over the clock. But the difference goes further. Take Jer 18:2, which talks about clay that is spoiled in the potter's hand, whereupon the potter reworks it into another vessel. "O House of Israel, can I not do with you as the potter has done?" asks God. "Behold, like the clay in the potter's hand so are you in my hand, O House of Israel" (Jer 18:6). In other words, Israel is a pot that is still being fashioned on the wheel. There is no finished product. God's involvement with creation is a continuous and passionate relationship that can be called off at any moment. If the hands of God cease to work at the wheel, then the clay will collapse into a stodgy mess. Creation will return to chaos. Implicit in this imagery is a view of continuous creation. There is no distinction between creation and maintenance—God's creative activity is what maintains the world in being; without that activity the world would cease to exist. Another analogy taken from St. Augustine makes this clear.

God as Creator III: Tunes and Creation Out of Nothing

In his *Confessions*, St. Augustine uses a different model of creation. Instead of a pot made by a potter, he suggests a tune sung by a singer. It is as if God did not make us and then leave us to fend for ourselves, but rather is constantly singing us. Augustine wrote:

> For in time we do not first utter formless sounds without singing and then adapt or fashion them into the form of a song, as wood or silver from which a chest or vessel is made. Such materials precede in time the forms of the things which are made from them. But in singing this is not so. For when a song is sung, its sound is heard at the same time. There is not first a formless sound, which afterward is formed into a song; but just as soon as it has sounded it passes away, and you cannot find anything of it which you could gather up and shape.[5]

The analogy between the creation of the world and the singing of a tune makes two things very clear. In the first place, we have a clear expression of the idea that the world is not brought into being and then left to continue in a self-sufficient state like the completed watch or the finished pot. It exists only because of the singer's will to go on; there is no point at which the tune ceases to be completely dependent upon the singer's desire to continue singing (Augustine lived well before cassettes and recording studios). An image such as this effectively questions the distinction between creation as an initial act and then the act of maintaining or sustaining in being the created universe. The singer/tune analogy suggests an act of continuing creation as the world exists in unending dependence upon the God who makes it. As was pointed out above in the quotation from Jeremiah, Israel is a pot that is still being fashioned on the wheel. If we are like potter's clay, then we are like clay that is constantly struggling against the God who is ever molding us anew; we are a tune that God chooses to go on singing, but at any moment God may stop the music.

The second implication of the singer/tune analogy is that the materials for God's creative activity do not predate the act of creation. God does not look for something to make a world from in the way that the potter looks for some clay and a wheel or the clockmaker searches around for wheels and cogs. This is reflected in the doctrine of creation out of nothing—*ex nihilo*.

There has been considerable debate about whether creation out of nothing is the biblical view of creation (and, of course, there may well be more than one biblical view). Some biblical theologians think that the famous account of creation in the first book of Genesis can be read as

5. Augustine, *Confessions*, 7.29.

consistent with creation out of nothing (for instance, by taking "the heavens and the earth" of Gen 1:1 effectively to mean everything, a view supported but not required by the fact that the Hebrew word for "create," *bara*, is used only of activity carried out by God), while others think that it merely points to God's ordering role in bringing a cosmos out of a chaos.

Yet whatever the reception history of the Genesis narrative, there is a certain logic to Augustine's insistence that creation must be out of nothing, since God could hardly be constrained by the properties of the material God had to make do with, working up a sweat trying to make the clay pliable. One can see why theologians are drawn to claim that God is not acting upon preexisting matter that is older than creation itself. "There is not first a formless sound, which afterward is formed into a song," says Augustine in the passage quoted above.[6] Nor, one might say, is there a potential big bang waiting to happen when God lights the blue touch paper.

Augustine's singer/tune transforms our idea of what God's creative activity might be and, by implication, our idea of what God might be. It rejects the idea that God is creating works upon materials external to Godself—the clay, the wheel, the metal instruments, the formless chaos.

Augustine's image brings out the continuing dependence of the world upon God, but it does so in a particular way. Consider another model that certainly emphasizes the world's dependence on God, that of the myth of Atlas. The mythological story of a world held in place by the titan Atlas (although Atlas was originally condemned by Zeus to hold up the sky to prevent it from reestablishing its primordial embrace of the earth) certainly presents a model of the world as continuously dependent upon there being a god to hold it up. But the image of Atlas represents a world that is dependent upon something *outside* itself. In the tune image of Augustine, it is more that the world is being spun from within as the singer gives voice. The world may be given a certain autonomy, a certain character as a finished product, the physical universe that in the Genesis story God saw to be good and then rested after making, but it is not an autonomy that can be conceived as taking it outside God.

In a figurative manner, this can be seen in the case of potters and watchmakers too. Imagine the exhausted sculptor who, having finally chipped to perfection, remarks: "I put all of myself into that work." But the prevailing sense of those images, unlike that of the tune, is still of a separate finished product, now self-sufficient while it ticks away, or stands being admired on a tabletop.

---

6. Augustine, *Confessions*, 12.29.

Something more than the dependence portrayed by the image of a universe held up on Atlas's vast shoulders is implied by passages in the Bible like Jer 23:24—"Do I not fill heaven and earth?" The point is that God is sustaining the world *from within*. One of the traditional attributes of God, after all, is "omnipresence," and God can hardly be omnipresent without being down here as well as up there. "Do I not fill heaven and earth?" This cannot be the absent God (however enabling through absence) of deism.

We therefore come to the following conclusion. When the idea of creation is freed from its Enlightenment straitjacket, it can be understood in a very different manner. The universe is no longer an independent finished product, which is the impression one easily gets from pots and watches. Just as the tune depends on the singer's desire to sing on, so the world depends upon God's desire to go on creating and sustaining it. Whatever truth there may be in the idea that God gives creation relative autonomy, allowing human beings to sin and reject their Creator, there remains a need for God's constant creative and sustaining activity in order for the universe to continue in being. God does not stop at the edges of the world, because without God the world would not continue to be.

The tune image gives God an immediacy that pots and clocks deny. The song cannot be separated from the singer (at least in Augustine's day) in the way the pot can be separated from the potter. The tune image stresses the immanence, the "within-the-worldness," of God, without whose constant presence the world would no longer exist.

God as Creator IV: Time and Space as Part of Creation

Augustine made another point about creation that is profoundly significant. In book 11 of his *Confessions* he says that it is crucial to understand that creation is not in time because time itself is a part of creation. This is the mistake, Augustine argues, of those who ask what God was doing before creation, as if there was some kind of empty stage that remained bare and unused until God arrived to fill it with light and scenery. It is also the mistake of those (like Hawking) who thought of creation as something that happens in the first few minutes (or nanoseconds) with some kind of big bang.

It is easy to imagine the time before creation in terms of a moment when all is quiet on stage. The curtain has not yet gone up. But there is still a stage there, still a curtain, still lights waiting to go on and actors waiting to tread the boards. There is an expectant audience there too. Even if it is said that creation is out of nothing, it is all too easy to make nothing into an almost tangible void where something is about to happen, an empty receptacle into which God is about to move to perform the great act of creation.

However, creation was not something that God brought along to the darkened stage on which some strange preexisting forms waited expectantly for the play to begin. All the forms that emerged with creation emerged alongside space and time, which were *part of* that creative activity. Time and space exist only in relation to the things that happen "in" them. There was nothing before creation, because "before" makes sense only in the context of creation itself: there is nothing "outside" what God has created, no heavenly realm "above" it, because "outside" and "above" make sense only in the context of the created world. There are no two realms, because realms exist only where there is creation and as a part of the created universe.

Augustine's idea that time and space are part of God's work of creation, rather than some kind of eternal backdrop to God's first intervention, does not fit well with Newtonian science or with the classical physics of the Enlightenment. However, it fits much better with Einstein's theory of relativity, as several recent and contemporary theologians have pointed out. Thus, Professor T. F. Torrance argues that to throw off our Enlightenment shackles we must give up a "receptacle" view of space and time. Torrance explains that when we talk of our planet or solar system as being in space, we all too easily think of space as a gigantic container inside which the planets orbit around each other like flies in a jam jar. He even suggests that "there may well be at work here a substitute symbolism arising out of post-natal desire for the security of being at home in a container and anxiety at being thrust out into the open world."[7] Be that as it may, the receptacle view creates difficulties—for instance, in being able to cope with the obvious question of what is "outside" the container. It also means that we commit ourselves to a view whereby our activities inside space are believed to be entirely independent of space itself. The same is true of time, which we are also said to be "in." Time becomes a backdrop to our activities, which is entirely unaffected by those activities themselves. Time and space are separated from what happens inside them—precisely the sort of separation that lures us into supposing that into a quiet world in which nothing was going on God suddenly appeared with a box of tricks in order to set off the big bang. The Creator comes along to the eternal, preexisting jam jar and pops in a few flies.

Modern science (as Torrance understands it) can change the whole narrative by rejecting this receptacle image according to which God creates something external to Godself and is then seen as constantly meddling in it. We need an approach in which there is no perforating or interfering from

---

7. Torrance, *Space, Time and Incarnation*, 22.

"outside," not because of some presumption that God thinks it better not to interfere or doesn't want to trouble us with miracles but because "outside" belongs only to the created order. The point is that space and time are wrapped up in the events that go on inside them; the events are wrapped up in space and time.

This analysis of creation does have an indirect bearing upon the sort of questions discussed in part 2, when discussing whether God in some way interfered in the workings of the universe, guiding it through some surreptitious touch on the tiller or coming in under the radar in order to act at the quantum level. That sort of understanding of what a special divine action might mean was rejected. But there is a wider point to make, which is that as soon as discussion turns to the question of special divine actions and, related to that, to the plausibility of miracles, there is a tendency to return to the "two realms" idea, to a God above and a universe below and then to the question of whether the divine hand ever reaches down in order to affect the way things are going here below. The discussion of chaos theory and quantum mechanics in part 2 centered upon the question of whether God could intervene without supplanting any law, enabling one to keep faith in the inviolability of laws of nature while leaving room for divine intervention. But we can see that there is a further question of whether, by thinking in terms of two realms, we are misconceiving in a fundamental manner God's relation to the created universe, which can never be seen as if it referred to two different realities set side by side with one another, the question then turning to whether the divine reality could in some manner reach out to the human. One is forced to the sort of considerations that, for a few extraordinary months sixty years ago, seemed to grip the popular mind on publication of John Robinson's *Honest to God*,[8] namely the unacceptability of any God up above looking down upon a distant and separate earth, the "God up there," as Robinson put it, as opposed to the God who was the "ground of our being" (a phrase used by the theologian Paul Tillich) or the "beyond in our midst" (a phrase of Dietrich Bonhoeffer, another influence on Robinson's book). The rest of part 4 examines these phrases more closely.

---

8. Queues formed outside bookshops. The prime minister of the United Kingdom, Harold Macmillan, presumably loathe to join the queue himself, sent for a copy to be delivered to him. By the end of 1963, SCM Press, having published *Honest to God*, was already rushing out another paperback called *The Honest to God Debate*.

Conclusion

It is as part of trying to establish a viable framework for a kenotic understanding of Christ that this chapter has looked at the doctrine of creation. It began with a view according to which God simply starts a process that then develops of its own accord. God winds up the watch or finishes the pot and puts it onto the shelf. This might be seen as a long-rejected form of deism, but if so it remains a common fallacy, one that clearly represented Stephen Hawking's understanding of creation when he talked about it to Pope John Paul II (who, it must be said, seemed to have the same idea).

The chapter then moved on to insist upon creation being a continuous activity of God rather than something that applies only to some notion of lighting the touch paper or firing the starting pistol. Augustine's notion of a tune sung by God provides a beautiful illustration of the concept of continuous creation. God is singing us. We depend upon God's continuing the song. It is like the music of the spheres, and should it ever cease we will cease with it.

But Augustine's image suggests something else. It confronts us with the notion of creation out of nothing. Whether or not this is the biblical view based on the study of the text of Genesis, it appears to emerge naturally from the imagery Augustine adopts. The potter needs clay to work on and a wheel at which to sit and work. The watchmaker needs cogs, wheels, a powerful eyeglass, and a studio. The materials would seem to predate the work of creation. But the singing of a tune suggests something different.

At this point we move beyond the idea of continuous creation being something like God's continuously sustaining the world from outside it, holding it up like Atlas. The notion of creation out of nothing, of creation without having to reach for available materials, suggests a world spun from within like a song. It makes the point that God's work of continuous creation does not take place outside God, for there is nowhere that is outside God.

These reflections strengthen the idea of God's self-giving love, which is at the heart of a kenotic theology. God does not make something and then leave it to fend for itself. God not only remains passionately committed to its welfare but is constantly in the process of making and sustaining it. God gives it relative autonomy—otherwise, creation would be no more than a mere extension of God, an "emanation" as some early theologians saw it. Yet it remains a universe sustained in being only through the fact that God permeates it with God's presence. Images of God as "light" and as "being" make this point in their different ways (as part 4 will develop further). So does the idea of God as "transcendent and immanent," which means to say not that God somehow alternates between being down here and being up there but that it is precisely as transcendent that God is continuously present with us on earth. All that one wants to say about God loving the world, being involved with it to the point of being continuously hurt by it, and seeking its redemption as a process inseparable from realizing God's own eternal nature as love is contained in the idea that creation was spun from within and exists in being only because God determines to continue singing what is at once a song of joy in creation and a condition of maintaining the created order in being.

The final reflection in this chapter was that if there is nowhere "outside" God and nothing like the "right time" for God to begin the work of creation, we have to understand how space and time are themselves part of creation rather than being some kind of backdrop for God's creative activity. The advantage of this approach is that we are forced away from thinking of space and time as a preexistent framework within which divine beings buzz up and down between heaven and earth. This may help us when we try to approach the specific question of a kenotic Christology. Even from a kenotic perspective, we must not be misled into thinking in terms of a salvific skydive from heaven down to earth. The kenoticist who adopts such an approach differs from other more supposedly orthodox interpretations only by wondering whether the skydiver takes all his equipment with him when he leaves heaven or whether he chooses to leave some of it behind—or perhaps he takes it with him, keeps it concealed about his person, and then refuses to use it. Part 5 looks at this more closely.

There may be in the language of the creeds much that suggests movement up and down, but we don't want to end up treating salvation history as an account of the traffic between two realms. Then when we try to make sense of the notion that "God was in Christ," it is more as if he becomes increasingly aware that his own life as the son of a carpenter can be seen in other terms, as God making room for Godself on earth, God becoming wrapped up in the specificities of creative forms like time and space, the light illuminating the world in the power of a single beam.

Nothing this chapter has said directly addressed the question of God's actions in the world, particularly those we associate with miracles. What it has tried to do is challenge the picture of two realms, the divine above and the earthly below, which seems to provide the background for discussing what sort of interference can come from one to the other and whether such interference is either scientifically credible or morally acceptable. By looking at the doctrine of creation, we have found a God who is an eternally sustaining presence rather than an observer from above. God's action in creating never ceases, so it is inappropriate to talk about whether God intervenes "from time to time." No action of God can be understood as a movement "from outside," as if God shared with men and women a common framework of space and time. By discussing the way in which God is traditionally thought of as both transcendent and immanent, the next chapter will attempt to make this point more clearly.

Chapter 12

God Transcendent and Immanent

This chapter takes up points made in the last chapter concerning the way in which a Creator God is related to the world. In the light of the discussion in that chapter, we can recognize three ways of understanding that relation. The first, which we associate with deism, sees the universe as something outside God, the pot on the shelf, or the watch in the workshop, or the heavy weight of the world pressing down on the shoulders of Atlas. This picture suggests a universe that somehow begins where God ends. Hence, it is recognized that such imagery makes the mistake of locating both Creator and creation in space.

The second way of understanding God's relation to the world is the opposite of deism. Pantheism is one form of theism that clearly understands God does not end where the world begins. There has already been a suggestion of this in the last chapter when it talked of a universe "spun from within." The idea arose in the context of denying that God worked on preexisting materials in creating. There is nothing outside God, nothing left lying around, as it were, for God to pick up and turn into a world. But does that mean that creation is something that happens inside God, a stage in the development of God's own being, if God can be thought of as developing? And if so, do we end up in a position where God and the world are one and the same thing? By running from the Scylla of deism, which placed God and the world apart from one another, do we end up in the Charybdis of pantheism, where they become identical to one another?

The Charybdis of pantheism may sound implausible, but it has a certain attraction when it comes to making sense of acts of God. For if on the basis of an analogy with our own actions we see the world, for instance, as God's body, then at least we get away from images of a distant God operating various levers and pulleys from above. These images remain dominant if we see the actions of God as mediated—as if God makes the world go in the right direction, in the way someone might drive a car in the right manner. But if the actions are direct rather than mediated, then some of the problems concerning acts of God seem to disappear. God's decision to part the Red Sea or to turn water into wine becomes no different from my decision to raise my arm. Acts of God are legitimized without in the process reintroducing all the ancient baggage of two realms and a designer forever muscling in on the scene in order to put things right.

Grace Jantzen's book *God's World, God's Body*, written in 1984, was a defining early work in this vein, followed by books such as Sallie McFague's *Models of God*, subtitled *Theology for an Ecological Nuclear Age*, which contrasted patriarchal and monarchical ideas of God as a distant father with different models of God such as mother, lover, and friend. These concerns alone show how discussions of the nature of God can raise issues related to the divine vulnerability and self-giving that appeals to a kenotic approach. It was already clear how the world had moved on from the confident "white heat of technology" within which John Robinson wrote his *Honest to God* in the early 1960s, toward a more sophisticated insight into the ways in which human beings were in danger of destroying their planet. The development of feminist writing in those intervening twenty years had also linked the image of God as separate from the world to the idea of God conceived in terms of patriarchal images of the sovereign lord. The God above, who remains in his heavenly realm, becomes the standoffish male who bars the way to his office or study.

Eastern religious traditions that have been glibly associated with a simple form of polytheism that believes in deities roaming the world like the gods of Homer wandering down from Olympus are more properly understood within this perspective, their gods being seen as manifestations of some more general divinity or world soul (Grace Jantzen's book discussed this in detail).

Pantheism therefore helps us to value the world around us—for this is God herself as "Mother Earth." And when the alternative seems to be the vacant God of deism, which everyone seems to abjure in principle but easily becomes sucked back into affirming, the pantheist God seems even more attractive. We find ourselves able to make sense of God's omnipresence. God is everywhere in the sense that I am wherever my body is. We find ourselves able to make sense of acts of God as no more problematic than my lifting a finger.

The pantheist position has clear benefits from a kenotic perspective. An external God looking down upon creation is one thing: a God who is the "soul" of creation is another. The God who says from above "I feel your pain" is less endearing from a kenotic perspective than the God who can say: "Your pain is mine." Though the whole point of the doctrine of incarnation is to say that God assumes humanity, and in this sense its pain definitely becomes God's—hence *The Crucified God*, the book already referred to by Jürgen Moltmann—a pantheist interpretation makes every part of the earth's fragile being, and every pain that the people suffer in it, a pain at the heart of God.

However, there are problems with the pantheist position too. Where is the equivalent to a central nervous system in the universe? More importantly, I am vulnerable as a body, may suffer injury, and eventually will die. God is surely not vulnerable in the same way, forced into being by a big bang and out of being by a big crunch! It is not clear that even God the mother or God the lover (models explored by Sallie McFague) can avoid the sort of difficulties that a pantheist interpretation is bound to land itself in.

It is important to recognize that the same tradition associated with Augustine, which denies that there is anything outside the omnipresent God, also argues that God is not identical with the world. While the world would not exist without God, God would exist without the world. However evocative pantheism may be, and however welcome a recall from the departed, self-banished, haughty, absentee male of patriarchal tradition, there remains the difficulty that, to put it crudely, crunch time for the universe is not meant to entail crunch time for God. To return to a point made by Augustine, the world minus God is nothing, but God minus the world is still supposed to be God.

Naturally Jantzen, McFague, and others were alive to this criticism. The question is whether they really answered it. McFague took the point up in an article entitled "Imaging a Theology of Nature: The World as God's Body."[1] She essentially drew on the idea that I might survive the death of my body (certainly, traditional understandings of immortality would agree with her). In a similar manner, she suggests, God might survive the death of the universe.

However, such an argument depends upon adopting a very conservative view of body and soul in order to avoid a very conservative view of God and the world. The patriarchal tendencies of a God who remains disdainfully above the world are avoided by adopting a very patriarchal view of the human self (not to mention one which raises enormous philosophical difficulties), the immortal soul apparently able to spread itself at will in and out of bodies, while remaining essentially independent of the physical constraints

---

1. To be found in Birch et al., *Liberating Life*, 201–27.

they impose. It is difficult to avoid the view that dualism at the level of the human person becomes the prop for avoiding dualism at the level of God and the universe. The trouble with *God's World, God's Body* is that the world can only be God's body, and God can only be the soul of the world, on the basis of a body/soul dichotomy which arguably restores the very separation which it seeks to undermine. Hence some writers have looked for a more nuanced way in which to undermine the "two realms" idea, and that brings us to the third option concerning God's relation to the world.

We might try to claim immunity from two extremes by insisting that our position is "panentheism," defined by saying that God is in the world but not identical with it (just as God will eventually be "all in all" but is not identical with all that is), or as Bradford McCall puts it, "Panentheism seeks to stress that the infinite God is as ontologically close to finite things as can possibly be thought without dissolving altogether the distinction between Creator and created."[2] In principle, panentheism is a desirable position to adopt. God is in the world, or the world is in God; the two are not identical, but they are never apart. However, panentheism is a term, not an explanation, and the definition offered above, using phrases like "ontological closeness," needs clearer definition. We can accept that God cannot sit above the world looking down, surveying what happens on the human pitch from some director's box in the sky. We can also accept that God cannot just be turned into another name for all that is. But it is the meaning of this God who is in the world but not identical with it that we must make sense of. If we are going to be panentheists, we need to be able to explain precisely what we are becoming. Rather than searching for the right form of words in a definition, we address this question indirectly by looking at a familiar image of the divine being, that of light.

The Image of Light

We know that scientists are more than willing to describe the fundamental makeup of reality using metaphors. They have their membranes and strings, their wormholes and black holes, their Higgs bosons in the form of champagne corks or Mexican hats. They need images. The theologians also need imagery, and there is one important and very traditional image that has frequently been used to describe God, that of light.

In the Greek Bible (New Testament), 1 John 1:5 has the famous words: "God is light and in him is no darkness at all." In John 8:12 Jesus tells his disciples, "I am the light of the world," and in Matt 5:14 he tells them, "You

---

2. McCall, *Modern Relation*, 30.

are the light of the world," reminding them that a light is not to be "hidden under a bushel" but exposed in the open in order to illuminate others.

The idea of light is an integral part of Judaism. In the Hebrew Bible, Ps 27:1 contains the famous words "the Lord is my light and my salvation," while the book of Samuel (2 Sam 22:29) talks of the Lord as "a lamp turning darkness into light." The imagery of 2 Sam 22:12–13 has a striking image of God making darkness "his canopy around him—the dark rain clouds of the sky. Out of the brightness of his presence bolts of lightning blazed forth."

The imagery of light has fed through into both Jewish and Christian religious tradition, whether it be the eternal flame of God's presence in the temple in Jerusalem or the tradition of lighting candles in churches. Hanukkah in Jewish religious tradition, an eight-day holiday that partially coincides with the Christian Advent season before Christmas, is also known as the Festival of Lights and celebrates the miraculous eight days in which a one-day supply of oil kept the flame alive in the temple. In Christian tradition the famous words of the Song of Simeon, commonly known as the *Nunc dimittis*, speak of Christ's salvation as "a light to lighten the gentiles and the glory of my people Israel," words that are so familiar from Anglican evensong, from Orthodox vespers, from the night office of Compline, and from the Eucharist.

There is no doubt that the development of Christian thinking was also affected by the imagery of light in powerful traditions from the Hellenistic world such as Platonism. Plato's *Republic* contains one of the most famous illustrations in the history of philosophy, the so-called "allegory of the cave," where we are asked to imagine people sitting by a fire in a cave. They are in chains, unable to turn around and watch what passes the entrance to the cave directly, but they see the shadows of people or objects going by thrown onto a wall of the cave by the light of the fire. They therefore have only indirect knowledge of what is real, being forced to focus their attention on a shadow world. Plato's myth uses light as a means of explaining how (though philosophers may be able to break the chains and obtain a direct understanding) we can know what is most real (the Forms) only indirectly, in the half-reality of the world we are forced to make do with.[3]

Why is the idea of God as light so attractive? The moral connotations of "light" and "darkness" play a part, the sort of traditional imagery that has made white knights and white witches benevolent and white lies excusable. There is also the association of light with intellectual as much as moral conversion—"seeing the light," being enlightened, the era of "Enlightenment"

---

3. See Plato, *Republic*, 227–35.

after the "dark ages" of superstition. But light is an important way of describing God for other reasons.

Light conveys both God's unapproachability and God's omnipresence. It is therefore an image that helps us to make sense of the definition that this chapter intends to explore, namely that God is both immanent and transcendent. On the one hand, light allows all the different parts of the world to be recognized. If you want to see an object clearly, you say: "Can you hold it up to the light?" The light enables it to be seen as it is. The light is not a part of it. The light is not a separate object that supports it, like a table on which it rests or a rope that holds it in the air. The light is the omnipresent enabler, the environment within which things can stand out and be what they are.

At the same time, light also reflects the unapproachability of God. To look directly into the light is dangerous. You can lose your sight by doing so. To try to turn away from the world and hunt God down in the brilliance of heaven is to burn one's eyes by hunting the sun. God is to be found here, in the ordinary things of the earth, and is not to be sought out as something separate from them.

Light or imagery connected with it, such as flames and fire, is often used to make this point. Take the following famous extract from the book of Exodus, the story of the burning bush:

> Now Moses was keeping the flock of his father-in-law, Jethro, the priest of Midian, and he led his flock to the west side of the wilderness and came to Horeb, the mountain of God. And the angel of the Lord appeared to him in a flame of fire out of the midst of a bush. He looked, and behold, the bush was burning, yet it was not consumed. And Moses said, "I will turn aside to see this great sight, why the bush is not burned." When the Lord saw that he turned aside to see, God called to him out of the bush, "Moses, Moses!" And he said, "Here I am." Then he said, "Do not come near; take your sandals off your feet, for the place on which you are standing is holy ground." And he said, "I am the God of your father, the God of Abraham, the God of Isaac, and the God of Jacob." And Moses hid his face, for he was afraid to look at God. (Exod 3:1–6)

"He was afraid to look at God," as one might shield one's eyes from the sun. There is the dual role of light as life giving and illuminating on the one hand and as dazzling and blinding (when looked at directly) on the other. The words of God to Moses in Exod 33:20 ("You cannot see my face, for man shall not see me and live") have to be taken alongside the many passages that point to the willingness of God to be revealed.

To sum up, calling God "light" is an attempt to illustrate that God suffuses all things while remaining essentially beyond definition. It is an image conveying the idea that God cannot be isolated from the things of this world and seen separately from them, but it also expresses the idea that God cannot be identified as a part of them, or as their basic ingredient, or as the microscopic building block (the Higgs boson as the "God particle"?) from which they are constructed. The theologian Dietrich Bonhoeffer is famous for his description of God as the "beyond in our midst,"[4] one of the definitions of a God who was not simply "up there," which John Robinson reached for in *Honest to God*, but it is important to stress that it is *only as beyond* that God can be in our midst.

The image of light portrays God as the omnipresent enabler, allowing objects to be the things they are, letting them come into being. It is this that the idea of "holding things up to the light" helps to convey.

It is easy to slip into a view of the universe as a huge, self-sufficient collection of objects like a gigantic warehouse. It is this that brings us back to the "two realms" fallacy. For by thinking of the universe in these terms we give it a certain self-sufficiency, which enables us to think of God as something outside or above, the maker who looks down on us and adopts the lucky ones for a future in heaven above. We then forget the point made so clearly by omnipresence, namely that God is everywhere. Naturally the question then becomes "Everywhere as what? I can't see God." The image of light provides the response, since light is not an object but that in which all objects come to be recognized for what they are. The term "omnipresent enabler" attempts to make that point.

The idea of "transcendent yet immanent" must never be understood in terms of alternative or even successive modes of being for God. God does not cease to be transcendent when God is immanent in the world. The "beyond in our midst" of Bonhoeffer's conception never ceases to be beyond when in our midst, just as the light that enables all things to be seen remains dazzling and blinding, forcing us to turn away, if we try to grasp it directly—to see into transcendence. The approach being made through the image of light is therefore not to strip the universe down to some essential ingredient, like atomic structure, but to understand how it is constantly being sustained from beyond itself. If it is understood that this is what the panentheist is trying to say, then some of the difficult terminology of writers who have attempted to represent a Thomist vision in the modern day, such as Karl Rahner's "transcendental" or "supernatural" existential,

---

4. Letter of April 30, 1944, in Bonhoeffer, *Letters and Papers*, 282.

may begin to make sense.[5] The omnipresent enabler is not made visible by deconstructing the universe as if it was a huge object and then identifying its fundamental constituents (this will be considered below in the context of examining Heidegger, whose influence on Rahner was considerable). To recall Augustine's image of the world as a tune sung by God, the music of the spheres exists only because the Creator desires to keep singing. A misleading self-sufficiency has been imposed upon the physical universe, and this has made it difficult for us to make sense of its character as created and as a world in which God is eternally present even while remaining transcendent.

The Problem of the "God Particle"

A theistic understanding of the world is bedeviled by the presumption that it is like a huge collection of self-supporting and self-sufficient things overseen by a benign deity. The fatal division between heaven above and earth below comes easily to us because we tend to think of a world of solid objects, things made of other things, which in turn are made up of other things, until we can see no more and rely on microscopes to go further, and then on complex methods of particle detection until we end up below the level of atoms, among neutrinos and the strangely named "God particle" (Higgs boson), which has been so much in the news in recent years. This strange microworld of quantum mechanics, as discussed in part 2, may or may not operate according to different laws, or even no laws at all, but however complex the divisions may be, and however far they stretch the laws we apply to the world we can actually see, we are still misled into thinking in LEGO terms of bits of stuff being assembled in various combinations, a view that fits in with the idea of God as the one who first assembles the pieces or perhaps puts them all into the box for us to assemble them ourselves. This is how Sean Carroll, a theoretical physicist at the California Institute of Technology, put it in 2013 in a section of his book *The Particle at the End of the Universe* entitled "A Big Universe Made of Little Pieces":

> Legoland is a lot like the real world. At any moment, your immediate environment typically contains all sorts of substances: wood, plastic, fabric, glass, metal, air, water, living bodies. Very different kinds of things, with very different properties. But when you look more closely, you discover that these substances aren't truly distinct from one another. They are simply different arrangements of a small number of fundamental building blocks. These building blocks are the elementary particles. Like

---

5. See "Transcendental Theology," in Rahner, *Encyclopedia of Theology*, 287–89.

the buildings in Legoland, tables and cars and trees and people represent some of the amazing diversity you can achieve by starting with a small number of simple pieces and fitting them together in a variety of ways. An atom is about one trillionth the size of a Lego block, but the principles are similar.[6]

Two and a half millennia ago, philosopher-scientists struggled in a similar manner with the question of what the "little pieces" looked like. Carroll supports their approach, feeling that it requires updating rather than changing:

> The hope that we can understand the world in terms of a few basic ingredients is an old idea. In ancient times, a number of different cultures—Babylonians, Greeks, Hindus, and others—invented a remarkably consistent set of five elements out of which everything else was made. The ones we are most familiar with are earth, air, fire, and water.[7]

When you reduce reality to its basics, you supposedly unearth the "original building block" of the universe as the pre-Socratics tried to do over two millennia ago. Anaximenes identified air as the fundamental constituent, which could be rarefied as fire or condensed as earth and water. Thales opted for water and Heraclitus for the ethereal fire from which all else comes and eventually goes in a final conflagration.

Or perhaps no one element is the fundamental one. It might be, as Empedocles, another of the pre-Socratics, claimed, that different combinations of the four elements produced the different kinds of stuff we observe around us. The four elements were combined in order to make things much as painters combined different pigments in order to make shades and tints. Others thought they saw objects resolve themselves into the four elements, for instance, when fire burned green wood. Above the flames (fire) the smoke rose and disappeared (becoming air), while drops of moisture were boiled off from the end of the wood (water) while it turned into ashes on the ground (earth). The images came and went as they do today, when string theory and wormholes are paraded as scientific breakthroughs.

Nevertheless, it seemed tidier to suppose that the four elements were somehow different combinations of one single element. This was the notion that emerged through Leucippus and Democritus (later to be presented by Epicurus and Lucretius) who arrived at the idea of the "atom," the word meaning "indivisible," or that which you arrive at when you've cut and cut

---

6. Carroll, *Particle at the End*, 9.
7. Carroll, *Particle at the End*, 10.

and cut and can cut no more. These atoms would vary in size and shape to produce the different things we observe (as in LEGO).

We do not think of atoms as indivisible today. The nineteenth-century chemist John Dalton made use of the term to describe the constituents of chemical elements, and our thinking has moved on since then. But Carroll's argument is that the idea of a basic, indivisible something has remained. The difference is simply one of terminology:

> What we now think of as an atom is not indivisible at all—it consists of a nucleus made of protons and neutrons, around which orbit a collection of electrons. Even the protons and neutrons aren't indivisible; they are made of smaller pieces called "quarks."
>
> The quarks and electrons are the real atoms in Democritus's sense of indivisible building blocks of matter. Today we call them "elementary particles."
>
> Two kinds of quarks—known playfully as "up" and "down"—go into making the protons and neutrons of an atomic nucleus. So all told we need only three elementary particles to make up every single piece of matter that we immediately perceive in the environment around us—electrons, up quarks and down quarks. That's an improvement over the five elements of antiquity, and a big improvement over the periodic table.[8]

Carroll admittedly goes on to assure us that "boiling the world down to just three particles is a bit of an exaggeration" and proceeds to discuss twelve different kinds of matter particles.[9] Indeed, his reference to "five" elements of antiquity reminds us that some people added the elusive "ether" to earth, air, fire, and water. Yet his "elementary particle," a subatomic particle with no substructure which is not composed of other particles, still seems to conform to the LEGO approach as the modern version of the basic building block.

In recent years there has been interest in the so-called Higgs boson, named after a physicist called Peter Higgs. Much as astronomers who observe a new star or comet might have it named after them, so discoverers of the infinitesimally small receive the same treatment. Halley's comet becomes Higgs boson. In 2009, *The Guardian* launched a competition to find the best way of describing the Higgs boson that avoided the term "God particle," a description that was coined by Nobel Prize–winning physicist Leon Lederman. Yet the search for a way of describing this particle arguably showed that the thinking of the pre-Socratics two and a half millennia ago, searching for the fundamental building block from which the universe was

---

8. Carroll, *Particle at the End*, 11.
9. Carroll, *Particle at the End*, 11.

made, had been replicated by *Guardian* writers and readers in the twenty-first century while they were struggling for an appropriate image for the Higgs boson and ending up with billions of invisible champagne corks or Mexican hats (the two most favored descriptions of the boson).

It might seem as though the "God particle" has to do with some theistic presumption behind the scientific work being done. In fact, it is nothing of the kind (Higgs himself is not a theist). If theistic ideas arise at all, it is because those investigating the Higgs boson seek to understand what was happening when the universe began, in the first trillionths of a second after the so-called big bang, and this is often described as the first moments of creation. We are back at Hawking's discussions over the origin of the universe with Pope John Paul II as discussed in the last chapter, but as pointed out then the idea of creation as referring to what happened "in the beginning" is a mistake. Creation refers to the continuing dependence of the physical universe upon God who holds it in being and sustains it.

Time and again those who write about creation think in terms of what happened "in the beginning," and because studying the particle called the Higgs boson means studying—or trying to replicate—the very first moments when the universe was being born, it is tempting to think of this in terms of getting back to the moment where God lit the blue touch paper and a world exploded into being. A lot of the data on which the study of the Higgs boson depends is provided by sophisticated machinery like the Large Hadron Collider at the European Particle Laboratory at CERN in Switzerland, where protons are made to collide in an attempt to achieve a concentration of energy that supposedly recreates conditions prevailing in the universe during the first trillionth of a second after the big bang. By doing so it is hoped to find evidence of the elusive boson, whose existence would help to explain how particles acquired mass. But scientific popularizers like to conjure up a picture of God appearing in order to ignite some incredible firework display, the embers of which are still with us to this day. Even the tongue-in-cheek words of Lederman himself in his opening chapter, "The Invisible Soccer Ball," suggest as much:

> When you read or hear anything about the birth of the universe, someone is making it up. We are in the realm of philosophy. Only God knows what happened at the very beginning and so far she hasn't led on.... The nothingness exploded. In this initial incandescence, space and time were created.
>
> Out of this energy matter emerged—a dense plasma of particles that dissolved into radiation and back to matter.... Particles

collided and gave birth to new particles. Space and time boiled and foamed as black holes formed and dissolved. What a scene![10]

And so on. Lederman and his cowriter Dick Teresi themselves boil and foam with excitement as they anticipate the findings of the Large Hadron Collider. But there remains a philosophical question that is arguably more fundamental. It is whether the post-Socratics hunting down the Higgs boson are heirs to the pre-Socratics, chasing down the fundamental building blocks with the aid of sophisticated modern machinery. In which case the question remains as to whether they are simply repeating the error of treating the universe as something brought into being by God and then left to its own devices. If there is to be a theistic dimension to the process of making sense of the universe, it has to be able to reflect *the universe's continuing dependence* upon the Creator, so that it is constantly sustained in being like the tune in Augustine's *Confessions*.

The "solid objects beneath God" view attaches itself very easily, as the discussion of God's creation has tried to show, to metaphors based on watches and watchmakers or pots and potters. It also persists in the LEGO approach to creation and the search for some kind of fundamental constituent upon which the whole is somehow erected, the champagne cork or Mexican hat simply an updated version of the pre-Socratics' earth, air, fire, and water. The approach being made through the image of light is entirely different. It suggests that instead of deconstructing the universe as if it was a huge object and then identifying its fundamental constituents, the point is to understand how the universe is perpetually sustained by an indefinable other. The music of the spheres exists only because the Creator desires to keep singing. A misleading self-sufficiency has been imposed upon the physical universe by the LEGO-ist approach, and this is above all what has hindered us in making sense of its character as created and as a world in which God is eternally present (immanent) even while remaining transcendent.

God and Being

When we move from light to the notion of being, we find the same point being made about the relation of God to creation, but it is presented in a more structured and analytical manner. We know what it means to say that light is everywhere, but of course, as a common saying has it, there are places where the sun doesn't shine. However, being is omnipresent and therefore appears

---

10. Lederman and Teresi, *God Particle*, 1–2.

to be a more effective way of trying to make sense of God as the omnipresent enabler. Everything has being, after all, insofar as it exists. The question is: What exactly are we saying when we say that something "exists"? Does the concept of being enable us to make sense of the idea that the universe is sustained only from beyond itself in a relation of constant dependence upon God?

We might be tempted to treat "existence" as if it was another quality to add to all the others that characterize something we are trying to describe. But this is something that many philosophers say we can never do—as the philosophical debate about the so-called ontological argument makes clear. The argument was originally formulated (assuming that it was actually intended to be an argument for God's existence) in the eleventh century by Anselm, who in his *Proslogion* defined God as that-than-which-nothing-greater-can-be-thought.[11] Since it is greater to exist than not to, Anselm suggested, and since God is that-than-which-nothing-greater-can-be-thought, then it is impossible to think of God save as existing. Hence God must exist. A later formulation by Descartes suggested that God must contain all perfections, and since existence was a perfection, the same conclusion could be drawn, namely that God must exist.

The argument has always been disliked in the sense that other attempted proofs of God—for instance, from design or causation or morality—though they may not hold water, are at least based upon claims about the world of experience. They at least get out of the front door into the real world, whereas the ontological argument is seen as one which tries to play with words in order to squeeze God's existence out of a definition alone. It is generally seen (despite continuing to find advocates such as Alvin Plantinga) as having been effectively demolished by Kant in an argument that is summed up in the sentence: "Existence is not a predicate."[12]

Kant's argument points out that existence is not an additional quality to add to all the others in describing something. One can say that a ball is round, hard, and orange. If one then says that it "exists," one does not in doing so add a further characteristic as one would if one said that it had green spots. One says that there is at least one object that fits the description. What one does *not* do is change the description itself.

The philosopher Bertrand Russell reformulated Kant's argument through a distinction between first-order and second-order predicates. First-order predicates attribute a property to an object—roundness,

---

11. See the translation with introduction by M. J. Charlesworth.
12. Kant, *Critique of Pure Reason*, ch. 3, sect. 4, of the Transcendental Dialectic, 500–507.

hardness, and orangeness to the ball, for instance. Second-order predicates are so called because they attribute a property to first-order predicates rather than to objects. To say that a ball is not only round, hard, and orange but also "exists" is to say that there is at least one instance of round, hard, and orange objects. It is not to add another property to the object itself.

Kant and Russell have been seen as providing a complete and even obvious demolition of the argument. And yet, while it is generally accepted that no proof of God's existence can be offered by this route, there is still a feeling that existence is not quite so easily disposed of in this way. G. E. Moore offered some reflections on this theme in a famous essay about what we mean when we say that "tame tigers exist" as opposed to "tame tigers growl." He felt compelled by the logic of Bertrand Russell's philosophy to agree that although to say "tame tigers growl" is to add to a description of what they are like, to make the further point that "tame tigers growl and exist" adds nothing to the description. It tells us no more about them than "tame tigers growl" tells us. He knew that this was crucial to the rebuttal of the ontological argument, since the rebuttal insists that existence is not a further quality to add to (in the case of tigers) growling or being stripy. And yet it made him uncomfortable to accept this, since he felt that it made perfectly good sense to say "Tame tigers might not have existed," and if it made perfectly good sense to say that, why should it not make perfectly good sense to say "Tame tigers exist"?[13]

The issue is whether, though existence is certainly not a predicate in the way that roundness, hardness, and spottiness are, it may still be a predicate in some other way, because of the lingering sense that existence, even if not a quality itself, is something that manifests itself through the qualities. It appears to be another case of an elusive and omnipresent enabler, like the light that cannot be directly gazed upon and yet is everywhere around, letting things be what they are. Moore clearly feels that there is something about existence that we fail to realize because of the unique way in which it makes its presence felt. Perhaps the question of being needs to be looked at more carefully than other philosophers thought.

Some philosophers have devoted a great deal of attention to it. The question of being was at the heart of the writings of the philosopher Martin Heidegger. "Being," Heidegger's *Sein und Zeit* (*Being and Time*) begins, is the question that "has today been forgotten" ("today," of course, being the 1920s), and he intended to explore it in a systematic manner.[14]

---

13. Moore, "Is Existence a Predicate?"
14. Heidegger, *Being and Time*, 2.

The question of being is forgotten, Heidegger suggests, because being cannot be conceived as an entity and is therefore indefinable. At the same time, it is self-evident, since it is implicit in any assertion that we make: we make comments such as "the sky is blue" all the time. Self-evident but indefinable seems to return us to Moore's puzzlement at being confronted by a tame tiger whose existence must mean something. We find ourselves using the concept all the time without being able to say what we mean by it, and for Heidegger this more than justifies us in raising the question of being again:

> The very fact that we already live in an understanding of Being and that the meaning of Being is still veiled in darkness proves that it is necessary in principle to raise this question again.[15]

We necessarily see only things as they appear to us, but Heidegger talks of "something which *hides* itself in that appearance—an emanation which announces."[16] Once we recognize that the meaning of being is veiled in darkness, we can proceed to what Heidegger calls the task of "ontology," which he defines as "to explain Being itself and to make the Being of entities stand out in full relief."[17] Our approach must be "phenomenological," by which he means we must go "to the things themselves"—looking at how they are rather than engaging in free-floating constructions. The trouble, as we have already seen, is that making the being of entities stand out is a much more complicated task than merely isolating it and then focusing our intellectual lens on it. It becomes an exercise like chasing our own shadow.

Heidegger tries to catch the shadow through observing the linguistic churn created by the always indirect presence of being in the reality we can observe. He shows how the complexities of being are played out in language through terms like "logos," "appearance," "phenomenon," and, of course, "being" itself, which was the subject of discussion in various fundamental texts of classical philosophy such as Plato's *Parmenides* (one of his most difficult writings), Aristotle's *Categories*, and his *Nicomachean Ethics*. Heidegger absorbed these texts thoroughly (he recommended that his students spend at least a decade familiarizing themselves with Aristotle).

The dense prose of *Sein und Zeit*, written in German and dealing with key terms from ancient Greek and Latin, makes for a very difficult text even when mediated through a very careful English translation like that of John Macquarrie. An honest appraisal of Heidegger (better minds than mine will

---

15. Heidegger, *Being and Time*, 23.
16. Heidegger, *Being and Time*, 54 (emphasis original).
17. Heidegger, *Being and Time*, 49.

not have to be so modest) would be that one is drawn to him by the sense that he's saying something important without being able to identify precisely what it is, an approach that is perhaps rather appropriate to the intended message of the work itself. For arguably that is precisely what Heidegger is saying about his own search for being. Language pushes us toward recognizing the presence of something we are unable to identify. Being is the elusive presence that cannot be defined—precisely what we might expect of the omnipresent enabler.

It is not that if we are sufficiently sensitive to language or penetrate deeply enough into reality, we shall have a glimpse of God somehow hidden beneath all the outer layers created by bad linguistic habits. The point is not that if you look hard enough and deeply enough you will be able to come upon lost traces of God, like the shards of the broken vessel in the myth of the *tikkun*. This story, mentioned in part 3 above, tells of how God contracted the divine self to create space for creation, a tale with an obvious kenotic resonance. In the process, divine light became contained in special vessels, some of which were unable to sustain the pressure and shattered. As a result, the light was scattered, and though most of it returned to its divine source, some light remained attached to broken shards of the vessels and became the basis for the material world. But Heidegger's exploration of being is not like a treasure hunt or a game of hide-and-seek designed to discover behind which particular use of language, like a hidden piece of that scattered light, God has somehow concealed Godself. It is an attempt to show how something at once self-evident and indefinable reveals itself in an environment where direct observation is impossible.

Being in Aristotle and Aquinas

Given that Heidegger himself recommended a decade of studying Aristotle, it would help at this point to mention Aristotle's writings, as well as the use made of his thought in Aquinas and the later tradition of Thomism.

For Aristotle, objects are the outcome of a process through which matter combines with form in order to produce this or that particular thing. Matter refers not to bits of stuff but to "pure potentiality," something that comes into being only when realized in objects that always take one form or another—tables, frogs, human beings, and so on. Only through a meeting of matter and form can individual things exist—in other words, they can be (come into being) only by being *something*.

But that is the point—how do they "come into being," as we say? When matter combines with form, it is not like a naked person slipping into a shirt or a dress. It is like the appearance of a composite that cannot be broken down into parts. We cannot chisel away at the outer layers of reality in order to find the fundamental building block of all that is. For Aristotle, things are the outcome of a process by which indefinable matter takes form as one thing or another. Matter is realizable only in the forms and cannot be separated out so that we can identify the pure matter—the atom or the Higgs boson—out of which everything is constructed.

It was Aristotle who provided the basis for Aquinas's theology and the Thomism that has had such an enormous influence upon later Christian thought. Aristotle gave Aquinas a vital clue about how we could all have being, whether as human beings or other lesser beings, without any sense that being was like the basic component out of which the whole universe is built up, the pre-Socratic earth, air, fire, and water. Indefinable matter became indefinable being and, since God was being itself, it became the indefinable God, the transcendent who was also immanent.

Aquinas suggests that it is insofar as things have being—insofar as they are—that they participate in God and are held in being by God. "In so far as they are *what*?" it might be asked. "Insofar as they are what they are" is the answer. Insofar as they are held up to the light, without themselves containing it. For they—and we—can have *being* only by being *something*. In McCall's words, "For Aquinas, extricating existence from life is absurd, because things do not simply exist—they exist as certain types of things, with particular types of operations."[18] And as Heidegger recognized, we cannot separate out or somehow distill the being. It is not as if there is some substance of which we can see slight traces in animals, larger quantities in ourselves, and somehow conceive of as existing in pure form in God. This is a misconception that supposes us to be somehow diluted versions of God, more diluted than angels but less diluted than animals or vegetables.

Given this understanding of being, it is important to stress that the so-called "analogy of being"—*analogia entis*—which has certainly proved a controversial idea in Christianity, needs to be very carefully defined. The "analogy of being" must never allow the idea of God as being itself to be diminished by treating being as if it is some kind of rare substance like gold that is discernible only in traces inside the lesser reality of human bodies. In defense of Thomism, one can surely argue that the attraction of Aristotle's notion of matter and form, together with Aquinas's use of it, is that it drives us away from thinking of a universe built like LEGO out of little bits, be they atoms or Higgs bosons. The idea of matter as something that can never be captured in itself but only recognized in the forms of which it is an essential

---

18. McCall, *Modern Relation*, 108.

but eternally elusive ingredient is that it undermines that idea rejected earlier of the material universe as a huge, self-sufficient object, infinite in its complexity but basically self-sufficient in being a finished work of creation. For that reason, Aquinas is able to call God being itself without being ending up as another name for the basic piece of LEGO. It can never be directly observed. Like light, it is everywhere but cannot be grasped, though precisely in its inaccessibility it enables things to be themselves. As being itself God is omnipresent without sacrificing God's transcendence.

Conclusion

The last two chapters have focused in different ways upon a challenge to the idea of two realms, the divine one above and the earthly one below. The first chapter examined this in the context of the doctrine of creation, insisting that creation neither concerned the first few moments in which the universe came into being nor the production of something that was somehow to be set beside God and made the subject of two-way traffic between the heavenly and earthly realms. The second chapter tried to look more closely at what it meant if God was not to set side by side with (or above) the created universe, but somehow interpenetrating it while remaining separate from it. Hence the discussion of a panentheist theology, one in which God is neither identified with the world (pantheism) nor somehow separate and adjacent to it (deism).

When it came to making sense of panentheism, the chapter turned to a familiar image, that of God as light. Images are useful—as the scientists would be the first to concede with their wormholes, membranes, and strings. Light does more than describe something associated with moral goodness or intellectual insight. It helps to convey a complex theological idea.

In the first place, it asserts God's unknowability and transcendence. The light that blinds when looked at directly warns us off thinking that God could ever be an object within our intellectual grasp.

Second, it asserts that God is nevertheless—even as transcendent—at the same time omnipresent, though not as something like the fundamental building block out of which the universe is constructed. If anything is knowable of God, it is that God is the enabler of all else—the things that are "held up to the light." Light is omnipresent not as an ingredient of the things we see, but as what enables them to be seen for what they are. Light helps to elucidate Bonhoeffer's famous description of God as the "beyond in our midst," the traditional theological idea of God as both transcendent and immanent.[19]

When we deal with God's immanence or presence in the world, we can do so only in negative terms, because God makes God known through the inability of what we know to sustain itself, something that makes Heidegger explore the notion that our language seems to be constructed around something it cannot adequately define. All this is consistent with the idea that we can say only what God is not. The *via negativa* is preserved. We can note the way in which God determines everything we know and at the same time say that God is beyond all knowledge.

And if this is the theological position that makes sense, isn't the whole search for the "God particle" a fool's errand, based on the strange idea that somehow, when we unearth the fundamental constituent of all that is, we will finally discover a slice of the divine essence or perhaps something that can help us to explain what happened "in the beginning"? There is no "God particle" to be unearthed somewhere as the basic constituent of the universe, a modern version of the pre-Socratic hunt for the fundamental ingredients of reality. The presence of the divine nature remains the presence of the indefinable other, the God that is everywhere present and on whom we depend for our being, but who can be neither observed nor defined. It is not as if a part of God is concealed within the fabric of the created order. It is not as if some kind of diluted divine essence has spread itself through the created order, as some understandings of the "analogy of being" suggest. In their different ways light and being indicate that the created order is sustained only by the God who is present, not by surrendering God's transcendence but by realizing it.

---

19. Bonhoeffer, *Letters and Papers*, 282. The letter was written to Eberhard Bethge on April 30, 1944. Bonhoeffer writes that "God is the beyond in the midst of our life. The church stands not at the boundaries where human powers give out, but in the middle of the village." The quotation comes from a very important letter, in which Bonhoeffer explored the idea of "religionless Christianity" that gave rise to many books on Christianity in a secular age. Editions of *Letters and Papers* have varied numbering, but the passage can be found by concentrating on the date of the letter.

Chapter 13

God as Trinity

The third chapter of part 4 connects what has been said about God as Creator and about the idea of God as both transcendent and immanent, to the notion of God as Trinity. It seeks to link the triunity of God to the way in which God both embraces and is set apart from the natural universe, as suggested in the first two chapters of part 4.

This chapter does not try to survey the complex history of the doctrine of the Trinity or the difficulties in making sense of the different words and expressions used, particularly in terms of the crossover between Latin expressions like *persona* and *substantia* and Greek terms like *prosopon*, *ousia*, and *hypostasis*. Though much that is useful can be learned from the struggle to find suitable language with which to express and make sense of the doctrine, the focus here is upon what the doctrine of the Trinity says about the nature of God.

Orthodox Christian doctrine speaks of "three persons" in "one substance." God is three but God is also one. How is this to be understood? It is a doctrine that has vexed theologians. In the Latin West there was an emphasis upon the oneness or unity of God, which ran the risk of denying the distinctness of the three persons, while in the Greek East the danger was more of losing sight of the unity and falling into tritheism (a belief in three gods) by emphasizing the distinctness of the persons.

The illustration often cited for the Western outlook is that of Augustine, who compares the three persons to mind, knowledge, and love (*mens, notitia, amor*) or to memory, intelligence, and will (*memoria, intelligentia, voluntas*).[1] It is not difficult to see why this was seen as undermining the

---

1. Augustine, *On the Trinity*, 23–60, bks. 8–15. Augustine refines his analogy as he

distinctness of persons. After all, it is not clear that distinct faculties (and are they even examples of three distinct faculties—is mind a faculty?) provide an adequate illustration of the distinctness of the divine persons, when they represent to some extent an arbitrary dividing up of the mind and in any case suggest different aspects of a single human person.

In the East, the illustrations were couched in more straightforward terms, by drawing a comparison between the general and the particular, between the species (for instance, goat) and three individual examples of it (Billy 1, Billy 2, and Billy 3). However, the idea that Father, Son, and Spirit might be instances of a particular species like three goats or humans obviously smacked of tritheism. Moreover, this was always something Christians were sensitive about, since their opponents liked to portray their language about the deity of Christ as a sign of their polytheistic beliefs. If they spoke of the Son as divine as well as the Father, surely they were committed to at least two gods. Now they appeared to be moving even further down the road to polytheism by claiming three. How many would they believe in next week? Twenty-six?

An attempt was made early on in patristic theology to distinguish between the "immanent" and "economic" Trinity, as if any apparent split inside the godhead portrayed by the latter could be overcome by an assertion of the implacable unity guaranteed by the former. But this raised the problem of identifying the precise relationship between the "economic" and the "immanent" Trinity. The point appeared to be that "economic" Trinity referred to the way in which the divine nature was revealed in the work of salvation. But this turned one problematic Trinity into two. Did God change when God became involved in the work of salvation? Was the economic Trinity a dumbed-down version of the true nature of God for humans? The problem was transferred to the "immanent" Trinity, which guaranteed the unity of God but whose nature remained unclear.

A better approach would be to find a way of suggesting that in the case of God, unity and inner diversity could be brought together in a way that didn't make sense at the human level. The sense of a higher unity in the case of the divine persons was captured in a book based on the Croall Lectures given by Leonard Hodgson as long ago as 1942–43.[2] Hodgson argued that as one followed the process of evolution one found a combination of greater inner complexity and at the same time a greater unifying power. As one moves from the amoeba to the vegetable to the animal to the human, for instance, one discovers a wider range of attributes and functions held

---

goes along, so it is best to read both chs. 9 and 10.

2. See Hodgson, *Doctrine of the Trinity*.

together by the increased organizing power of individual examples of the species. An individual animal can move where an individual plant cannot. An individual human can reason where (some would say) an individual animal cannot. And so on. By extrapolation, Hodgson wants to suggest, God can maintain unity through an inner diversity that from the creaturely perspective must clearly break apart. Hence at the level of divinity triunity is possible, where from our human perspective there is only tritheism.

Enough has been said in part 2 to reflect our suspicion about evolutionary trees and escalators. Hodgson's analogy is too suggestive of some kind of unimaginably complex multitasking deity who can hold together in one system of management the countless obligations of being divine. But where Hodgson has a point is in the suggestion that the persons of the Trinity are interconnected and mutually dependent in a manner that we cannot expect to be replicated at the human level. There is evidence of such an approach in both Eastern and Western traditions.

For instance, Gregory of Nyssa tries to link the divine persons to their activities by arguing as follows (the translation is unfortunately punctuated as a single sentence, but the meaning soon becomes clear):

> Perhaps one might reasonably allege as a cause why, in the case of men, those who share with one another in the same pursuit are enumerated and spoken of in the plural, while on the other hand the Deity is spoken of in the singular as one God and one Godhead, even though the three persons are not separated from the significance expressed by the term "Godhead," one might allege, I say, the fact that men, even if several are engaged in the same form of action, work separately each by himself at the task he has undertaken, having no participation in his individual action with others who are engaged in the same occupation.[3]

As Brown points out in quoting this passage, when we speak of a group of people acting together—for instance, a mob—we tend to use the singular. The separate individuals become one through their common purpose. But Gregory in the quotation above suggests something more. It is not just that the divine persons have a complete unity of purpose that is lacking in human beings, even when they are in complete agreement. By saying that human beings, even if they are working on the same project "work separately each by himself at the task he has undertaken," Gregory suggests that in the case of the Trinity the three persons participate in a more direct manner in the actions of each.

---

3. From Gregory of Nyssa, *Ad Ablabium quod non sint tres dii* (To Ablabius on why there are not three Gods); quoted in D. Brown, *Divine Trinity*, 279.

This attempt to make sense of the complexities of divine coworking is significant because it bears upon the doctrine of the incarnation, which is the focus of part 5. In particular, it raises the question of how far the incarnation is an act of the Son and how far it involves all three persons of the Trinity. In an essay on the relation between the doctrines of incarnation and Trinity, MacKinnon warns theologians not to make too much of the distinction between "the Western emphasis on unity expressed e.g., in the Augustinian invocation of psychological analogies in treatment of persons and processions, with the Greek (Cappadocian) preoccupation with the three *hypostaseis*."[4] He points instead to the established axiom of Trinitarian theology associated with both West and East that *omnia opera Dei ad extra sunt opera totius indivisae Trinitatis* (all actions of God toward the outside world are actions of the one undivided Trinity). This proves very important for making sense of the incarnation. For once we assert that all three divine persons are involved in the work of each, the incarnation becomes not simply a special action of the Son but something that involves the Spirit and the Father too. The other two persons were intimately involved in the process, even though only the Word became flesh. They did not simply remain on the sidelines in heaven while the Son popped off for a tour of duty on earth.

However, if one asserts that all three persons are involved in the work of each, there may be a problem identifying the grounds for distinguishing between them. If they are not distinguished by having special areas of competence unique to their particular roles, then how are they to be distinguished at all? If all actions of God toward the outside world are really actions of the one undivided Trinity, then presumably the ground for differentiating between them must lie somewhere in their internal nature. But what can that difference be, when they are said to be three persons in one substance? If we imagine a fourth-century Arian in the form of devil's advocate here, he or she would suggest that the different persons can be distinguished only if they are of different substances—hence the famous iota through which Arius affirmed that the Son and Father were "of like substance"—*homoiousios*—rather than "of one substance"—*homoousios*. Where else could one go in order to distinguish the three persons? The Arian could conclude that orthodoxy is forced to choose between three different substances and a single indivisible blob that it makes no sense to divide into separate divine persons.

Augustine cannot move from the category of substance to that of accident in order to rescue the distinction between the persons, since one could

---

4. MacKinnon, *Themes in Theology*, 156. This is a revised form of an essay that first appeared in McKinney, *Creation, Christ and Culture*.

hardly present Father, Son, and Spirit as a description of passing phases in the one God. So having rejected the Arian idea that the persons are different (however similar) in terms of substance, and also the idea that they differ in terms of accident, he brings to the fore the concept of relation, arguing that the distinction between the persons is grounded in their eternal relations to one another. According to the Nicene Creed the Son is eternally "begotten" of the Father, the Father by implication is the eternal begetter, and the Holy Spirit eternally "proceeds" from the Father and from the Son (the famous *filioque* clause "and from the Son" that was a source of controversy between Western and Eastern approaches).

There is, of course, every reason to wonder what exactly "begetting" and "proceeding" amount to and even how they differ from one another. Brown tries to present Augustine's approach in the most general possible terms:

> It is the Father who alone relates and is not related, the Son who both relates and is related and the Holy Spirit alone who is related but does not actively relate.[5]

It is clear from this summary of Augustine's view how important the *filioque* clause was. Only if the Holy Spirit proceeded from both Father and Son could the distinction be made between the Son who "relates and is related" and the Spirit who "is related but does not actively relate."

Whatever the neatness of the distinction, it is hard, as Brown himself admits, to give it meaning, besides which it would be reasonable to want to know much more of what exactly begetting meant and how it differed from proceeding. And yet the interest in the concept of relation as the key to understanding the Trinity persisted in Western thought. It was a concept that offered to make sense of the close connection, the "perichoresis" or *circumincessio*, Greek and Latin words suggesting a "going around" each other as in a dance, the mutual indwelling of the divine persons whose separate being was exhaustively defined by their relations to each other. This remained an important principle whatever one made of begetting and proceeding.

MacKinnon refers to Aquinas's *De Trinitate* (*On the Trinity*), in which "the relations with which the persons of the Trinity are identified are characterized as quasi-substantial."[6] Human beings are partly constituted as themselves through their relations to others. The notion of "substantial relations" suggests that each of the divine persons is not partly but wholly constituted by their relation to the other two. The self-giving is so complete

---

5. D. Brown, *Divine Trinity*, 282.

6. See Aquinas, *Summa contra Gentiles*, 4.1–26; Aquinas, *Summa Theologiae*, 1.27–43. Discussed in MacKinnon, *Themes in Theology*, 156.

that there is no residue of individuality that can continue without the others. The self of each is exhaustively contained in its relation to the other two. MacKinnon quotes a passage of Régnon's *Etudes sur l'histoire du dogme de la Trinité* to this effect:

> Whoever says "father" says "father of a son." Whoever says "son" says "son of a father." To be a father is to have a son, to be a son is to have a father. I know that among men paternity is something added, as a man must be constituted a human being, before he can be a father. But in God the person of the Father is made up of nothing else than being a Father.[7]

Aquinas's idea of "substantial relations" provides a powerful image of the mutual self-giving of the three divine persons and the willing vulnerability of each in being dependent on—indeed, on being formed through—its relations with the other two. If a father loses a son, he may well say that "a part of me has died." But if the father was constituted only through his relation to the son, what kind of unimaginable grief must the death of that son impart? In this sense the idea of substantial relations allows us to make some sense of Moltmann's observations on the crucifixion as presented in Moltmann's *The Crucified God*, where he comments that "the grief of the Father is just as important as the death of the Son."[8] We see from this that in the light of the mutual indwelling of the three persons the kenotic "self-emptying," with its suggestion of freely willed vulnerability, is not confined to the Son but is shared by all three persons of the Trinity and reflects the divine nature as such.

The Trinity and the Vulnerability of God

As part 5 will examine in more detail, those attracted to a kenotic theology are inspired by an overwhelming sense of divine self-giving and self-sacrifice demonstrated in the life of Jesus, a self-giving that the kenoticists are prepared to affirm whatever the metaphysical consequences. For precisely this reason, David Brown in *Divine Humanity* presents many of the kenotic theologians as highly orthodox in their overall theologies and yet driven by the kenotic impulse almost beyond their own inclinations. He cites John Austin Baker's *The Foolishness of God* (1970) and William Vanstone's *Love's Endeavour, Love's Expense* (1977) as examples of powerful works that find

---

7. MacKinnon, *Themes in Theology*, 156–57. See also appendix C, 165–67, for the original text by Régnon in French.
8. Moltmann, *Crucified God*, 206, 243.

in the kenotic idea the means of ensuring that we appreciate the cost to God of what happened in the life of Christ.[9] The poem "Hymn to the Creation," with which Vanstone ends his book *Love's Endeavour, Love's Expense*, concludes by reminding the reader that God is not a monarch "thron'd in easy state"[10] but one with arms of love that ache with the strain of sustaining the world.

The more it is emphasized that God was indeed in Christ as he lived and suffered on earth, the more it makes sense to talk of those aching "arms of love" or the foolishness (perhaps that of the "holy fool") of one who gives himself for others. Not that this is anything particularly new. As Brown points out, one can find similar language in the hymns of Charles Wesley, and Vanstone's powerful poetic language could be matched by Wesley's:

> He left his Father's throne above—
> So free, so infinite his grace—
> Emptied himself of all but love,
> And bled for Adam's helpless race.[11]

However, there is a problem with this approach, however powerful. If we look again at Charles Wesley's hymn, we see the reference to "He left his Father's throne above." It is hard to dispel the image of the Son being sent to earth on a kind of mission impossible. Brown points out that one of the concerns that John Austin Baker had about kenoticism, despite the obvious way in which he was influenced by kenotic ideas in *The Foolishness of God*, was the manner in which it seemed to be separating out one person of the Trinity from the others, as though God was, as Baker puts it, "a committee, one of whose members can be detached to serve on a foreign posting."[12] The arms of love appear to be those of the Son alone. It is precisely in order to avoid such an interpretation that the doctrine of the Trinity needs to be grounded, as emphasized by MacKinnon above, upon the idea that "all actions of God toward the outside world are actions of the one undivided Trinity."[13]

If this principle is forgotten, then the "way of the Son of God into the far country," as Barth put it in his *Church Dogmatics*, is seen as the action of one person of the Trinity alone, almost a form of absconding.[14] It is as if he

---

9. See the discussion in D. Brown, *Divine Humanity*, 159–68.
10. Quoted in D. Brown, *Divine Humanity*, 165.
11. D. Brown, *Divine Humanity*, 31.
12. Baker, *Foolishness of God*, 320.
13. See MacKinnon, *Themes in Theology*, 156, who describes this principle as "fully in accordance with orthodox tradition."
14. See Barth, *Church Dogmatics*, 4.1:157–211.

goes off leaving behind important business for the other two persons of the Trinity to take up, like fellow members of some triumvirate keeping shop while one of them is temporarily indisposed. Such a misguided approach leads Wolfhart Pannenberg, for instance, to ask in his famous *Jesus, God and Man* what might otherwise seem to be a bizarre question, namely how, if the earthly Jesus didn't want to be almighty, he "rules the world as the Logos in the meantime."[15]

In an article entitled "The Strange Persistence of Kenotic Christology," whose title well reflects its overall perspective, Professor S. W. Sykes highlights what he considers to be the problems of a kenotic approach, citing William Temple's criticism of H. R. Mackintosh's *The Person of Jesus Christ*:

> The difficulties are intolerable. What was happening to the rest of the universe during the period of our Lord's earthly life? . . . To say that the Creative Lord was so self-emptied as to have no being except in the Infant Jesus is to assert that for a certain period the history of the world was let loose from the control of the Creative Word.[16]

Sykes continues by quoting D. M. Baillie, arguing thirty-five years later (in *God Was in Christ*) that "the challenge had gone unanswered."[17] But is this a fair assessment and are the difficulties really "intolerable"? What is meant by "for a certain period the history of the world was let loose from the control of the Creative Word"? Is it as if by becoming incarnate the Word has to take his hand off the wheel of the ship and go to sort out a problem down below while the ship is left to careen around at will?

One way of trying to deal with this problem has been to assert a division within Christ himself. This is the position taken in what Lutheran scholastics of the seventeenth century were to dub (perhaps unfairly) the *extra calvinisticum* of the Reformed tradition. This argued that the Son maintains two centers of consciousness, one in heaven where he continues to perform his role up above, never removing his hand from the wheel of governance, and the other on earth where he takes flesh. He kept his hand at the wheel while his double, as it were, went off to become incarnate. It is difficult to see how such a bifurcation can maintain the unity of Christ's person. Though it may say that one of his two "natures" remains in heaven while the other appears on earth (based on the christological formula that Christ is "two natures in one person," it is an argument that would appear to make sense only in terms of two persons. There is a problem maintaining the unity of

---

15. Pannenberg, *Jesus, God and Man*, 353.
16. Sykes, "Strange Persistence," 357.
17. Sykes, "Strange Persistence," 357.

Christ as "two natures in one person," just as there is a problem maintaining the unity of God as "three persons in one substance."

Rather than trying to imagine something akin to two Christs, one on earth as Jesus of Nazareth while the other keeps control of the wheel up above, it would be better to understand how all three persons of the Trinity are directly involved in the work of incarnation, even if only one becomes flesh. The argument of this chapter is that the difficulties Temple saw as intolerable were so because of a failure to grasp that Father, Son, and Spirit were nothing like three essential crew members steering the ship or (to recall an earlier analogy) the three members of a triumvirate empowered to manage an empire like that of ancient Rome. The divine nature cannot be turned into a committee, even by those who make use of the doctrine of the Trinity. To do so would indeed be to develop a form of tritheism. The three persons then become three gods, two of whom stay running heaven while the third is sent to earth. To avoid this, the life of Jesus has to be seen as part of the eternal life of the triune God and not just a special task set aside for one part of it. It involves them all.

The doctrine of the Trinity prevents us from bracketing off the life of Jesus as the responsibility of the Word alone. The incarnation is not some kind of unpleasant task for which the three persons draw straws and the Son's proves the shortest, leading to his being temporarily evicted by the family *ad extra*. It is not assigned exclusively to the Son while the others promise to cover for him while he's gone. The doctrine of the Trinity enables us to present the incarnation as an essential part of the internal life of God. It is for precisely this reason that the Trinity provides the metaphysical scaffolding around the incarnation.

There are suggestions of this in the New Testament texts, though part 5 will examine this in more detail. In Mark 1:11-12 we read:

> And a voice came from heaven, "You are my Son, the Beloved; with you I am well pleased." And the Spirit immediately drove him out into the wilderness.

These verses make clear that Father and Spirit are intimately involved in the life of the Son; they are not sitting up in heaven "minding the shop" while he is away.

At the same time, merely to say that all three persons are "involved" is not enough, for the three persons are not simply a triumvirate working together. Though orthodox Trinitarian theology rejects tritheism, we easily find ourselves thinking in terms of three separate people helping each other out, so that in the passage cited above (Mark 1:12-13) we think of the Father blessing from above, the Son receiving from below, and the Spirit then pushing him on to the next task of being tempted in the desert. There is even a certain advantage in this perspective, since it prevents us from thinking that God created the world out of loneliness or as the expression of some kind of social need. Fellowship, we can argue, is already internal to the divine being in the differentiation of the three persons one from another. But this cannot be understood simply in terms of three separate people enjoying each other's company. The imagery explored in the previous section has tried to suggest a much closer relationship, a perichoresis, which is not simply an intimate dance but total self-determination through the other.

On the basis of what we have described in this chapter, we can draw from the doctrine of the Trinity an affirmation that the Father is definable only in terms of relation to the Son and the Spirit. In the same way the Spirit is definable in terms of relation to the Son and the Father, the Son only in terms of relation to the Spirit and the Father. Each has their distinct personhood only in relation to the others. This prepares us for the christological focus of part 5, because it makes clear that the incarnation does not involve the Son alone. It is an action of the Trinity itself, and the example from the biblical text above shows how both Father and Spirit are involved in the incarnate life (not to mention the death) of the Son. As for the kenosis, which is the focus of this book, self-emptying, in the sense of the giving of self to the other, is not one of the demands made of the Son in order to facilitate his journey down to the humans. It is a definition of what constitutes the divine persons, who realize themselves only through their relations to each other, and thereby show what is demanded of human persons who must also live for and through others. The self-humbling of kenosis, whatever our conclusions about the meaning of Phil 2:5–11 and its famous "christological hymn," is not simply an act of generosity on the part of the Son, or a decision to repeat the journey of the first Adam by showing the obedience that the first Adam did not show. It is primarily a statement about the nature of God, a statement about God's own nature as persons in relation, realizing themselves only through their eternal dance of mutuality. Though it is hard to make sense of this in terms of ideas like begetting and proceeding, these traditional creedal formulae suggest a mutual dependence in which each lives through the other—not through some kind of eternal subservience but through an eternal dependence in which each is fully realized only in relation to the others. Hence, MacKinnon's comment that "what is the doctrine of the Trinity if not the effort so to reconstruct the doctrine of God that this 'descent' [MacKinnon is referring to the *descendit de coelis*—he descended from heaven—of the creed] may be seen as supremely, indeed paradigmatically, declaratory of what He is in himself?"[18]

Conclusion

Perhaps it would have been better to follow Barth in beginning with the doctrine of Christ, as his *Church Dogmatics* does, and then moving to the doctrine of God that arises out of that definitive self-revelation. But this book has begun with a discussion of God as Creator, as transcendent and immanent, and as Trinity, in an attempt to provide the metaphysical scaffolding for the doctrine of Christ.

Chapter 11 examined the doctrine of creation. It emphasized that space and time are themselves part of creation rather than some kind of backdrop for God's activity in the world, whether as Creator or as Redeemer. We are therefore primed to be clear in part 5 that when God assumes humanity in the incarnation this is not like a trip through time and space, a thirty-three-year visit from heaven to earth.

Chapter 12 considered the nature of God as both immanent and transcendent and only immanent *as* transcendent. It explored the image of light and the concept of being in order to examine how we can meaningfully discern what is beyond knowledge in the things that make themselves known to us. The chapter considered what it means to say that God is woven into the interstices of reality in such a way that God can be recognized only indirectly, hidden in the linguistic churn that underlies so much of our language about being. Our guiding principle remains that transcendence does not go away when God is immanent. God is immanent only *as* transcendent. In this sense we have a "negative theology" even when talking about God's immanence. This is of crucial significance when we move on in part 5 to what can be known of God through God's self-revelation in Christ.

Chapter 13 focused on the doctrine of the Trinity. It helps to prepare for part 5 by emphasizing that the incarnation does not involve the Son going off alone, leaving the other two behind. It is an action of the whole Trinity, reflecting the way in which each person of the Trinity lives through and for the others. Hence when we finally come to Christology in part 5, we are not discussing a part of God or just one person of the Trinity.

This, then, is the metaphysical scaffolding around the idea that, as Baillie's book defined it, *God Was in Christ*. The God who was in Jesus of Nazareth was the triune God, not merely "one part" of the divine being. The God who was in Jesus of Nazareth was not a God who stands outside

---

18. MacKinnon, *Themes in Theology*, 160.

or above the world, but a God who is eternally present to the world, a God whose presence is recognized by the way the world carries within itself a perpetual dependence upon what can never be directly observed or defined. We see things when they are held up to the light; but our power of sight is destroyed if we try to face the light directly. God is not in the particles that supposedly form the basic LEGO blocks of a self-sufficient universe. God is the beyond in our midst, the God who never ceases to be beyond when in our midst, the God who is transcendent even when immanent, affirming an infinite qualitative difference between God and human beings even when God risks everything in the self-emptying of divine incarnation.

This was the Barthian bomb that a century ago, encased in his great commentary on *Romans*, exploded, as Karl Adam put it, "in the playground of the theologians,"[19] and now explodes in the playground of *Guardian* readers as they try to reconstruct God from champagne corks and Mexican hats.

---

19. Time, *Religion*, 4.

PART 5

The Uncertain Christ

The point is surely this: we cannot say what God is in himself; all we have is the narrative of God with us. And that is a narrative of "a journey into a far country" (to borrow Barth's powerful image itself of normative importance to McKinnon) a story of God's son as a creature and a mortal and defeated creature: the unity of God and his Son in this story is not, in the actual detail, moment by moment, of the story, desert temptation, Gethsemane, dereliction, realized for us as an unshakeable, already achieved thing. It emerges at last, when Christ goes to his Father risen and glorified, as the issue of a temporal process, with all its ambiguity, the uncontrolledness of its effects . . . the precariousness of its growth. That is what temporal process is for us. In other words, it is a story of "risk"; and only at Easter are we able to say, "He comes from God, just as he goes to God," and to see in the contingent fact of the resurrection–the limited events of the finding of an empty tomb and a scatter of bewildering encounters—that which is not contingent, the life of God as Father and Son together.

ROWAN WILLIAMS[20]

---

20. R. Williams, "Trinity and Ontology," 82.

Chapter 14

How the Logos Left Heaven Behind: The Unavoidable Focus?

The final part of this book will go to what is often regarded as the core of the problem of kenoticism and will attempt to flesh out a Christocentric perspective, taking account of what has been said in part 4 about the nature of God.

Two Natures in One Person

It is unrealistic to talk as if there is just one problem where Christology is concerned. However, there has traditionally been one orthodox formula used to describe Christ, namely as "two natures in one person." As generations of scholars have struggled to make sense of this idea, they have been rather like people struggling with an old-fashioned shower, twiddling one way to avoid something scalding hot and then immediately twiddling the other way in order to avoid something freezing cold, with the two extremes marked Antioch and Alexandria rather than hot and cold.

Rather than try to define the differences between these two schools of thought, this chapter will look at what have been identified as difficulties on the way to formulating an adequate Christology. Those who risk being scalded in the shower (broadly speaking, the Alexandrians) argue that the unity of Christ's person should not be compromised. They stress that the center of consciousness, even of the incarnate Christ taking human form, must lie with the divine person who assumes humanity. The criticism they then face is that they compromise the fullness of Christ's humanity. Sometimes their opponents accused them of allowing "taking human form" in the incarnation to mean something more like appearing human than being human. Hence the accusation of docetism. More subtly, the accusation was that they had a Logos-flesh or Logos-body rather than a Logos-man Christology, so that the divine Word or Logos effectively took the place of the soul in the person of Christ. The human body of Christ then became something like a container or sack that the Logos entered and used as an instrument of its divine will. The famous saying in John 1:14, "The Word became flesh," was turned into something more like "The Word clothed itself in flesh." For some philosophers at the time flesh as such, or even a body as such, required an animating principle, such as a soul, or else it was merely lifeless matter. According to a Logos-flesh Christology, the Logos would essentially supply the capacities that in someone else would have been supplied by the soul. This idea had an obvious attraction to those whose idea of the relation of soul to body was that the soul was essentially some kind of driving force inside its bodily covering.

One problem with the Logos replacing the soul in Christ was clearly stated by Gregory of Nazianzus: "That which is not taken is not healed, but whatever is united to God is saved."[1] The implication of the principle that what is not assumed is not redeemed was that if Christ simply replaced the human soul in Jesus, the human soul was not saved. Hence orthodoxy preferred the idea of indwelling Logos or Word, human soul and human body as an ungainly threesome constituting the person of Christ.

At times the orthodox position espoused by Athanasius and others could veer toward saying that the Logos took the place of the soul in Jesus, as it was clearly to do in the thinking of Apollinarius when Apollinarius insisted that there could only be one nature (*mia physis*) in Christ. On the whole, however, Athanasius and others were happy to acknowledge that Christ had a soul as well as a body, provided that the Logos was still the indwelling director of both. Hence in John 10:28 Jesus says, "I have power to lay my soul down and power to take it up again." So far as Athanasius was concerned, Jesus could have a human soul just so long as it was as much under the control of the Logos as his body was.

There was an advantage in this way of thinking when it came to dealing with Christ's passion and death. In the first place, it was believed that the suffering, uncertainty, and pain of the passion must be ascribed to the flesh only, if necessary by talking of "the will of the flesh" (a term used by Marcellus of Ancyra) in order to shield the Logos from such susceptibilities.

---

1. From Gregory of Nazianzus's famous "Epistle 101," which criticizes the ideas of Apollinarius.

HOW THE LOGOS LEFT HEAVEN BEHIND: THE UNAVOIDABLE FOCUS?

But in the second place, if the point was to maintain a shield between the incarnate Logos and the sufferings of the human condition, then adding a human soul to the person of Christ was a good way of strengthening the shield. One might even go so far as to say that there were two wills in Christ (dyothelitism). Where Jesus says in Matt 26:41 "Not my will but thine be done," it might be interpreted to mean that two wills inside the same body are agreeing who should be in charge of a particular decision. However much this seems to overload the person of Christ with centers of consciousness and threatens to break the unity of his person apart, it does at least add to the cladding around Christ to keep his physical sufferings and even his mental irresolution away from the steadfast and immutable nature of the indwelling divine Logos. As Aloys Grillmeier puts it:

> To avoid burdening the Logos with the suffering on the Mount of Olives, as happens in Arian argumentation, he (Marcellus) contrasts the divine will of the Logos with the human will of the flesh in Christ. This already seems to introduce the beginnings of a Word-man Christology.[2]

The will of the flesh became a shield to protect the Logos from sufferings that would otherwise have to be attributed to him. This was an advantage in challenging the Arians, the followers of Arius against whose challenge the Council of Nicaea met and produced the Nicene Creed in 325. Behind the attempt of Arius and his followers to express their belief that the Son was a little less than divine—for instance, the insertion of an iota to suggest that the son was "of like substance" (*homoiousios*) rather than "of the same substance" (*homoousios*) with the Father—was a desire to protect the Father by finding some way of inserting a wedge between him and the Son. They felt driven to find some way of protecting God from too much exposure to human sensibilities when present in the Son. Orthodoxy preferred an approach that kept layers of protection around the Logos in order to preserve the divinity from contamination. The idea of a second will, a will of the flesh, provided a suitable repository in order to avoid ascribing the more unsavory aspects of the human condition to the Logos.

Probably those who adopt a kenotic perspective will not feel too challenged by this apparent problem of exposing the Logos/Son too much to the human condition. From a kenotic point of view, it could be argued that no protective shield is necessary because God does indeed feel the emotions of Christ on the Mount of Olives, and all this is part of the self-giving of God as love, the outworking even of God's omnipotence if it is recognized

---

2. Grillmeier, *From the Apostolic Age*, 285–86.

to be an omnipotence of love (as discussed in part 3). There is no need for any shield to be put in place by attributing all these emotions to something separate from the Logos itself. The fixation on the flesh as a kind of tent to be occupied and then vacated by the Logos fails to see that in the incarnation the Logos does not travel to the Earth in a protective spacesuit designed to be worn in the emotionally troublesome atmosphere of the blue planet.

The attempt to separate the Logos from the will of the flesh is even more problematic when it comes to the death of Christ. Writing against the Arians, Athanasius declares that "the Lord, being himself immortal, had power as God to become separate from the body and to take it again when he would."[3] We can see here how closely allied the notion of the Logos inside the flesh is to the notion of an immortal soul inside an earthly body, leaving it behind at death as a snake might leave behind its sloughed skin. With the death of Christ, according to Athanasius's conception, the Logos apparently leaves the body of Christ in the tomb and visits the souls of the dead in Hades. We are far from the idea of the death of Christ as a death within God, as described in Moltmann's *The Crucified God*. Death applies to the body in which the Logos is contained, but it does not happen to the Logos himself, which continues on its way to visit the souls of the dead much as Plato imagined the soul to leave the body behind as a discarded shell. Such a view reminds us how important traditions of the empty tomb are to a Christology that recognizes the importance of Christ's body. It is not just a shell to be removed at death but becomes part of the resurrection. Resurrection is resurrection of the body, not the future life of an immortal soul that has escaped the body. This reinforces the claim from a kenotic perspective that just as the body is a necessary part of Christ's life after death, so bodily suffering and uncertainty are part of the experience of the incarnate Logos. The Logos cannot be separated from human suffering, any more than the human soul can be detached from the body.

"Becoming Flesh" and the Continuity Problem

It might seem that a preparedness to accept the idea of the Logos suffering pain and even death overcomes the christological problem faced by Athanasius. Athanasius's fear was that a Logos who suffered would thereby be less than divine, giving Arius his entry to deny the divinity of the Son. Only affirm from a kenotic perspective that the Son can indeed suffer without losing divinity and the problem is solved. It is all part of the "self-emptying" of the Son in becoming incarnate.

3. Athanasius, *Against the Arians*, discourse 3.

However, there is more to the problem of Christology than this. Athanasius is not just concerned about shielding the Logos from some of the less prestigious aspects of being human. He is unclear what can be meant by "became" in "the Word became flesh" (John 1:14). For one thing, he was concerned about the danger of imagining the Logos turning into something else. That would either introduce the *tertium quid*, some kind of half-divine, half-human mixture like a superior angel, or it would imply that the eternal Logos had turned into a human and for that reason was no longer the Logos. There were also various ideas of divine emanation around, as if the Logos came forth like a finger extended from heaven, but that was clearly problematic. Incarnation could hardly be cashed as divine extension. The idea of the Word "becoming" flesh seemed to avoid these two dangers if it meant something like taking flesh or indwelling flesh or using the body (and the soul, if necessary) as an instrument. It seemed logical to suppose that if the Logos was not to change into a *tertium quid* or a man, then assuming humanity must mean adding something, and that was precisely what seemed attractive about ideas of "indwelling" or even of putting the body on as a garment that could then be taken off in the tomb when his work was done. Anything else was in danger of becoming a metamorphosis.

Hence we see that protecting the Logos from suffering was not the only difficulty in making sense of the incarnation. There was also a problem of continuity between the divine Logos and the human Christ. This was another reason why orthodoxy moved rapidly in the direction of incarnation as a case of addition without division. Of course, this was difficult to defend. The idea of the *sarx* or flesh, or even an "ensouled" flesh, as some kind of tent for the Logos to dwell in during its earthly sojourn, raised all sorts of difficulties. A century after Nicaea, at the time of the conflict with Nestorius at the end of the 420s, the unsatisfactory nature of the lingering "tent" conception was still being emphasized:

> Before the beginning of the Nestorian controversy, Cyril had used the "indwelling formulas" unconcernedly with the rest of the tradition. After 429 they are either repudiated or expanded.[4]

Cyril of Alexandria accused Nestorius of a form of indwelling that indicated a merely accidental relationship, like the tent that is used for a while and then discarded. Cyril wanted instead to emphasize a "true, substantial" relationship between the Logos and human nature. Human nature, he insisted, was not a temporary addition, later thrown away. This was surely correct. For instance, Jesus undergoes a resurrection of the body rather than

---

4. Grillmeier, *From the Apostolic Age*, 477.

the disappearance of the Logos from the tomb, having discarded its bodily companion—a view that would be compatible with the body remaining in the tomb to decay while the followers of Jesus tried arguing that the divine Son had simply left this temporary article behind, like a parachute abandoned after a jump.

However, once we insist upon the avoidance of the body or even body-soul being viewed as a mere temporary home for the Logos, we have to face the continuity problem, that is to say, the problem of establishing that the Logos or Son does not change into something else by becoming flesh. We have to make clear that Cyril's "true and substantial" relationship cannot be seen in terms of a metamorphosis, as if the Logos changes into a human being much as, in Kafka's famous story of Gregor Samsa, a man changes into a beetle.[5] We can insist that the Logos does not simply put on humanity as if climbing into (and later, after death, out of) a tent, but if we then move toward some kind of mixing of the two, we end up with a blended being who is half-divine and half-human, the already-mentioned danger of the *tertium quid*. Cyril of Alexandria tried to express the point by saying "God the Logos did not come into a man, but he 'truly' became man, while remaining God."[6] This may not be a solution to the problem, but one can see what Cyril is trying to do.[7] In becoming flesh the Word cannot be said to change into something else, but it also can't be said to have simply put on humanity like a new set of clothes. It must be said to have both stayed unchanged as God the Son *and* to have become man in a more complete sense than donning a uniform. Cyril wants to avoid the two pitfalls of addition on the one hand and change on the other. But this is obviously a difficult circle to square where any meaningful notion of the unity of Christ's person is concerned.

Trying to square the circle produced a great deal of complex linguistic interweaving on the part of patristic thinkers. The idea of "two natures in one person" was developed in order to maintain their hoped-for position, but it was always in danger of falling apart. If you were going to stress that the divinity and humanity while conjoined (to avoid division) in no way blend together to form a "third something" that is neither divine nor human, you were in constant danger of splitting the two.

Cyril insisted that the two natures represented distinction rather than division. He used the word *hypostases* to describe the natures, a word that was also used to describe the separate persons of the Trinity, and which

---

5. See Kafka, *Metamorphosis*.

6. Grillmeier, *From the Apostolic Age*, 477.

7. See "Cyril of Alexandria, the Adversary of Nestorius," in Grillmeier, *From the Apostolic Age*, 473–84.

might well be thought to imply separate persons inside Christ. Yet we need to remember that it is difficult to analyze different philosophical understandings in terms of the choice of words, since the words themselves changed their meaning through time and in any case might mean different things in different contexts. A classic example of this is the word *prosopon*. It is generally accepted that *prosopon* originally meant something like an actor's mask or a face, although it later came to mean an individual person. But if at a certain moment both meanings overlapped, could someone play upon the ambiguity? Is this what Nestorius was up to, playing up the "individual person" when he wanted to protect the individuality of the two natures, and then playing it down when he was challenged over whether he could really claim to be maintaining the unity of Christ's person? The search for meaning has to take account of the possibilities both of deliberate obfuscation and of the natural change in the meaning of words over time.

It is best to say that the arguments over the use of words reflected a genuine philosophical difficulty. Despite the way in which words change their meaning and different meanings may well overlap, we can agree that the word *hypostasis* had a stronger sense of self-existent being than the word *phusis*, which is closer to essence. It was therefore a dangerous term to use, since it could easily be taken to mean that there were somehow two centers of consciousness in Christ.

Even leading scholars like Aloys Grillmeier and J. N. D. Kelly didn't always seem to offer very precise definitions. As Grillmeier put it, "The Godhead and manhood in Christ unite themselves in one combined appearance."[8] Such language avoids controversy by leaving all options open until one takes the scalpel to terms like "combined appearance" and tries to identify what lies within.

Incarnation and Reincarnation

In *Divine Humanity* David Brown mentions a growing interest in kenosis on the part of analytic philosophers at the end of the last century and the beginning of this one. He cites as an example the philosopher Peter Forrest, who published "A Philosophical Case for Kenosis" in 2000. Forrest hypothesizes "that Jesus had some memories of his pre-incarnate state."[9] Part of the reason for this is that he believes that some "awkward questions concerning personal identity" have been neglected.[10] How do we know that

---

8. Grillmeier, *From the Apostolic Age*, 492.
9. Forrest, "Philosophical Case," 129.
10. Forrest, "Philosophical Case," 134.

the divine Word and the human Jesus are the same person? We can hardly rely on bodily continuity. Forrest points out that while an amnesiac may lack any memories of a past life, there is "continuity of body image." But that is lacking in this case, as is what Forrest calls "continuity of routine behavior patterns, such as the way of eating, the way of dressing, the way of walking, and so on."[11]

The philosopher John Locke had a famous story of a prince and a cobbler.[12] Imagine a prince who wants a quiet life—perhaps he is afraid of being assassinated—and a pauper who would like wealth and status, even at the cost of extra risk. Each decides to become the other. The easiest way to conceive of this is to presume a dichotomy between soul and body and then imagine the prince's disembodied soul slipping into the cobbler's body and the cobbler's disembodied soul slipping into the prince's body. Swapping bodies becomes a bit like swapping clothes. Our souls are seen as detachable from their bodily shells, much as one might get in and out of a car.

For all its flaws, this analogy makes sense of the activities of the Word in one sense. The Word abandons the merc in heaven and pops down to earth for a spell chugging about in a battered mini. This is the attraction of the body as "shell" or "tent" discussed earlier in this chapter. Like the soul in Locke's story, the Logos moves into a human body and starts to direct it. Such an idea raises problems concerning Christ as an individual person, but it appears to make sense of the continuity of identity between the heavenly Word and the incarnate Word.

We find ourselves facing the sort of philosophical issues that are raised by those who hold a belief in reincarnation, where they are forced to consider what justifies them in saying that someone living now had a former life as someone else. For believers in reincarnation cannot go down the route of Locke's prince and cobbler. They do not suggest that the soul of one person can get into the body of another or even replace another soul with their own, rather like a cuckoo invading a nest. Another life begins only at birth. Therefore, the evidence of continuity has to come from elsewhere, and the usual technique is to suggest that for some reason a few memories of a previous life remain. It is as if the ritual bathing in the waters of Lethe that was supposed to take away all memories of another life had been inadequate and a few dry bits remained unaffected, like the heel that made Achilles vulnerable. Supporters of reincarnation stress the memory of a past life, claiming that some of the details were not made known to anyone else, and so their

---

11. Forrest, "Philosophical Case," 138.

12. See "Of Ideas of Identity and Diversity," in Locke, *Essay Concerning Human Understanding*, bk. 2, ch. 27.

recall shows that the person speaking about them must have had another life before their present one. Although it is true that Jesus makes claims about himself as one sent by God (one thinks of the parable of the vineyard, where the owner of the vineyard finally decides to deal with troublesome tenants by sending his son), it is not as if when challenged about those messianic claims he tries to say, in the manner of those trying to make a case for their having had previous lives: "I was in heaven a few decades back, and if you don't believe me let me tell you something about what it was like."

It is worth pointing out that similar identity problems can crop up after the end of Jesus's life, in the understanding of what happens to him through resurrection and ascension. If we take the view that the empty tomb shows, among other things, that whatever happened to Jesus at the resurrection involved his body, we are immediately removed from the sort of understanding that focuses upon a disembodied soul, which could have emerged from the tomb leaving the body behind. Therefore, we have to say that resurrection involves a transformed body, not a departed soul. Does this mean, then, that in its post-resurrection life the Word still has the body of Jesus with it, albeit a transformed body that can, according to the resurrection narratives, be difficult at first to recognize (on the road to Emmaus) and can suddenly appear in a room and just as suddenly vanish? It is not the body resuscitated, which would be Lazarus brought back to life but required to die all over again. It is the body raised to a new form of life. This transformed body would be an important context for understanding the ascension. If Jesus simply goes up like a rocket, then he is still subject to the limitations of space. But if what happens is more like the vanishing from the upper room referred to at the end of Luke's Gospel, then it simply reflects the fact that he is no longer confined by the spatiotemporal parameters that limit the rest of us. Forrest interestingly remarks that "Jesus did not go anywhere—by becoming omnipresent he went everywhere."[13] It was this belief that enabled Lutherans to maintain the view that he could be present in the eucharistic elements, even when communion was being celebrated in several different places at once.

Forrest concludes with these words, reflecting his conviction that bodily continuity in itself is not enough to guarantee continuity of identity in the case of the risen Jesus:

> It is only if the exalted Christ knows some things in the divine way and others in a human way that he can have the memories which seemed to be required for him to be identical with Jesus

---

13. Forrest, "Philosophical Case," 129.

rather than anyone else who came to share in the Word's project of reconciling humanity to God.[14]

Forrest's point is that unless the exalted Christ retains memories of being Jesus of Nazareth, continuity of identity is again put in doubt. But in the case of the resurrection/ascension, there is at least some form of bodily continuity. In the case of the skydive, the leap taken by the preexistent Word into the form of existence described as "becoming flesh," there is neither bodily continuity nor the memories Forrest insists upon even when there is such continuity.

The False Lure of the Skydive

How, then, are we to try to deliver a plausible understanding of Christ's person? What we surely have to bear in mind is the fact that much of the philosophical interest described in the last section stems from assuming that the kenotic approach is based on the self-conscious decision of the divine Word to embark on what Karl Barth called a journey into "the far country" and then the way in which he returned from it at the resurrection/ascension. The key problem arises when we start to imagine some kind of transformative dive out of heaven by the Logos or Son. At the risk of an Aunt Sally, let us imagine an initial heavenly state in which the divine Son has all his powers and is busy governing the universe at the right hand of the Father. We then imagine him being handed some kind of communication from his left side, a kind of mission impossible, requiring him to leave his position above and go down to earth, where he is to be born in a manger. Unsurprisingly, there will be a problem of identity. How do we know that the person at point A, up in heaven, is the same person as the mewling infant opening its eyes in the manger at point B? Lacking the usual means by which we feel entitled to assert continuity of identity, such as bodily continuity or memories of a past life, we may feel that we face a dilemma and therefore head for the idea of "addition." Hence the humanity of Jesus as a tent or clothing in which the divine Son chooses to wrap himself.

But can we do without the dive? In one sense, the dive is an idea that appeals to kenoticists. The divine Son stoops to conquer. The prince leaves the palace and goes off in disguise to woo the humble maiden (Kierkegaard's famous analogy).[15] Kenoticism emphasizes the idea, based on the so-called

---

14. Forrest, "Philosophical Case," 139.
15. See "God as Teacher and Savior," in Kierkegaard, *Philosophical Fragments*, ch. 2, esp. 26–30.

christological hymn of Phil 2:5–11, of the Son of God "emptying himself," and this inevitably sets up in our minds the notion of getting rid of something. Hence the idea that the Logos surrenders certain attributes—like omniscience—and becomes the human Jesus who can say, for instance, "of that day or hour no one knows, not even Son, only the Father" (Mark 13:32). In some versions of kenoticism, the incarnate Logos merely conceals his powers; in others, he gives them up. But in either case we have the sort of imagery where the incarnate Logos, like a parachutist waking up in the desert after a long and bruising fall, realizes that he no longer has all his equipment with him or remembers why he has chosen not to bring it along, or perhaps why, despite bringing it along, he cannot use it.

It is the false lure of the skydive that leads to the problem of continuity described in the last section. Once you assert that there is a divine being waiting in heaven for the right moment to plunge to earth, where he emerges into the world as a helpless human child somewhere in the Near East, one has all the problems of continuity of identity—between the Logos in heaven and the creature coming to consciousness in Bethlehem—which arise in the philosophical discussions we've tried to outline.

A recent chapter by John McGuckin concerning "Origen of Alexandria on the Kenosis of the Lord" points out that Origen was accused (by Jerome) of claiming that the soul of the Savior existed before it was born of Mary, and it was this preexisting soul that was "in the form of God and did not think it robbery to be equal to God but emptied itself taking the form of a slave" (Phil 2:7).[16] This became one of the anathemas aimed against Origen at the Second Council of Constantinople in 553. It may well have been a misrepresentation of what Origen believed, but one can see precisely why Origen might be drawn to say it. For if the christological hymn in Phil 2 is used in order to imagine something like a being in heaven deciding to make a journey to earth and later emerging as a baby in a manger, then there is surely bound to be a question of how the identity of that being is maintained. The idea of a soul continuing to exist through all these changes at least attempts to find a way of maintaining the identity of the Word through the process of leaving heaven and appearing on earth.

In reality, Origen's approach was not so different from that of Augustine when he stressed that in "emptying himself" the Son took what he was not rather than divesting himself of what he was. There is a similar concern about continuity of identity, but in this case through the emphasis upon addition, so that continuity is ensured by whatever the body was added to. Whether it is the soul adding a body (Origen as interpreted—perhaps

16. McGuckin, "Origen of Alexandria," 95.

misinterpreted—by Jerome) or the Son adding "what he was not" rather than divesting himself of what he was, there is at least an enduring subject through all the changes. Of course, as Kantzer Komline points out, Augustine recognized that addition produced its own problems. It cannot be like "acceptance of an extraneous, alien appendage," or in more down-to-earth language like putting on a set of clothes for the journey from heaven down under.[17]

As soon as the skydive becomes our dominant image, the person of Christ is imagined not as a human subject but as a self-conscious divine subject, one who from what is traditionally seen as a kenotic perspective is thinking of what has been surrendered or concealed by leaving heaven. Then we find ourselves forced to add this divine subject to the human nature of Christ, either from the very beginning at birth or as he grows up as a child and a young adult in and around Nazareth. If we do that, are we not bound to divide Christ into two persons, following the Nestorian heresy condemned by the Synod of Ephesus in 431? Will we not end up with two subjects, two centers of consciousness? Or else, will we not go to the other extreme and, by making the Logos the only subject, deny or at least undervalue the humanity, turning human nature into a mere appearance or ghost because its experiences are not the experiences of a human subject? And don't these problems, in reaching an adequate understanding of the "two natures in one person," reflect the problems described above of establishing the continuity of identity between the heavenly Logos and Jesus of Nazareth? We end up without any continuity of identity at all because we have two persons rather than one, or else we end up with one divine Word and a human being who isn't a person at all. One way or another we are surely forced in the end to ask ourselves: What sense does it make to say that the subject of the experiences of the central character in the New Testament narrative is any other than the human being Jesus of Nazareth?

Does not any other approach to that which makes the human being Jesus of Nazareth the subject of all the experiences of the incarnate Christ make the christological problem insoluble? Any idea of "he came down from heaven" immediately gives the impression of an incomer looking for somewhere to stay, even if the incomer "empties himself" by removing a lot of his heavenly baggage on the way. Can we maintain the insights of a kenotic perspective while developing our Christology, as it has often been expressed, "from below" rather than "from above," starting from what is happening in the life of Jesus and the way in which, as a human subject

---

17. See Komline, "Augustine, Kenosis," 108.

rather than a divine subject in exile, he tries to make sense of the situation he finds himself in? This is what the rest of part 5 will explore.

Conclusion

This chapter began by considering difficulties that have arisen with the idea that the subject of the incarnate Christ must be the divine Logos. Traditionally, one problem has been the apparent need to ascribe qualities like pain, suffering, and uncertainty to the Logos. But since the point of a kenotic approach is to admit that these very qualities belong to the heart of a God who freely accepts the weakness and vulnerability of being incarnate, the ascription of such qualities is not an insurmountable barrier to making sense of the incarnation.

More problematic is the continuity problem, that is to say, on what basis do we identify the divine Logos before incarnation with Jesus of Nazareth on earth? Where is the continuity of identity? We don't want to say that the Logos has been blended with humanity to produce some kind of half-human, half-divine mixture, the danger of the *tertium quid*. Nor do we want to say that the divine Logos has changed into something human like Gregor Samsa turning into an insect in Kafka's *Metamorphosis*. We therefore feel driven to maintain continuity by adding humanity to an unchanging divine subject—precisely the sort of approach that leads us in the direction of humanity as like a tent for the Logos to dwell in or a coat for the Logos to wear. Inevitably, the person of Christ becomes cluttered and the maintenance of one subject of Christ's experiences more difficult—or even impossible—to defend.

The conclusion of the chapter is that focusing upon the process of leaving heaven for earth may be a mistake. Once we start thinking of the process by which in the incarnation humanity is assumed by the Son in terms of a journey from the heavenly realm above to the earthly realm below, we seem to go wrong. If leaving heaven for earth is thought of in the way Locke presents his prince getting inside the body of a cobbler in order to live a new life away from the palace, we inevitably encounter problems. Should we stop trying to begin our analysis with speculation about what happened in heaven before the Word took the plunge and set off for the far country? The next chapter will examine whether a kenotic Christology can avoid being tarnished with the brush of the skydive.

Chapter 15

Avoiding the Skydive

There is a thorough examination of different kenotic models in Professor Coakley's "Does Kenosis Rest on a Mistake?" Coakley examines three kenotic models in patristic exegesis, which she associates with Cyril of Alexandria, Nestorius, and (her preferred option) Gregory of Nyssa. With Cyril she says that "the personal identity of Christ lies squarely in the preexistent Logos" who assumes human nature (without being "contaminated" by it, as she puts it, using a striking phrase concerning the dangers of "ontological leakage") for salvific purposes—recalling Gregory of Nazianzus's point that what hasn't been assumed cannot be redeemed.[1] This presents the divine Logos as firmly in control of the whole proceedings and is very much a Christology from above.

The second example she gives is Nestorius, who emphasizes that Jesus is the second Adam, a human being who retakes the path trodden by the first, but this time in obedience rather than disobedience, thereby making up for what went wrong in the case of the first Adam. There is emphasis on Jesus of Nazareth as a human being and therefore the picture is more one of conjunction than assumption, because such a clearly drawn human figure can hardly be presented as a mere outfit or appearance, which is the danger of assumption. But how does the divine nature fit together with the human figure? This threatens the unity of Christ's person, the problem that bedevils the Nestorian position. Moreover, conjunction simply means adding a focus upon the divine Word to a focus upon the human subject. It does not try to replace the former with the latter.

---

1. Coakley, "Does Kenosis Rest," 251.

Though Nestorius wants to ensure that the humanity is fully recognized, he is also very keen to stress that the two natures remain distinct. Paradoxically, it may be the Alexandrian approach, stressing an assumption of humanity, that has a more positive view of the humanity of Christ than the Nestorian conjunction of natures, because the Nestorian stress upon the full humanity goes along with a desire to keep the divinity from being "contaminated" by it. The assumption of humanity emphasized on the Alexandrian side may threaten to swamp the human nature with a divinity that effectively undermines it, but it may also elevate it rather than treat it as something to be kept at bay. There may be a more obvious role for the humanity in the Antiochene position, but at the same time it may be a more marginalized one.

Coakley's own preference is for Gregory of Nyssa's idea of a "progressive transfusion." As she puts it:

> Rather, what Gregory proposes is a real, but gradual, transfusion of divinity into the human, until, as he memorably puts it, the humanity is "absorbed by the omnipotent divinity like a drop of vinegar mingled in the boundless sea."[2]

One can see the benefits of this approach. On the one hand it avoids a standoffish approach where humanity and divinity face each other but remain distinct, even within the one person. On the other hand, it avoids a scenario of metamorphosis where something divine changes into something human, the incarnate Christ waking up like Gregor Samsa in the restrictive state of humanity (the equivalent of Samsa's insectitude). Progressive transfusion, even if a bit like meeting Dracula, at least conveys the idea that divinity and humanity do not simply confront each other but interrelate, the divine infusing the human "until it is fully restored to its proper perfection in the resurrection."[3]

"Progressive transfusion" allows the theologian to cope with the picture of even a mistaken, confused, and frightened Jesus brought out by modern biblical criticism. Coakley points out that Gregory of Nyssa's transfusion is not two way but the gradual filling of one container until there is no more it can take. Presumably on the way to receiving it Jesus maintains his human limitations—he is still in the state of being Popeye without enough spinach, and he receives the full tin only at the time of the resurrection.

However, what is noticeable about all three approaches is that whether the focus is upon the preexistent Logos assuming human nature without

---

2. Coakley, "Does Kenosis Rest," 257.
3. Coakley, "Does Kenosis Rest," 259.

being "contaminated" by it (Cyril), the human and the divine in some kind of close conjunction (Nestorius), or the divine nature steadily filling the human with its riches as the latter becomes progressively more able to receive them (Gregory of Nyssa), we keep thinking along the lines of a divine subject determining how to impart its virtues adequately to a human receiver (or even how to protect them from being "contaminated" by the human receiver). After all, the *communicatio idiomatum* (communication of attributes) in Coakley's presentation is one way only, from divine to human, rather than from human to divine. The Nestorian position avoids this, but its position of conjunction also runs into difficulties. It presents the divine nature struggling to find room for itself alongside the fully drawn human nature without expelling it, like the victim of the cuckoo, from the cramped nest of Christ's personhood. Whichever of Coakley's three options we decide for, we are still working with the divine subject in the foreground—and in control, a presumption that has led to some interesting criticism from feminist theologians.

Feminist Reservations about Kenoticism

Some feminist writings have highlighted the danger of a kenotic theology, glorifying self-abnegation or alternatively presenting a new form of male domination in the way a patriarchal God effectively manages the humanity in which he condescends to be incarnate.[4] It is as if the humanity is effectively commandeered from above and prohibited from interfering in the business of the incarnate Word or allowing anything effeminate like emotion to compromise the essential business of arranging human salvation, like a woman who finds herself forced to stay at home and keep out of her husband's affairs (doubtless in both senses of the word). The humanity becomes a prop for the Son, something for him to use in order to realize his incarnate design without actively contributing to the realization of that design. McCormack describes Apollinarianism as taking the Alexandrian position to its logical conclusion through the "complete instrumentalization of the human, with no independent, personal reality outside the Logos' own life."[5] Once the preexistent Logos is the christological subject, a truncated humanity follows.

Consider the well-known controversy that emerged between the creeds of Nicaea (325) and Chalcedon (451) over the *theotokos*, the notion of Mary as "God-bearer." Some theologians—for instance, Theodoret—were

---

4. For example, Hampson, *Theology and Feminism*.
5. See McCormack, *Humility of Eternal Son*, 39.

uncomfortable about acknowledging Mary as God-bearer, Man-bearer, or Christ-bearer, and for others, like Nestorius, discomfort led to heresy. What was the problem? The difficulty lay in the fact that if Jesus was God from birth and not from later in his life, then the impact of the human nature upon the person of Christ, being able through influence or association to weld it into the reality of God the Son incarnate, was bypassed. The divine nature alone provided the principle of unity in the person of Christ. This is what upset Nestorius. What about the burning bush, he asked, where fire and bush remain separate but form one thing together by some form of co-penetration? What about the Trinity itself, where God is one only by also being three? He wanted to say that Christ is God and Man only by a similar co-penetration, but in the *theotokos* we have the nature of Christ signed, sealed, and delivered by the divine Logos alone, emerging into the daylight through Mary, the role of whose own flesh is marginalized (even more so by the idea of the virgin birth). As "God-bearer," Mary is duly honored but also *dis*honored, since the God-*bearer* falls short of being a God-*maker*, and by having a ready-made deity emerge at birth (rather like the image of "a bun in the oven," which marginalizes the woman's role) she is denied significant influence upon his life. With a divine nature ready-made, there is no need for human nurture, and in a way that is not unnoticeable in the history of the Christian church, Mary is promoted away from being a significant player, like a troublesome politician rewarded with a peerage and sent to be unheard of among the ermine warriors of the upper house.

To return to Cyril of Alexandria for a moment, McCormack believes that "for Cyril, there is really no such thing as 'the man Jesus' in the sense of 'a human person,' an independent entity to whom the Word has conjoined himself."[6] Even worse from a feminist viewpoint, the Word makes human properties his own, in a sense, takes possession of them and owns them. It is as if the patriarch gives the woman a completeness she could never have on her own and achieves by surrendering entirely to being possessed by the male. When it comes to the communication of properties, the communication is all one way, from the vinegar to the sea rather than from the sea to the vinegar. The traffic flows in only one direction. It is hardly surprising if theologians were forced by their belief in two wills (dyothelitism) within Christ, the human and the divine, to claim that the unity of person could be maintained only by making one of the wills entirely passive. Nor is it surprising if a convenient model for such an active/passive combination of wills should have come from considerations of the relation between man and woman in a patriarchal society. Is there a way out of this dilemma?

---

6. McCormack, *Humility of Eternal Son*, 45–46.

Beginning with the Human Subject—The Two Natures in Reverse?

In *Divine Humanity*, David Brown suggests an analogy from method acting based on the ideas of Konstantin Stanislavsky. The actors become totally absorbed in the identities of the characters they are playing. Brown suggests that his analogy helps to explain how the two natures may be held together in one person. The problem with traditional two-natures Christology, he plausibly infers, is that the two natures end up "so minimally interacting that the notion of there being a single person involved makes no real sense."[7] His analogy, on the other hand, clearly avoids the sort of minimal interaction that so often weakens the force of a two-natures Christology (as when it is said that the human nature weeps for Lazarus, while the divine nature raises him). He also makes the point that the acting analogy need not turn the human nature into a passive script written by the divine Word. There is room for improvisation and even for Brechtian disruption (*Verfremdung*). This human actor takes the Word beyond what is in the script and into the challenges faced by conflict in society.

It is a powerful image, but it suggests that Brown is another kenotic skydiver. He reminds us of the capacity of great actors to become the parts they are playing, of great writers to bring to life characters that they recognize as having minds of their own, so that they almost take the story out of the hands of the author and write their own parts. At the conclusion of his book, he talks about the total absorption in the character's identity practiced by the method acting associated with Stanislavsky. Like the method actor, the incarnate Son enters into the experience of another while remaining aware that it is not his own. "If I may dare to put it like this," Brown writes, "it is not so much God with a human skin as God under our very skin."[8] But even for the greatest of actors we are clear that the subject of these experiences is the Logos, the one who left heaven behind in order to get "under our skin."

We have seen how, for fear of ending up with two subjects in the incarnate Christ, the human nature was forced into the position of being a mere passive instrument of the divine Logos. But suppose we turn this upside down. Suppose that in order to avoid ending up with two subjects in the incarnate Christ, and also to avoid making the human Jesus a mere instrument of the overwhelming Logos, the divine Logos is seen as a passive instrument of the human Jesus.

Consider Bruce McCormack's recent *The Humility of the Eternal Son*, a work that has caused theological discussions to toss around the phrase

---

7. D. Brown, *Divine Humanity*, 253.
8. D. Brown, *Divine Humanity*, 254.

"ontological receptivity." Cyril of Alexandria had secured a unified subject of the incarnate Christ through an active Word employing the human Jesus as its instrument. McCormack suggests reversing this by making the human Jesus the performative agent in the power of the Spirit. All the Logos does in assuming humanity is to take all that Jesus did and experienced as a self-existent human being up into his own life. It is not so much an act of passivity on the part of the Logos as receptivity, since "ontological receptivity" is an active relation. To quote McCormack's admittedly difficult description of Christ's person:

> A single composite hypostasis, constituted in time by what I will call the "ontological receptivity" of the eternal son to the "act of being" proper to the human Jesus as human.[9]

McCormack wants to avoid any sense of the humanity being instrumentalized by the divine Son. He notes that this does not happen in the case of the Spirit, which is always seen as inspiring. When Jesus is described as being "full of the Holy Spirit" (Luke 4:1), this is not seen as taking away his full powers as a self-existent being, despite the fact that, in Mark's version, the Spirit drives (Mark 1:12) Jesus into the wilderness. The Spirit's indwelling is seen as empowering rather than controlling and instrumentalizing.

"Ontological receptivity" is McCormack's way of saying that the assumption of humanity by the Son does not limit Jesus as a self-existent human being. How could it undermine the very human nature that orthodoxy assures us is in fact being exalted through the incarnation? Why is assumption by the Son, unlike the indwelling of the Spirit, somehow perceived as a steamrollering of the humanity? Not that the two should be seen as separate operators, like the nice and nasty policeman. Rather, it is precisely through understanding how Son and the Spirit work together (and indeed how God functions as a triunity) that we can understand that "the Son can only possess the absolute nature of God in the mode of receptivity"[10] and therefore can assume humanity while allowing the human Jesus the full autonomy of independent human existence.

McCormack's position has a similar sense to Brown of the need to stress that the indwelling Logos does not dominate and control the humanity, but rather allows itself to be determined by the humanity just as a great actor allows themselves to live only in and through the parts they are playing. McCormack similarly suggests that the assumption of humanity in the incarnation appears to be an effective takeover, turning the humanity

---

9. McCormack, *Humility of Eternal Son*, 45–46.
10. McCormack, *Humility of Eternal Son*, 252.

into the passive instrument of the indwelling Son, only because we fail to understand the true nature of the indwelling Logos. But he goes further than Brown in suggesting that the root of our failure to understand the true nature of the indwelling Logos lies in our failure to understand the nature of God, and in particular the mutual self-giving that informs the persons-in-relation who comprise the Trinity (as we examined in chapter 13). This means that the complete receptivity of the divine Son, which enables his indwelling in no way to override the self-existent being Jesus of Nazareth, is grounded in the complete receptivity of the Son to the Father in the perichoresis that characterizes the three-in-one God. The clue to why the Son does not override the humanity through assumption lies in the way the Son, Spirit, and Father coexist in the "ontological receptivity" that is the essence of Godhead. In this way McCormack provides an ingenious linkage between the doctrines of the incarnation and the Trinity, hoping to use this link in order to solve the problem of Christology.

Total Receptivity—MacKinnon Anticipates McCormack

MacKinnon says the following in his essay on the relation between the doctrines of the incarnation and the Trinity:

> Yet if Jesus is to reveal that "He is the revealer," thus disclosing that his significance is not in himself, and that where he is concerned, the most important fact is this, that he is the identifiable historical individual through whom God has addressed the world, we may claim that this is only possible through the realisation in his historical individuality of a total receptivity.[11]

In this passage McCormack's "ontological receptivity" is anticipated some decades before by MacKinnon. Both think in terms of a "total receptivity" (to quote MacKinnon), which is realized in the historical individuality of Jesus of Nazareth but at the same time represents the particular role of the Son in the eternal triunity of God.

The Catholic theologian Hans Urs von Balthasar described God's existence as in itself a kind of "super-Kenosis."[12] McCormack is drawn to this idea, quoting Balthasar's description of the "primal divine drama" (theo-drama) whereby God surrenders Godself without reserve and without losing Godself. By making this clear, McCormack believes that Balthasar manages to "establish the ontological ground in God of the Son's self-giving

---

11. MacKinnon, *Themes in Theology*, 144.
12. Balthasar, *Mysterium Paschale*, viii.

in time."[13] In other words, what happens in the incarnation is grounded in the eternal being of God. In the words of Christoph Schwöbel: "Is it necessary to assume a primordial kenosis, an Ur-kenosis, in the relation between the Father and the eternal Son in order to make the incarnation as kenosis real?"[14] If he answers yes to his own question, it is because Jesus receiving power from the Father is part of the eternal life of God as the mutual indwelling of three persons.

The emphasis of a kenotic approach ceases to be a particular interpretation of what happens when the Word descends from heaven. As David Fergusson puts it, "The thirty-three years of Christ's life and passion have been viewed as a *katabasis* that performs a divinely initiated rescue mission on a fallen world."[15] Instead of being a way of describing Christ's unique rescue mission to bring back fallen humanity, kenoticism should describe the way in which God is God, the eternal life of the Trinity. The self-emptying of which kenosis speaks has nothing to do with a surrender or loss of deity. It is an expression of deity. As Fergusson puts it, the divine humility is an essential attribute, not an expedient measure. And he adds that the latter view is a danger run by those atonement theories that present Christ's death as a necessary sacrifice in order to satisfy the supposed requirements of divine justice.

Both MacKinnon and McCormack suggest that a kenotic approach must connect the life of Jesus with the eternal life of God as Trinity. Jesus of Nazareth is drawn into a perichoresis of divine persons who exist in relation to one another and whose love flows from one to the other in a unity of mutual dependence. The Trinity is a means of enabling us to see how God was defined by the incarnation. It is when we understand how God is three in one that we have a clue about how God can be in Christ. One must, of course, avoid tritheism, which so easily slips into our thinking when we think, for instance, of the Son being driven into the desert by the Spirit while the Father approves from above—the incarnation turns into a sort of mission impossible carried out by a dynamic trio. The three persons of the Trinity do not have individual consciousness. The threeness of God is a way of describing the divine nature as one of eternal receiving through giving, a concept that makes sense only in terms of internal self-differentiation.

We return to MacKinnon's interest in Aquinas's notion of "substantial relations," where each person of the Trinity is exhaustively defined in terms of its relation to the others. The inner self-differentiation that is essential to God's being becomes a demonstration of divine love through each person's

13. McCormack, *Humility of Eternal Son*, 153; Balthasar, *Action*, 325.
14. Schwöbel, "Generosity of Triune God," 270.
15. Ferguson, "Kenosis," 204.

willingness to be determined by the others, so that the self-giving between the divine persons is so complete that they must be seen as constituting one being. McCormack quotes what he calls in his book one of the "post-Barthians," Eberhard Jüngel. In *Gott als Geheimnis der Welt* (*God as the Mystery of the World*), Jüngel describes how "God has himself only in that he gives himself away. But in giving himself away, he has himself. That is how he is."[16] In terms of the Trinitarian thinking that is inseparable from thought about the incarnation, it is only insofar as the persons of the Trinity give themselves to each other that they may have themselves. God remains other in God's givenness and is given in God's otherness.

This mutual giving and receiving that is the essence of God in God's Trinitarian being is the essential context for understanding how "the Word became flesh" (John 1:14). What is revealed to Jesus of Nazareth in his total receptivity to the Father is that he is part of the mutual giving and receiving of the triune God, the divine perichoresis. The divine love is defining itself through him. As an individual human being living in total receptivity to the Father, Jesus finds himself drawn into the giving-as-receiving of God in God's eternal triunity.

It should be noted that this is not adoptionism. If Jesus of Nazareth finds that his life is progressively revealed to be part of the eternal self-giving of divine love, then he also recognizes that this is not a reward for anything he has done. Adoptionism treats God as an external force, rewarding or blessing those whom it wishes to favor from above.

McCormack quotes Sergius Bulgakov in *The Lamb of God* locating the "primordial identity between the divine I of the Logos and the human I" in the nature of the eternally self-relating God.[17] It seems to me that what he discovers from Bulgakov is a way of turning the assumption of humanity by the Logos inside out. The eternally self-relating Logos comes apparently to assume but as a matter of fact in order to be assumed. Jesus of Nazareth comes to terms with the fact that God is drawing the constricted life of a human being into Godself and defining Godself through it. He is not being made into the passive instrument of the Logos, the tent or shell within which the Logos has chosen to dwell for a short sojourn on earth. Instead, the eternally receiving Logos has made itself the instrument of him, Jesus of Nazareth. Apollinarius has been turned inside out. Instead of the Logos moving in to replace the human soul in the person of Christ, it is the soul of Christ that has found itself drawn into the eternally self-relating God, becoming identified with the eternal receptivity of Son to Father in the Spirit. In a manner

---

16. Jüngel, *God as the Mystery*, 328.
17. Sergius Bulgakov, as quoted in McCormack, *Humility of Eternal Son*, 141.

that takes nothing from the mystery and transcendence of God, God has determined to be realized through a human being's earthly responses.

Conclusion

The last two chapters considered many different ways in which beginning from the Logos making his way from heaven to earth produces problems as well as yields insights. How can we identify the boy born in Nazareth with the divine Logos? How can we avoid losing any sense of unity of person in Christ if we simply try to add the two together? How can the assuming Logos not in reality be more of an overwhelming Logos for the humanity that is supposedly assumed? Feminist criticism has highlighted the implicit passivity of the assumed humanity and the way in which patriarchal ideas of female passivity before an all-powerful male colored those views of incarnation.

Focusing upon the process of leaving heaven for earth may be a mistake. Once we start thinking of the process by which in the incarnation humanity is assumed by the Son in terms of a journey from the heavenly realm above to the earthly realm below, we seem to go wrong. If leaving heaven for earth is thought of in the way Locke presents his prince getting inside the body of a cobbler in order to live a new life away from the palace, we inevitably encounter problems.

We should stop trying to begin our analysis with speculation about what happened in heaven before the Word took the plunge and set off for the far country. Instead, we should try to understand incarnation by focusing upon the human subject, Jesus of Nazareth. David Brown's emphasis upon Stanislavsky and the way in which method actors become the part they are playing is an interesting analogy, which can be compared to McCormack's notion of "ontological receptivity" (itself close to MacKinnon's "total receptivity"). However, MacKinnon and McCormack go further by linking their understanding of the incarnation to their understanding of God as a triunity. Their insights suggest that the self-emptying of which kenosis speaks is not primarily about a surrender or loss of deity. It is about an *expression* of deity. What we are concerned with in the incarnation is a demonstration in time of what God is in eternity. The eternal receptivity of Son to Father in the Spirit, which is the nature of God as Trinity, becomes united with the receptivity of a self-existent human on earth.

But what do we mean by the receptivity of a self-existent being on earth to God? Receptive to God? Receptive to others? How can we approach what is distinctive and unique about Christ in these terms? The next chapter will try to take these questions further.

Chapter 16

Beginning from the Human Subject

The last chapter linked the eternal receptivity of the divine persons to each other in the Trinity with the receptivity of Jesus. But what do we mean by the receptivity of Jesus? If we put aside any consideration of a heavenly backstory, we have a powerful image of a person who is able to feel suffering, pain, doubt, maybe even able to grow in goodness and question why people ask him if he's good since that is true of God alone (all three Synoptic Gospels refer to this).[1] Brown offers a portrait that not only highlights his physical weakness and embrace of suffering, but suggests that he might not have been good or at least might have had to learn goodness through the natural process of childhood development from a self-centered approach to one accepting of others. Jesus tells the Syrophoenician woman: "It is not meet to take the children's bread and cast it to the dogs" (a derogatory term for gentiles). She replies: "Even the dogs under the table eat the children's crumbs" (Matt 15:26–27; Mark 7:27–28). Brown suggests:

> As part of his own learning process, his vision had now begun to extend beyond his own nation.[2]

We have a Jesus whose receptivity lies not only in his steady acquisition of knowledge but in the way he has to mature in a moral sense. His goodness has to be learned through others. His being a product of a particular age and time extends to the way he understands right and wrong. Brown refers to a painting by the surrealist Max Ernst entitled *The Blessed Virgin Chastising the Infant Jesus*, in which Jesus is spanked by his mother while three people

---

1. Mark 10:18; Luke 18:19; Matt 19:17.
2. D. Brown, *Divine Humanity*, 216.

look on. The painting was highly controversial at the time, but Brown points out that a less saccharine presentation of Jesus experiencing the travails of growing up was nothign new. He refers to a German mediaeval craftsman who on a roof boss in the Frauenkirche at Nuremburg presents the reluctant Jesus being dragged to school by his mother, who holds a strap in her hand, while an angel anxiously looks on. Not many, perhaps, would go this far in portraying the warts and all humanity of Christ, but it does at least bring out the significance of those around him, who can easily be relegated to bit parts in the narrative if Jesus is presented as the divine controller on earth. The Jesus presented here has need of others, not least the women around him, including his mother. They are not props for his performances but the essential means by which he develops the self-understanding that enables him to carry out his mission. The idiosyncrasies of patriarchal interpretation find no clearer expression than in the idea that the "Mother of God" might have had no need to scold Jesus or in the insipid manner with which the church promoted her out of all real influence upon the life of her son.

What stuns Jesus of Nazareth as he goes into the wilderness to pray before his ministry begins is the growing sense that his life is not what he thought it might be. It is not as if he becomes aware of something else struggling to get out or of an alter ego rising slowly through the depths of his consciousness. He is not God the Son coming to terms with life outside the heavenly trio. He is one individual human being in Palestine. What is at stake is the realization on the part of an individual that there is an alternative way of viewing his own life. It is one that might make sense of certain abilities that he has, but it doesn't take away his uncertainty or his fear that he is deluded. The focus is on a single human being trying—and feeling driven—to understand himself.

There is even more to the limitations of being part of a particular time and place than an inability to sympathize with someone from another culture. It is not just certain assumptions born of a necessarily specific background (not least in being of a particular gender and race). The inevitable conditioning determined by time and place can be described in even more general terms, as MacKinnon does when he writes:

> What it was for him to be human was to be subject to the sort of fragmentation of effort, curtailment of design, interruption of purpose, distraction of resolve that belongs to temporal experience. To leave one place for another is to leave work undone; to give attention to one suppliant is to ignore another; to expend energy today is to leave less for tomorrow. We have to ask ourselves how far this very conformity to the complex discipline of temporality, this acceptance of the often tragic consequences

that spring from its obstinate, ineluctable truncation of human effort, belongs to the very substance of Jesus's defeat.[3]

If we put these various observations together, it is not only a question of seeing Jesus's encounter with humanity in terms of the requirement to understand his own situation and mission in society (after all, his ministry does not begin until he is thirty). It is also a question of the strain imposed by having to realize that mission under the inevitable limitations imposed by the parameters of existence in space and time, moving from one thing to another, recognizing the opportunity cost of every action taken and the human suffering that simply cannot be dealt with because there is a limit to how much one person can do, whatever their gifts. Perhaps he has miraculous powers, but we also get a sense (for instance, from the opening chapters of Mark) that he was hounded from place to place and had to ration the attention he gave to people. That, too, was part of what it meant to be human.

It might seem that what we are doing now is moving from a Christology from above to a Christology from below. But the point is more that we have to start with what we know—and that is the human subject, Jesus of Nazareth, though there are limits to our knowledge even about Jesus as a merely human figure. Yet one thing becomes clear from the description we have given of Jesus's life. Everything a kenoticist wishes to assert about the exposure to pain and uncertainty taken on board by the incarnate Word is understandable without any recourse to a backstory involving his descent from heaven.

We are thinking of a person who becomes increasingly aware that in his life God is playing out God's eternal triune being. He has to come to terms (perhaps reluctantly) with a growing understanding that in his life as a human being God is opening up the Godhead itself. He is beginning to perceive that God, who once walked with the first humans in the garden of Eden, is now walking with him. We could say that Jesus grew up as a fully conscious human being. We could affirm that he had absolutely no sense at all of having descended from above, with or without his various divine attributes. He was aware of no backstory. He couldn't refer back to his experience inside the security of the heavenly trio. What he had to come to terms with, as he matured, a carpenter's son in a distant outpost of imperial Rome, was not that he had departed from his heavenly origins. It is not as if we are ever, where the understanding of Christ's earthly existence is concerned, in the realms of reincarnation and the slow dawning of the realization that he had a past life.

---

3. MacKinnon, *Themes in Theology*, 162–63.

This could be Coakley's "transfusion" in the manner of Gregory of Nyssa—but only as seen from the side of the human recipient, who has to understand for himself that heaven is opening up to him and through him. It could even be said that the transfusion goes the other way. The divine sea is preparing itself to receive the human vinegar.

What troubled him, what perhaps delayed his mission until the age of thirty even though he is described as being able to preach in the temple from the age of twelve, what drove him into the desert to pray and to try to understand his own calling and convince himself that he was not yet another deluded fool (many, after all, were saying that he could cast out devils only because he had demonic power himself, and one should not underestimate the debilitating effect of the mockery that attended his life and eventually his dying), was the steadily growing conviction that his own human story was part of the inner life of God. If this led him to talk in terms of being an emissary sent from God, or as in the parable of the vineyard to talk about the Father sending his own son rather than one of the servants, it was not because he could recall anything about his heavenly preexistence. It was a growing sense that the life of God was being played out in his awareness of his own development as a human being, something that, as we shall see, was not foreign to the religious tradition in which he was raised.

Jesus of Nazareth, as he grows up, eats, drinks, watches his father at work doing carpentry, mixes with his family in ways we know nothing about, and tries to understand what is happening to him as a maturing human being and why he feels that what is happening to him is the eternal being of God concentrated and defined at a time and place in history. What gave him this extraordinary idea? It was the Jewish tradition to which he belonged, and which had all the resources for understanding how the sons of God might be reunited with their maker. He needed the synagogue and its tradition, he needed to know that this had been foretold by the prophets—how else could he shake off the suspicion of being deluded?

When Jesus begins to understand the nature of his ministry, he does so by being a young Jew who goes to the synagogue to discover the tradition into which he has been born, as a young man on his way to adulthood. In his *Christian Origins*, Professor Rowland remarks:

> Indeed, it may be the case that early Christianity may itself offer testimony in its Christological reflection more to the theological complexity already inherent within contemporary Jewish religion rather than to the unique inventiveness of its adherents.[4]

---

4. Rowland, *Christian Origins*, 36.

In other words, one should not start with the presumption that the building blocks for understanding the claims of Jesus of Nazareth must lie outside Jewish tradition, so that one must reach out to various available -isms—Stoicism, Middle Platonism, Hellenism, and so on—in order to find the necessary tools for constructing an imposing christological edifice able to do justice to its central figure. The tendency to do that has been associated with an anti-Semitic aversion to the Jewishness of Christ. However, it is also a reflection of the sort of misunderstanding that the heavenly backstory and the skydive from heaven tend to encourage, namely the idea of something utterly different from the environment in which it lands falling to earth. He descends from heaven and then looks around for a way of dealing with his arrival in strange parts.

In *The Crucified God* Moltmann quotes the Jewish writer Franz Rosenzweig's *The Star of Redemption* in order to give a perspective on self-differentiation in God through the Shekhina.[5] He quotes Rosenzweig saying: "God himself separates himself off from himself, he gives himself away to his people, he shares in their sufferings, sets forth with them into the agony of exile, joins their wanderings."[6] Not only does this suggest the sort of linkage between the incarnation and the mutual indwelling or perichoresis of the Trinitarian God suggested by MacKinnon and McCormack, but it also enables Jews to make sense of the idea that God joins their wanderings. The Son of Man has nowhere to lay his head, says Jesus (Matt 8:20). He lacks a bed and the indwelling God has also known times when there was no temple to rest in. It is not so very difficult to imagine that Jesus might have grown up to the realization that his imminent roving ministry was somehow linked to the restless indwelling of a God who remained faithful to the people of Israel. It does not need a special leap from heaven by the preexistent Logos. The special leap was made on earth, in the mind of Jesus of Nazareth.

Jesus does not understand his mission by reflecting upon his nature as something other than a self-existent being. He is not the second person of the Trinity who has metamorphosed into a human. What he had to come to terms with, as he matured, a carpenter's son in a distant outpost of imperial Rome, was not that he had departed from his heavenly origins. It is not as if we are ever, where the understanding of Christ's earthly existence is concerned, in the realms of reincarnation and the slow dawning of the realization that he had a past life. The subject of whatever experiences take place as he matures is not the Logos, aware of what it has taken upon itself,

---

5. Moltmann, *Crucified God*, 143–44.
6. Rosenzweig, *Star of Redemption*, 409.

but a human being seeking to understand while full of uncertainty—like any young person—his way in life.

Jesus Has No Power "in Himself"

In Matt 26:53, when one of Jesus's companions strikes a servant of the high priest who has come to arrest him and he orders his companion to put his sword away, he goes on to say: "Do you think I cannot call on my Father, and he will at once put at my disposal more than twelve legions of angels?" It should be noted that this is a power Jesus can call upon rather than one he actually possesses. The same is true of his afterlife. He does not have within himself the means to survive death. He does not possess an immortal soul. Rather, he relies on the external power of the Father to raise him. He is raised from the dead; he doesn't raise himself. The divine power comes from without; it is not kept concealed inside his pocket, like the attributes that concerned "old-style" kenoticists when they worried about what the Son could take with him on his journey to the world and disputed whether these powers were to be brought out in emergencies or even discarded altogether.

After his resurrection, in Matt 28:18–20, Jesus appears to his disciples and declares, "All authority in heaven and on earth has been given to me," before enjoining them to make disciples of all nations. Once again, it is power given rather than displayed from within. The same can be said of the power to perform miracles. In John 10:37–39 Jesus comments, "If I am not doing the works of my Father, then do not believe me; but if I do them, even though you do not believe me, believe the works, that you may know and understand that the Father is in me and I am in the Father." John calls the miracles "signs," signs of divine activity and of the coming kingdom of God. But one would not conclude from this that the divine nature suddenly swept to the fore, pushing its fallible human companion aside and taking over the reins for a display of power. We should note that with his opponents, the issue is not whether Jesus performed miracles but where the power to do so came from. Did it come from God, or was it derived from the dark powers (according to Luke 11:15, "Some of them said, 'He casts out demons by Beelzebul, the prince of demons'")? It can be said that the miracles authenticate Jesus as a prophet of God, and as the one ordained by God to initiate the kingdom. Hence in Luke 11:20 he argues that "if it is by the finger of God that I cast out demons, then the kingdom of God has come upon you." But the reference is away from himself. His power comes from beyond, even when he responds to inquiries about his authority. As John 14:10 puts it, "The Father who dwells in me does his works."

The most difficult aspect of this concerns the way in which we can suppose it impinged upon Jesus himself. He grew up in an insignificant part of the Roman Empire, of no more intrinsic significance than the planet he lived upon, a tiny speck in a minor galaxy located in the boondocks of the physical universe. If he swept away praise and denied his goodness, it was because he knew that he had nothing special *in himself*. He was just the carpenter's son—and he didn't have to remind others of this fact because they reminded him in their turn, causing him to observe that a prophet was without honor in his own country (Mark 6:4; Matt 13:37). Refuting the accusation of having ideas above his station, he had to emphasize that everything he possessed he had received from the Father, the Father who was greater than he, the Father who alone was good.

Jesus's Focus Is on the Future

Earlier in the chapter we quoted Professor Rowland's *Christian Origins*:

> Indeed, it may be the case that early Christianity may itself offer testimony in its Christological reflection more to the theological complexity already inherent within contemporary Jewish religion rather than to the unique inventiveness of its adherents.[7]

Rowland's own theological position is built around one central principle. He rejects any tendency to interpret Jesus's message in terms of delivery *from* the world rather than transformation *of* it. He points out that "the whole association of Jesus with the kingdom of God is by itself sufficient to make a Christological claim of great weight without any recourse to the titles."[8] Jesus's role in proclaiming the kingdom of God should be the focus for understanding his person and trying to unpack the significance of terms like "Son of God," "Son of Man," "Messiah," and "Prophet."

It is the stress upon the eschatological dimension that attracts Rowland to the book of Revelation in contrast to the Gospel of John, though, of course, the former is not set in opposition to the latter as a contrast of right and wrong. On the one hand, there is the idea of a Christ who descends from the realm of light to that of darkness and plucks the children of light from their prison. Their eyes are focused on heaven above. On the other hand, there is the idea of a process begun through the life, death, and resurrection of Christ that will lead to the establishment of a messianic realm on earth—indeed, Revelation speaks of a "new heaven and new earth." Here the

---

7. Rowland, *Christian Origins*, 36.
8. Rowland, *Christian Origins*, 171.

eyes are focused on the kingdom of God on earth, where sorrow and sighing will flee away.[9] In his commentary on Revelation, Rowland writes:

> In the present age heaven stands over against earth. That is not part of the permanent order of things. God wishes to walk again in paradise in the cool of the day and tend the garden of the created world.[10]

Hence the importance of the vision of a new heaven and a new earth in Rev 21:1—22:5, where Rowland describes the vision of God's tabernacling with humanity as "the climax of the eschatological drama."[11] Behind this vision is the idea expressed in the book of Genesis that Adam and Eve, shortly after the fall when they had eaten the forbidden fruit, heard the Lord God walking in the garden in the cool of the day (Gen 3:8). In other words, the eschatological expectation is of a return of God to be with human beings once again on earth, a God who will once again be "all in all" (1 Cor 15:28). The focus is forward, toward the kingdom of God on earth, rather than upward, to a heaven above into which the redeemed are led by their Savior.

What Rowland sees is that the belief that characterized the first century of the church's life, namely that the Messiah was coming back to reign on earth, at least made clear that a transformed earth was the focus of Christian hope, not departure into a better world above. This point needs to be recognized when one is tempted to see belief in the imminent return of Christ as a simple mistake. It is true that Christ did not return before the present generation had died out (consider, for instance, Matt 24:34), but the advantage of believing in that return of Christ was that it kept the emphasis upon what happened on earth and the potential for its transformation, rather than upon anticipation of getting away from earth altogether and being lifted up to heaven. Rowland's concern is to maintain the focus upon the transformation of this world rather than escape to another. His Christology is built upon this foundation. His worry about the "Word made flesh" becomes a concern that the emphasis will be upon personal identification with the one who has come down from heaven and promises to take the redeemed back to heaven with him. As he puts it:

> The hidden logos amidst the flux of a decaying world becomes a more compelling paradigm in late antiquity than the "Son of Man," vindicator of the downtrodden, or the prophet of the Kingdom of God, proclaiming the imminent overthrow of

---

9. Rowland, *Christian Origins*, 255.
10. Rowland, *Revelation*, 47–48.
11. Rowland, *Revelation*, 153.

empire and the establishment of a divine commonwealth on earth.[12]

One can see how the emphasis upon a heavenly backstory to the life of Jesus can easily become tinged with Gnosticism. The Son agrees to a mission impossible and goes to rescue the "trapped" souls on earth. A Christology that is focused upon the life of Christ rather than his supposed preexistence is more likely to prevent his followers becoming wrapped up in thoughts about their own postexistence away from earth. Christians look forward not to their movement up to heaven from the earth beneath as they head off to "a better place," but for God to complete the work on earth that was interrupted by human sin. It is therefore insofar as that future hope has already been realized in Christ that one can speak of God having already come down to be with God's people in him. Christology becomes an anticipation in Jesus of Nazareth—the first fruits of the resurrection—of what is to be expected at the end of all things. Rather than referring backward to what happened when the Logos abandoned heaven for earth, it refers forward to the moment when God is all in all.

Rowland gives his own interpretation of the "christological hymn" in Phil 2:5–11. In his commentary on Revelation[13] he suggests that in Phil 2:5, when Paul refers to equality with God as not being "a thing to be grasped," he has in mind the divine snatching up to heaven spoken of in Rev 12:5 ("And she gave birth to a son, a male child, who is to rule all the nations with a rod of iron. But her child was snatched away and taken to God and to his throne") and elsewhere in Scripture, for instance, in 1 Thess 4:17, when the elect are caught up to meet Christ at the parousia (the so-called "rapture"), or in 2 Cor 12:2, when Paul talks of being snatched up to paradise. The point is that for Jesus there is no divine rapture which might enable him to avoid the pain and suffering of death. His "emptying himself" refers not to his willingness to leave heaven for earth in the incarnation, but to his willingness when already on earth to accept the harder path. The christological hymn refers not to a decision of the preexistent Logos to don the mantle of living like the humans down below, but to the decision of one down below not to take the easy way out by running back above—summoning legions of angels who, as he reminded those who taunted him (Matt 26:53), will at once be put at his disposal should he ask for them. If the world as we knew it was about to end in Rowland's thinking, it was because it was being transformed into what, from the perspective of the "visionaries and subversives,"

---

12. Rowland, *Christian Origins*, 255–56.
13. Rowland, *Revelation*, 104.

it was always meant to be.[14] There is nothing in Rowland's thinking to suggest abandoning the world for the heavenly lifeboats as if it was a sinking ship. The mystics, subversives, and visionaries strove for heaven on earth. It was those who feared their presence who sought to pack them off to a safe haven above along with their dangerous ideas.

Jesus the Visionary and Subversive

By removing any backstory of descent by the divine Word and focusing on the human subject, Jesus of Nazareth, this chapter has tried to convey the limitations of Jesus's humanity, not only in terms of the natural constraints that come from being born in a particular time and place but in terms of the need to mature through contact with others and understand, over time and in a manner that was steeped in the tradition from which he came, the nature of his mission. If he worked miracles, it was understood that the power to do so came from outside him. If he had the "total receptivity" of which MacKinnon spoke, it expressed itself in the complete and freely given dependence upon the Father that characterized his life.

But is this enough to do justice to the claims about him? It seems to me that it is enough if we recognize that his overwhelming sense of God could also be understood as a movement from God to him. In that way the "ontological receptivity" McCormack speaks of is inseparable from the mutual indwelling and self-giving that characterize the divine being and into which Jesus of Nazareth is drawn through his own response.

In a memorable piece of theological writing entitled "Cyril of Alexandria and the Sacrifice of Gethsemane," Katherine Sonderegger describes the way Jesus is "God intoxicated, eaten up by zeal for the Father's house." She goes on to say:

> The beatific vision for Jesus Christ meant something unique for this Son of Man, something that drove him out into the hills, long nights alone in prayer, something that filled him with the conviction that he must be rejected by his own, betrayed and killed, something that turned his steps always and unmistakably to Jerusalem, the holy city of his holy death. That something in him terrified his disciples. . . . Something in him, the evangelists tell us, made his opponents adamantly at war with him; it made his own family consider him out of his mind. He was like all of them, they knew that. Yet he was actually unlike, a terrifying,

---

14. See Rowland, *Radical Prophet*, subtitled *The Mystics, Subversives and Visionaries Who Strove for Heaven on Earth*, that is to say, not for a route out of earth to heaven.

majestic and royal figure, to whom one goes down on one's knees. Go away from me, Lord, for I am a sinner![15]

That "something in him," Sonderegger suggests, was the beatific vision:

> I believe that Jesus Christ, in his own human inwardness, saw the reality of God, its rationality or Logos, in its fiery descent into the world, its utter lowliness.... What Jesus saw, or better, what he was, in his own unique person, was the holy fire who is God, cascading down the ladder between heaven and earth, a molten divine Son, who will make his own flesh the sacrifice to be burned to ash on the world's altar. Jesus Christ in his humanity looks on this, this fiery burning, and he understands that he is to live this terrible descent as his very own life, his very own death.... It is God acting, God willing, God lowering and bending down, the eternal generation of the Son, that is seen in all its terrible relentlessness by Christ's inward eye. Just this is what it means for God to save. Just this is what it means for Christ in his person to be sacrifice.[16]

Sonderegger's language is influenced by Cyril of Alexandria's comparison, in *On the Unity of Christ*, of the coming together of two natures in Christ to the contact between iron and fire. On the one hand, it can be said that this is an attempt to restore an orthodox Christology in which there is emphasis upon the divine subject, the "molten divine Son" who is descending to earth—cascading down the ladder between heaven and earth. Yet the focus remains upon the human subject, which is in no way turned into a tool or prop of the invading, controlling Logos. Sonderegger talks about what "is seen in all its terrible relentlessness by Christ's inward eye."[17] Jesus is being dragged into the presence of the light that blinds, the fire that consumes (even as it turns an iron bar into molten malleability). Rather than becoming a prop, he is touched by a vision that determines his unique, unsettling life, a mystery to his friends and family who even wonder about his sanity, and even a mystery to himself.

Sonderegger's presentation does two very important things. On the one hand, it demonstrates that a Christology "from above" may still be focused upon Jesus of Nazareth as a self-existent being affected by the uncertainty and even the sense of failure discerned in his life. He is still a human being trying to understand his way. He is not taken over by the incoming Word but driven by a vision that inspires him as a human being. Second, if

---

15. Sonderegger, "Cyril of Alexandria," 134–35.
16. Sonderegger, "Cyril of Alexandria," 135.
17. Sonderegger, "Cyril of Alexandria," 135.

indirectly, theology must do justice to the concern of feminist theologians that "an excessive stress on kenosis will encourage a culture of suffering in silence, victimhood and acquiescence in abusive practices."[18] Sonderegger shows that theology can do this by not letting its stress upon the self-emptying spoken of in Phil 2 justify a presentation of Christ as somehow unwilling to challenge oppression, whether male or more generally societal. But this should not be hard to do. For what on earth has the life of Jesus got to do with suffering in silence? Jesus confronts his opponents, argues with them, antagonizes them, and in the end leads them to do away with him. He upturns the tables of the money changers. Where is the acquiescence in abusive practices? It may not be clear what abusive practices are being referred to, but words such as "I say to you that everyone who looks at a woman with lust has already committed adultery with her in his heart" (Matt 5:28) hardly suggests a toleration of the objectification of women, while "it would be better for him to have a millstone hung around his neck and to be thrown into the sea than to cause one of these little ones to stumble" (Matt 18:6) hardly suggests any kind of acquiescence in the mistreatment of children. It is arguably not an excessive stress on kenosis but a false understanding of the nature of Christ, the superimposition of a "gentle Jesus" upon the angry and uncompromising original, that is at fault here.

In a similar manner, we find Professor Sykes in "The Strange Persistence of Kenotic Christology" suggesting that "the danger of the metaphor of kenosis . . . is that it should be thought that the new higher life of loving and humble service has no point of contact with the necessarily structured life of ordinary society or that involvement in society can be conducted on higher principles."[19] It is difficult to connect this with what we know of the life of Jesus, whether or not presented by kenotic theologians. The whole point of Jesus's engagement with the authorities, whether in terms of the deliberate challenge to the economic basis of society in upturning the tables of the money changers or the obvious challenge Jesus posed—and accepted—to the rulers of his day, was precisely to enable a "higher life of loving and humble service," to make contact with the structured life of ordinary society, and to suggest how it desperately needed to be *re*structured. Coming at the problem from different directions, both Sykes and Hampson seem to think of the kenoticists as creating a weak-willed, subservient, acquiescent Christ. But this is nothing to do with the Christ of the Gospels, and it is nothing to do with the point being made by the kenotic writers.

---

18. Hampson, *Theology and Feminism*, 155.
19. Sykes, "Strange Persistence," 371.

They are not trying to remove the anger and conflict from the life of Jesus. They are trying to present that anger and conflict as part of the challenge God makes to Godself in God's eternal selving. There is a confusion of terms here. If kenoticists talk about humility, they do not mean abasement. If they talk of vulnerability, they do not mean passivity. If they talk about weakness, they do not take one bit away from the righteous anger of the incarnate Son. And if they talk of love and of failure, in the last resort they are suggesting that God builds into the divine nature itself a limit upon God's saving capacity that is even more of a final barrier to salvation than the harshness of an imperious patriarch.

Conclusion

This chapter has put aside any heavenly backstory. Instead of beginning by considering how the divine Logos when incarnate can assume humanity, it tried to begin from below, from the human subject Jesus of Nazareth. It followed MacKinnon and McCormack in arguing that the eternal receptivity of Son to Father in the Spirit, which is the nature of God as Trinity, cannot be separated from the receptivity of a self-existent human being, Jesus of Nazareth, on earth. The question remains what exactly that receptivity consists of.

Hence, the chapter focused upon a human being, Jesus of Nazareth, able to feel suffering, pain, doubt, maybe even able to grow in goodness. This was a person faced with the uncertainties and limitations of being human rather than someone receiving the assurance and security of a divine takeover.

How does Jesus of Nazareth make sense of what is happening to him? He reaches for the Jewish tradition to which he belonged, the synagogue and its tradition, the evidence that what was happening to him had been foretold by the prophets—how else could he shake off the suspicion of being deluded? The building blocks for understanding the claims of Jesus of Nazareth did not have to be found outside Jewish tradition. Within that very tradition Jesus grew into the realization that his own wandering ministry as the Son of Man with nowhere to lay his head was linked to the restless indwelling of a God who remained faithful to the people of Israel. This God, who remains beyond all understanding, is the God who burns those who come too close with the glory of God's presence. But this is also the God whose indwelling (Shekhina) is fundamental to Jewish tradition, the God who says, "I will dwell in the midst of the Israelites" (Exod 29:45), the God who goes ahead of God's people as the pillar of cloud by day and the pillar of fire by night. This is the God who dwells in the ark of the covenant and after the destruction of the city and temple by the Babylonians, goes with God's people into exile and humiliation. This is the God whom the predecessors of Jesus encountered in the desert, in the ark of the covenant—even in the garden—never once shedding transcendence but rather shaking the contours of human existence with God's presence.

The chapter has emphasized the way in which Jesus knew that he had nothing special *in himself*. He denies that he is good. He rejects worship directed at himself. He accepts his lowly origins, and plenty of people are there to remind him of them. He is a prophet without honor in his own country. He can call upon extraordinary powers—he can work miracles—but these are not like special tricks hidden inside his person.

It became increasingly clear to Jesus that he had a mission going beyond even that of the prophets. It involved a concentration of God's power in himself, but even this was no more than a development of Jewish tradition. The God who was in the ark without a temple would be in the Son of Man with nowhere to lay his head. It was completely unnecessary to suppose that he had somehow parachuted out of heaven as something other; through the tradition he was born into he came to an understanding that he was the fulfillment of God's promise on earth. God walked in the garden with Adam and Eve, dwelt with God's people in the desert, dwelt in the temple and in the ark of the covenant, dwelt with the people in exile, and now (so he began to recognize, though perhaps with surprise, wonder, and even uncertainty) dwelt in the man Jesus.

If he is willing to think of himself as the Son of God, it is because he has an overwhelming vision. The fire and molten iron analogy taken from Cyril and used by Sonderegger is more effective than the vinegar and sea analogy mentioned earlier. In the latter case, the vinegar simply dissolves in the sea, doubtless invigorating it like an additional spice in the stew but hardly changing its nature. The iron, however, is visibly transformed into molten form without ceasing to be iron. We should not use Sonderegger's language about the "molten divine Son cascading down to earth" in order to suggest that Jesus of Nazareth is somehow turned into a passive instrument of a fiery divine person who descends upon him. The overpowering vision described in terms of the melting malleability of iron forged in a furnace takes nothing away from the centrality of the human subject and nothing away from a life that was the very opposite of passive in its preparedness to confront both individuals with their personal failings and institutions with their destructive impact on the people they manipulated.

However, rejecting the heavenly backstory and concentrating upon the human being Jesus of Nazareth does not mean that the christological problem is solved. Faced with the traditional understanding of the being of Christ expressed in the title of Pannenberg's classic *Jesus, God and Man*, we have to be clearer about what it means to say Jesus is "God." Some of what has been said, both in this chapter and earlier in the book, is relevant to that. It has already been argued that God's omnipresence and the whole fallacy of the "two realms" idea shows that God must not be perceived as a purely external force up above, the God up there attacked in John Robinson's famous *Honest to God*. This chapter has suggested that the Jewish tradition into which Jesus was born was perfectly familiar with the idea of God's presence on earth, although by being present God never ceased to be beyond human understanding. God was immanent as well as transcendent, but immanent *as* transcendent. But these are points that argue for God's presence in a general way. They do not address the question of how God is *uniquely* present in Jesus of Nazareth. The next chapter will address this.

Chapter 17

The Mystery of God

The last chapter sought to lay stress upon the nature of Christ as a self-existent human being. It emphasized the manner in which he had to make his own way in the world, limited in his understanding and his abilities by the circumstances of his birth. It stressed his dependence upon the Father for his miracle-working powers, which were certainly not powers that he simply carried with him as part of the armory of one who has arrived in hostile terrain from beyond. It emphasized the focus he had upon transforming the world rather than escaping it. It laid weight on the powerful vision that sustained him, though it didn't remove the uncertainty from his life.

Is this enough to justify the description in the title of Donald Baillie's famous book, *God Was in Christ*? Can it capture the uniqueness of Christ? Or is it no more than a description of another prophet, another Isaiah or Jeremiah with an overwhelming vision of God and a rough response from those who heard his message? Clearly the book wants to affirm the uniqueness of Christ. It wants to claim that the "total receptivity" of Jesus became part of the mutual indwelling of the divine persons. It is less God was in Christ than Christ was in God. It is as much a movement from the human into the divine as of the divine to the human. Jesus finds that his human life is being taken into the life of God and is even defining it.

The point of McCormack's "ontological receptivity" is that the incarnate Word is not designed to overwhelm the humanity but to allow itself to receive from it. The humanity does not become a mere instrument or prop for fulfilling the divine purpose. It becomes the defining factor in determining whether the divine purpose is carried out. Where Jesus of Nazareth is concerned, it is more being saddled with a huge responsibility than being told to obey. For God is defining God through human beings. The mutual self-giving that characterizes the Trinity is absorbing the self-giving of the Nazarene and determining its own nature through the Nazarene's response. "Not my will, but thine be done," says Jesus when he realizes that he is to die an agonizing death (Luke 22:42). Yet God is ordaining that God's will and that of Jesus shall be one. The Word assumes flesh, and yet in such a way that it is as if the flesh assumed the Word. That is surely the point of "ontological receptivity." Under the constraints of "ontological receptivity" the Stanislavsky actors referred to in David Brown's *Divine Humanity* would find that they had to do far more than immerse themselves in their parts.[1] They would find that their parts are taking wing and writing the lives of the actors themselves. This is the vulnerability of the kenotic God, where the mutual self-giving of the triunity absorbs humanity into its own continuous self-giving.

Yet however much the emphasis is upon the self-giving of God in Christ, that does not mean a compromising of God's transcendence. Nor does the emphasis in Jewish tradition upon the presence of God on earth and in God's sons on earth remove the transcendence of God, which is not an alternative to God's presence but the form it takes. God remains unknown, even when in Christ.

In the Acts of the Apostles, St. Paul makes a famous speech to the Athenians at the Areopagus. In it he says:

> For as I passed along and observed the objects of your worship, I found also an altar with this inscription: "To the unknown god." What therefore you worship as unknown, this I proclaim to you.
> (Acts 17:23)

In his interpretation of Paul's words, Karl Barth argues that this "unknown God" is not simply like a spare god to be brought out if anyone needed an extra one besides the dozen or so already available. It is that this God "who made the world and everything in it, being Lord of heaven and earth, does not live in temples made by man" (Acts 17:24). Paul does not tell the Athenians that his God is unknown in the sense that they haven't yet come across God. He is saying, Barth believes, that his God is in principle unknowable because God is beyond our clutches and did not in the incarnation become graspable, but rather proclaimed the ungraspability of God among us. From Barth's point of view, we cannot grasp God (the double sense of the word is appropriate — to grasp what is meant by "God" would also be to grasp in the sense of greedily seizing hold). Were we to

---

1. D. Brown, *Divine Humanity*, 250-51.

grasp God, we would reduce God, we would force God to be accommodated to the limits of what we can know, much as Kant had argued that the "thing-in-itself" cannot get past the forms of our understanding and therefore can appear to us only on our terms. We would find that whatever we had in our grasp was less than God, an intellectual idol, made not with our hands out of the mistaken supposition that God could live in a temple like a carved statue but with our minds, out of the mistaken supposition that we could contain God by arriving at an understanding of God through our powers of intellectual reasoning.

It is this making known of the unknowable that is presented most starkly in Barth's great commentary on Romans, even in the substantially altered second edition by which it is usually known. It is the essence of Barth's negative dialectics in that work, suggesting that our establishment comes only by way of dissolution, salvation by way of cross and revelation, through the denial of this world that has been left in separation from God and its reestablishment beyond that dissolution in a form that cannot now be perceived. The second edition of the commentary is a dialectical critique that self-confessedly has as its fundamental principle the "infinite qualitative distinction" between God and humanity, which can be overcome only eschatologically. The ultimate establishment of the human person can be only beyond the dissolution of this world order, a life through death, the establishment of the not-I, the nonexistence of our nonexistence. God's yes is only ever uttered in and through God's no. The antitheses come thick and fast like hammerblows.

Barth introduces a colorful metaphor probably not uninfluenced by the long war out of which Europe had just emerged:

> The effulgence, or rather, the crater made at the percussion point of an exploding shell; the void by which the point on the line of intersection makes itself known in the concrete world of history is not—even though it be named the life of Jesus—that other world which touches our world in Him.[2]

Barth's revelation discloses only insofar as it explodes. It is the intrusion of absolute otherness, the revelation of a different reality that cannot be inserted into history in the Hegelian way as a stage in its development.

It is when theologians try to consider the implication of Barth's theology for their understanding of incarnation that they often find themselves in the most difficulty—and this despite the fact that the fundamental principle of Barth's theology, and the reason why his great *Church Dogmatics*

---

2. Barth, *Epistle to the Romans*, 29.

deals with the doctrine of the word of God in volume 1 and the doctrine of God in volume 2, is that a dogmatic theology must always begin from Alfred N. Whitehead's "tremendous fact of Christ."[3] Commenting on Rom 1:3–4, which speaks of Jesus "born of the seed of David according to the flesh," Barth affirms that the years AD 1–30 are "the era of revelation and disclosure" (*Offenbarungszeit und Entdeckungszeit*).[4] But what exactly was revealed? What exactly was disclosed? Is Barth in danger of excluding divine self-giving along with human self-assertion? Does the incarnation not disappear with the rejection of an idolatrous God by humanity? If Barth is committed to the unity of God and humanity only in terms of an eschatological realization beyond the present world order, what sense can be made of their unity in the incarnate Word *within* that order? Critics assert that his theology would not only exclude the pretentious claim of humanity to humanize the divine, but also the voluntary self-giving of God in taking humanity to Godself in Jesus Christ. The separation that cannot be overcome from the side of humanity in possessing God would also exclude an action to overcome it from the side of God through God's initiative to make Godself present in the incarnation.

But it may be that Barth's position can be justified. It is presented in its starkest form in *Epistle to the Romans*, in a passage where he declares that "in Jesus God is known as the unknown God."[5] Now it might be asked: Is this any sort of revelation? Or is Jesus in fact simply disclosing that God cannot be disclosed? Does the revelation of God in Jesus Christ become no more than the declaration no revelation is possible? Does the paradox of Christ become no more than the revelation that there can be no revelation, in which case it is not really a paradox at all? For surely the real paradox, it could be argued, is not that Jesus proclaims the unknown God, but that he proclaims the *knownness* of the unknown God.

But Barth's point is that nothing can be taken away from the unknowability of God when God is identified with Jesus of Nazareth. "God was in Christ" does not mean that God had suddenly become a recognizable object in space and time. It is perfectly reasonable to say, as Barth does, that "in Jesus God is known as the unknown God,"[6] so long as it is recognized that it is *in Jesus* that God is known as the unknown God. Everything that is unknowable about God passes through the prism of this Nazarene struggling to understand his life.

3. Whitehead, *Religion in the Making*, 51.
4. Barth, *Epistle to the Romans*, 29.
5. Barth, *Epistle to the Romans*, 114.
6. Barth, *Epistle to the Romans*, 114.

The human being Jesus of Nazareth and the divine Word are identified as one in Christian tradition without—as earlier chapters in part 5 have tried to show—any sense of a voyage from above that can somehow be traced back to its divine starting point. But to say that takes nothing away from the *content* of revelation, since Jesus of Nazareth is a figure from history with a specific message and a specific fate, not to mention concrete actions attributed to him, whether in the form of teaching or miracles or actions like upsetting the tables of the money changers in the temple. This cannot be contentless revelation, because it concerns a human life about which we can claim to know a great deal (though never, as part 1 emphasized, with certainty).

There is therefore no need to worry about "contentless revelation." The tremendous fact of Christ can be analyzed by biblical critics, historians, and theologians for what it was, the short life of a man in Nazareth. Theology then tries to construct an understanding of how this figure can be linked to the unknowable God. Based on the type of kenotic approach advocated in this book, we can try to consider what sort of God would be identified with this historical figure. We can perfectly well agree that "the incarnation is first and foremost an expression of who God is."[7] But this does not mean that the incarnation enables us to define the indefinable God. When it comes to understanding revelation, the process in one sense is perfectly clear. It is a matter of trying to understand the life and teaching of a figure in history. But the God with whom this human being is associated remains unknowable. There is therefore no reason to fear that the supreme being would deliver God to our understanding only by being changed into something less.

If Jesus recognizes an identity between his life and the life of God, it is without being able to see what is happening from the side of God. His uncertainty, his sense of possible delusion, does not go away. Jesus's "beatific vision" draws him into something that it is beyond him to fathom or make sense of—hence the troubled, uncertain character of his life. Revelation is not a reductive act providing a humanly accessible deity; it is a reaffirmation of the unknownness of God in the soul of the receiver—as it was for Jesus himself, even in the face of an overpowering vision that drove him forward. He can only be pulled along in the wake of what is happening. He is drawn into something that remains beyond him, the God whose immanence in a particular place and time does not negate but only affirms God's transcendence. God's kenotic self-giving may mean that God has chosen to be

---

7. Nimmo and Johnson, *Kenosis*, 307.

defined through the life of a human being, but still God is not stripped of the transcendence that cannot be taken away even by revelation.

The Sea and the Wave

Even if God surrenders nothing of transcendence in being revealed through the life of a single human being, is there not still a need to understand how that transcendent God has become uniquely identified with this particular person? Jesus of Nazareth, one person among millions of others, one who is enough like other human beings to be able to slip through a crowd and get away (Luke 4:30), nevertheless becomes the location of God's eternal process of being God. He has been called the "concrete universal," where the simple specificity of an ordinary human life encounters the eternal life of God. The most powerful images are those that try to capture this. Rather than Gregory of Nyssa's drop of divine vinegar in the human sea, we might consider a similar but more revealing metaphor that originates with Hans Urs von Balthasar and is mentioned by Edward T. Oakes in an article on the descent into hell. Oakes is discussing Jesus's claim in John's Gospel to be "the way, the truth, and the life":

> In effect, this claim means the following: one product of the universe also claims to be its substrate, or in Balthasar's image, the wave is the sea, a claim that is on the face of it not just paradoxical, but absurd: and the response to that claim is bound to result in outrage and rejection. For whatever else Jesus is, he is a human being "born of woman" (Galatians 4:4), and thus the product of the universe out of which he came and to which he is destined to return at death.[8]

This is a classic statement of the so-called "scandal of particularity." The scandal of particularity concerns a single human being, born of woman like all others, one of a hundred billion or so births around the world, one wave in the ocean, the man who can get lost in the crowd, Jesus of Nazareth. Yet this single individual "is the sea"—is God.

How can we cope with the idea of the sea being contained within a single wave? It is worth recalling Thomas F. Torrance's discussion of time and space as part of creation in part 4, where he emphasized that the incarnation is less something "in" time and space than something that takes time and space with it.

---

8. Oakes, "He Descended into Hell," 234.

In the short work entitled *Space, Time and Incarnation*, Torrance talks about Christ's "whole space-time track in the cosmos"[9] and of how in Christ "the infinite Being of God penetrates into our existence and creates room for himself within the horizontal dimensions of finite being in space and time."[10] We saw in part 4 how space and time are inseparably related to the events that a "receptacle" notion of space would see as merely containing them (events "in" space and "in" time). Instead of the "receptacle" view, Torrance proposes a "relational" view of time and space. The infinite being of God, in Torrance's words quoted above, "creates room for himself" in the incarnation.

Though analogies are always dangerous, Torrance's use of relativity may help us in trying to make sense of the uniqueness of Christ. Imagine someone who tries to question the idea that it is impossible to go faster than the speed of light, 186,000 miles per second. The person tells us that such a figure appears entirely arbitrary, a speed limit imposed by a tired imagination. They concede that there are not yet spaceships that can go that fast—or anything like it. It may take decades or centuries to build one that can. But it is ridiculous, our skeptic continues, to say that 186,000 miles per second is possible but 190,000 will never be.

Think of the time, the skeptic goes on, when travel was determined by the speed of a galloping horse. No one had ever exceeded fifty or sixty miles per hour, from the period of ancient civilization through to that of the stagecoach. But then the iron horse came along and faster speeds became reality. A hundred years after that came the jet engine and planes that could break the sound barrier. That was something else that many considered to be impossible at the time, and yet in the end it proved possible to break the sound barrier and the supersonic age began. One day, the skeptic concludes, spaceships will break the light barrier, too, after which we shall be able to visit other planets as easily as we visit other continents today.

To defend the idea that it is impossible to exceed the speed of light, we would probably argue as follows. In the case of going faster than the galloping horse, it is improvements in technology that are needed. Viewed from this perspective, talk of a barrier provided by the speed of light sounds like a foolish, almost Luddite piece of resistance to what technology can do.

However, we would continue, 186,000 miles per second is a speed limit based on entirely different principles to those that hampered our ability to go faster before the development of steam engines and jet planes. The reason we are justified in thinking it impossible to go faster than light lies not in the fact that we lazily assume that no supersonic jet could ever manage to cover

---

9. Torrance, *Space, Time and Incarnation*, 85.
10. Torrance, *Space, Time and Incarnation*, 75.

distance in so short a time. It lies in the fact that objects approaching that speed undergo significant changes in mass. And as they get very close to 186,000 miles per second, they approach infinite mass. That is why 186,000 miles per second is a real speed limit rather than just one imposed by our failure to see as yet how we could go any faster. As it approached the speed of light, the mass of a spaceship would increase, and time would slow. At the speed of light, it would acquire infinite density and time would stop. This is what makes the speed of light an effective barrier rather than simply a milestone on the way to further technological improvements in the design of spaceships to make them move faster.

Torrance, one of the few theologians to have a strong background in science, asks whether the insights of relativity can help us to understand the claims made about Christ. Is there a parallel between the sort of understanding that supposes we will always find a way of going faster than our predecessors, until eventually we find a way of going faster than the speed of light, and the sort of approach that wonders, for instance, why Christ should be considered not just good but the one in terms of whom goodness is measured? If approaching the speed of light means acquiring almost infinite mass and time slowing to a stop, it is as if what we have taken to be the context of, or backdrop to, events on earth, space, and time, have been turned inside out and now find themselves emerging from the very events they were supposed to put into context.

Thus, instead of Jesus of Nazareth being placed alongside other instances of saintly behavior as an example of a good life, we have the idea that the notion of goodness derives from this human life. Someone who was better than Jesus becomes as impossible as someone going faster than light, for in terms of him alone can goodness be measured. One analogy MacKinnon liked to give was the standard meter in Paris, with which all other measurements had to correspond. Christ became the moral equivalent of the *mètre étalon*, a small shelf of marble installed in Paris after the French Revolution. It made no sense to ask whether this shelf was a meter in length, since it alone determined what a meter was. The goodness of Christ is not a conclusion drawn from observing (for instance) how keen to help the poor or infirm he was but is part of the "tremendous fact" (to return to Whitehead's phrase) from which one derives a sense of what goodness is. Christ is not good because he helped the poor and infirm. Helping the poor and infirm is good because it conforms to the nature of Christ.

MacKinnon also used to point to that passage of Matthew (Matt 25:31–40) in which the sheep are divided from the goats and are told that they did (or did not) feed him when hungry, visit him in prison, and so on. Those he addresses have no recollection of having done so (or having not done so). But Jesus claims that "insofar as you did it to the least of these my brethren, you did it unto me" (Matt 25:40). In other words, the fact that Christ is the measure of goodness can be seen from the fact that all acts of charity (or neglect) toward others can be understood as acts of charity (or neglect) toward him.

Torrance argues that as the divine agent in our midst, God is shaking the contours of our existence and demanding that we adjust our ideas to the nature of the object they are dealing with. What he means is that we cannot make sense of that action of God if we insist upon placing it "in" time and "in" space, locating it as another event against the backdrop of a particular place (Nazareth) and a particular time (first century CE). Light, too, has its particularity: 186,000 miles per second. Not 187,000 or 185,000. We can, similarly, suggest that Jesus was not born on the other side of the Mediterranean or of the Atlantic. But there is no point in saying: "Why this man? Why not a woman? Why not in another century? Why not in another part of the globe?" The scandal of particularity is unavoidable.

Having a particular speed does not prevent light from being an absolute barrier beyond which it is impossible to go, because time is brought to a stop and objects acquire infinite mass. Similarly, suggests Torrance, Jesus draws in his wake the things that are supposed to be simply the sentries acknowledging his coming. He is making his "space-time track" in the cosmos because he is not heading for a particular place and time that await his coming but is turning the universe inside out, making time and space serve that very coming in which at the same time he accepts a particular placing, just as light accepts a particular speed and makes it absolute.

I am very conscious of the fact that this is no more than an analogy and perhaps a very bad one. But even if it fails it provides some clue as to what we should be doing in trying to make sense of Christ's uniqueness. Just as the speed of light seems to pluck a particular number and turn it from the "latest fastest" into a limit that marks the way in which the whole universe of space and time is determined, so the incarnation plucks a particular human being (and not as a tent or shell for "something divine" to get inside) and turns him into the criterion in terms of which all human lives are to be measured.

Incarnation and Eucharist

When at the climax of his ministry Jesus gathers his disciples for a Last Supper and declares that "this is my body, this is my blood," he is reenacting what happened in his own life. As a limited form of human experience bound by time, place, and circumstance, it nevertheless became the locus of God's self-giving. And that is the mystery that is repeated in the act of communion. The Eucharist is not just an expression of Christian fellowship. The Last Supper is an attempt on Jesus's part to share the meaning of what has happened to him. In that last meal Jesus is communicating to his disciples before he departs something of the mysterious presence that he has been struggling to make sense of all his life.

The bread and wine in the Eucharist mark out a similar assumption of ordinary things by God. One can, of course, talk of the importance of fellowship and ritual bonding just as the church has down the centuries as a community of the faithful. But the idea of the real presence goes further than this. If Jesus of Nazareth has to come to terms with the idea that in his ordinary human life, one among millions and, like every human life—bound by the particularity of gender, upbringing, and location—God chose to realize God's nature as God, then the idea of a real presence in the eucharistic elements follows from this. The real presence in them follows from the real presence in him. The celebration of the Eucharist becomes more than the weekly meeting of the friends of Jesus. The Eucharist is the reenactment of God's decision to take humanity and make it part of God's eternal celebration of deity. Flesh and blood became part of God's eternal self-realization. Jesus of Nazareth did not know how that was so. It was beyond his comprehension—he was not being slowly admitted into the secrets of deity and he was not remembering the way in which he had dropped out of heaven for a while. In the invitation to the Last Supper, he invited his disciples to be part of a reality whose meaning was beyond their comprehension too. Bread and wine become where Christ is. They are not just pieces of food and drink, just as Jesus of Nazareth was not just flesh and blood but became the place where God is uniquely present. These are the ordinary things that become charged with the glory of God. The real presence in the bread and wine is an extension of the real presence in a wandering Galilean.

Conclusion

MacKinnon often quoted a remark by Alfred North Whitehead that whereas Buddhism was "a metaphysics generating a religion, Christianity was a religion perennially in search of a metaphysics,"[11] a religion which, confronted by what Whitehead called, as we have said, the "tremendous fact" of Christ, has to erect around this christological center a metaphysical structure that will allow it to stand. This chapter tried to make one or two suggestions in

---

11. Whitehead, *Religion in the Making*, 50–51.

this regard. Could sense be made of the idea that the incarnation, rather than being an event in which space and time did no more than stand sentry upon the coming of Christ, saw them borne in its wake as if derived from the act of incarnation itself? Is this one way in which theology can make sense of the concrete universal that Balthasar described in terms of the sea and the wave? And in a similar way, do not (as MacKinnon suggested) the efforts to measure whether the life of Jesus demonstrates how far one can move in the direction of moral goodness ignore the fact that one's understanding of goodness derives from the very example one is supposedly trying to measure? The criterion of goodness, the moral absolute, has been located in the life of one individual. Insofar as you have shown compassion toward others, you have shown it toward me. Here in this concrete instance of a particular human life lies the criterion with which to judge good and evil.

Christianity, like Judaism, has to struggle constantly with the overpowering sense both of God's presence and of God's transcendence, and one can see this in the life of Christ. Jesus asserts an identity between his life and the life of God, but without being able to see what is happening from the side of God. His uncertainty, his sense of possible delusion, do not go away. He is drawn into something that it is beyond him to fathom or make sense of—hence the troubled, uncertain character of his life. Revelation is not a reductive act providing a humanly accessible deity; it is a reaffirmation of the unknown God in the soul of the receiver—and was so for Jesus himself, even as he received an overpowering vision, for a vision is not an explanation.

Chapter 18

MacKinnon's Warning

This book has been broadly supportive of the approach to kenosis offered by McCormack in his recent *The Humility of the Eternal Son*. Like McCormack, it has tried to make clear that kenoticism needs to adopt an approach that is different from that which characterizes the controversies that are traditionally associated with it. In the first place there was the seventeenth-century *krypsis-kenosis* controversy between the Lutheran theologians of Tübingen and Giessen, concerning whether Christ concealed his use of divine powers or whether he abstained from their use for the duration of his earthly ministry. Then there was the later controversy over kenotic Christology in the nineteenth century, between Gottfried Thomasius, Wolfgang Gess, and others, over whether in the incarnation the Word abandoned some (Thomasius) or all (Gess) of the divine attributes. But in each case the focus was upon what I have called the heavenly backstory. The argument of this book is that a kenotic approach has been trapped into focusing upon this backstory because it wants to support (rightly, in my view) the self-renunciation inherent in the divine nature and displayed in the incarnation. It has not been sufficiently aware of the fact that in order to understand the self-renunciation in the incarnation, one has to be able to associate it with the eternal process of mutual indwelling-in-vulnerability that is the essence of the triune God. As Nimmo says of the incarnation, this event "corresponds perfectly to the being of God, and it is grounded in the eternal obedience of the son to the Father."[1]

Jesus of Nazareth was confronted by the overwhelming and hardly bearable idea that the God who was in every human being, in every son of

---

1. Nimmo and Johnson, *Kenosis*, 188.

God, was in him in a way that was definitive. In him, another wave in the ocean, the whole sea had contracted to a point and defined itself. God was everywhere, but in Jesus of Nazareth God was defined forever. In recognizing this Jesus lacked the comfort blanket of a heavenly backstory to which he could have immediate recourse. That is why we are easily misled—not least by kenoticists enthused by Phil 2:5–11 and the notion of "self-emptying"—into thinking in terms of a salvific skydive from heaven down to earth, something that the maturing child Jesus of Nazareth could grasp hold of in order to get an immediate understanding of "why he was sent here." This is not what we should be thinking of when we consider how he became conscious of his identity and mission.

As Rowan Williams pointed out, "The existence of Jesus is not an episode in the biography of the Word."[2] In other words, we mustn't make the mistake of dividing the life of the Son into stages during which he is first in heaven, then "humiliates" himself by journeying to earth, then goes through the suffering and death of a martyr's life, and then is exalted to the right hand of God—as if these were all part of Williams's biography of the Word. Similarly, Paul Nimmo argues, when discussing Barth's *Church Dogmatics*, that "the movements of humiliation and exaltation are not predicated successively of the person of Jesus Christ but simultaneously."[3]

Christianity too often tries to set itself apart from Judaism by presenting the sudden eruption of something new into the world, the dive into the Jewish environment of the divine other. This is a misrepresentation. God is already there, in a differentiation Christians later called that of the Father and the Son in the Spirit, but which self-differentiation was implicit in Jewish tradition too. The divine perichoresis was apparent in what Moltmann, referring to Rosenzweig, calls "the homecoming of the departed Shekhina to the fullness of the One God."[4] Rosenzweig's *The Star of Redemption* is certainly a remarkable book, and it is worth quoting part of "The Wanderings of the Shekhina" from book 3, in which Rosenzweig alludes to the myth of the *tikkun* mentioned earlier in this book, the story of how God contracted the divine self to create space for creation:

> The Shekhina, God's descent upon men and his sojourn among men, is pictured as a dichotomy taking place in God himself. God himself separates himself from himself, he gives himself away to his people, he shares in their sufferings, sets forth with them into the agony of exile, joins their wanderings. . . . The idea

---

2. R. Williams, *Arius*, 44.
3. Nimmo and Johnson, *Kenosis*, 185.
4. Moltmann, *Crucified God*, 143–44.

of the wanderings of the Shekhina, of the sparks of the original divine light being scattered about the world, this casts all of revelation between the Jewish God and Jewish man, and thereby anchors both God as well as the remnant, in all the depth of revelation.[5]

The self-differentiation of God as a way of understanding God's embrace of the earth is a Jewish tradition that Christianity developed in its own particular way.

But what was its way? McCormack sees a difference between his position and that of Barth. He suggests that Barth will not let the human Jesus (in the power of the Holy Spirit) be "the performative agent of all that is done by the God-human in his divine-human unity."[6] Why will Barth not let this happen? Why must the Logos always be the acting subject and push the humanity, as it were, to one side? Because, suggests McCormack, Barth cannot see that the humility and obedience of Jesus concretize what he describes on the same page as "a humility and obedience that are essential to the Son."[7] In other words, if one understands the ontological receptivity of the Son, one will understand why the human Jesus *can* be the acting subject, precisely because that is the form the assumption of humanity must take if it is to be true to the nature of the Son himself as displayed in his relations within the Godhead.

But is McCormack fair on Barth? In a sense, one might say no. It might be said that Barth comes close himself to a position of "ontological receptivity." Cambria Kaltwasser stresses (based on a close reading of Barth's *Church Dogmatics*) the way in which Jesus's humanity not only determines but is also determined by that of others. She quotes the following passage from the *Church Dogmatics*:

> There is not in Him a kind of deep, inner, secret recess in which He is alone in himself with God, existing in social calm or mystic rapture apart from his fellows, untouched by their state or fate. He has no such place of rest. He is immediately and directly affected by the existence of His fellows.[8]

By such means the patriarchal Son who remains untouched by his encounter with humanity turns into the considerate man who is open to the other. She points out how much of what Jesus does is in response to

---

5. Rosenzweig, *Star of Redemption*, 409–10.
6. McCormack, *Humility of Eternal Son*, 119.
7. McCormack, *Humility of Eternal Son*, 119.
8. Kaltwasser, "Kenosis," 240.

others—the woman who tugs at his garment, the Canaanite woman asking for her daughter to be healed, even his mother asking for wine at the wedding in Cana. He does not move through the world oblivious to those around him, at one and the same time saving humanity and saving himself from it. His life on earth shows that God intends shared governance, which Kaltwasser defines as "a matter of God's allowing and enabling us to co-determine God's actions."[9] Moreover—and this, she would say, is the whole point of kenoticism—"God's reciprocity with us poses no threat to God's sovereignty,"[10] thereby emphasizing the central point that kenoticism is actually about our understanding of the nature of God rather than the way in which Christ manages the process of becoming incarnate. We will be covenant partners of God, who in prayer achieve what Barth calls "a genuine and actual share in the universal lordship of God."[11] Rather than the dangerous process of self-abnegation before the divine controller, prayer becomes a kind of Zoom meeting with an invisible deity to discuss how best to run the world.

However, as has often been pointed out in criticism of Barth, this divine willingness to open up to a cooperative venture with human beings could turn out to be more apparent than real. Kaltwasser quotes a revealing passage where Barth writes that "permitted by God, and indeed willed and created by Him, there is freedom of the *friends of God* concerning whom He has determined that without abandoning the helm for one moment He will still allow Himself to be determined by them."[12] Without abandoning the helm for one moment? Isn't the whole point of a kenotic approach that God does indeed abandon the helm and that this is precisely what the self-emptying expressed through kenoticism means? God cannot share without becoming vulnerable—that is the cost to God. And arguably such vulnerability is, from a feminist point of view, precisely what men in relationships find it most difficult to accept. After all, if God has not abandoned the helm there doesn't seem to be much cash value in all this shared governance that Barth likes to talk about. Kaltwasser spends much of her chapter discussing what she calls Sarah Coakley's "deeper motivation . . . to recover a useful model of power-in-vulnerability that she believes lies at the heart of Christology."[13] But arguably it is at the heart of Christology only if it is at the heart of *the*ology, and only if God is willing to abandon the helm and risk failure.

9. Kaltwasser, "Kenosis," 243.
10. Kaltwasser, "Kenosis," 243.
11. Barth, *Church Dogmatics*, 3.3:285; quoted in Kaltwasser, "Kenosis," 244.
12. Barth, *Church Dogmatics*, 3.3:285; quoted in Kaltwasser, "Kenosis," 244.
13. Kaltwasser, "Kenosis," 233.

Is this divine willingness to put God at risk through a cooperative venture with human beings any more apparent in McCormack, or is there a similar resistance to the idea of divine vulnerability in McCormack himself? He writes that he was approached by Jürgen Moltmann after he gave a paper in 2015 and asked why he couldn't simply acknowledge divine mutability. McCormack's response was interesting:

> I tried to answer his question on the basis of a justifiably confident hope, that is, with the confidence of the Christian not only in God's faithfulness but also in God's capacity to achieve a complete victory over evils, both natural and of human origin, and the suffering they bring in an eschatological future that is free of both. It is not enough, I suggested, simply to posit such a complete victory; faith requires an understanding of why such hope is reasonable. . . . "Mutability" in God introduces an element of the "arbitrary" into God's work ad extra—of ad hoc reaction to events as they unfold. A truly mutable God cannot fully anticipate what he will "become" in response to events in history. All too often, whether the "becoming" of God is that of the process theologians or that of the "post-Barthians," the promised future seems to hang in the air, without adequate foundation. And that does indeed undermine hope.[14]

McCormack's writing is, as ever, full of scare quotes, but the point seems clear. For all the emphasis upon ontological receptivity, McCormack wants to make sure that God is suitably armor-plated in relation to the created order. God must achieve a complete victory over evils. God cannot be put into a position of reacting to events. The future mustn't hang in the air—does McCormack mean that it must be predetermined? This would conflict with what this book has put forward in terms of God's willingness to limit God's own powers, to the point of being able neither to determine the future nor to know what it will be. McCormack's ontological receptivity seems to be interwoven with iron control. In a curious way, with his concern about divine mutability, he seems to have returned to the sort of concern about the Logos becoming too tainted with the human condition that characterized the patristic writers, with whose concerns about protecting the Logos part 5 began.

McCormack essentially offers us a passive-aggressive Logos. On the one hand we are told that because of his very nature the Son can possess the absolute nature of God only in the mode of receptivity. Yet this receptivity is never allowed to threaten the predetermined course of salvation-history.

---

14. McCormack, *Humility of Eternal Son*, 194.

Complete self-giving is never allowed to take away complete control. In the end that is bound to make us wonder whether this is self-giving or some kind of disguised remote control, whereby the Logos assumes humanity with the utmost modesty while nevertheless firmly controlling all possible outcomes.

The Failure of Christ

Jesus has power only from outside himself. He exists in a relation of what we have seen McCormack call "ontological receptivity." It is only through the eternal relation of Son and Father, the giving and receiving that is at the heart of the divine being, the mutual indwelling that is the divine triunity, that Jesus of Nazareth carries out his ministry on earth. This means that the suffering and vulnerability illustrated in Jesus's life is innate to the very Godness of God. That vulnerability reaches its climax in Jesus's submission to the cross and with it his acceptance of failure.

In John 11 there is the story of the raising of Lazarus. It is this that, the Gospel writer tells us, leads to the plot to get rid of Jesus.

> So the chief priests and the Pharisees gathered the council, and said, "What are we to do? For this man performs many signs.
>
> If we let him go on thus, everyone will believe in him, and the Romans will come and destroy both our holy place and our nation."
>
> But one of them, Ca'iaphas, who was high priest that year, said to them, "You know nothing at all;
>
> you do not understand that it is expedient for you that one man should die for the people, and that the whole nation should not perish."
>
> He did not say this of his own accord, but being high priest that year he prophesied that Jesus should die for the nation,
>
> and not for the nation only, but to gather into one the children of God who are scattered abroad.
>
> So from that day on they took counsel how to put him to death.
>
> Jesus therefore no longer went about openly among the Jews but went from there to the country near the wilderness, to a town called E'phraim; and there he stayed with the disciples. (John 11:47–54)

Now in one sense this must appear to be a somewhat strange reaction. For if Jesus was performing signs that included bringing someone back from the dead, why did the authorities think that they could do away with him? And why did he react to the news by making himself scarce, retreating to the outskirts of the desert and remaining in the company of his disciples alone? Effectively he becomes a fugitive in hiding.

A challenge is offered at the foot of the cross:

> He saved others; he cannot save himself. He is the King of Israel; let him come down now from the cross, and we will believe in him. (Matt 27:42)

Of course, if one rejects the idea that Jesus brought someone back from the dead, then although it might be more difficult to explain the concern of the authorities, one can at least understand their confidence that they can arrest and kill him (and his feeling that he has to go into hiding). One need simply say that rumors spread about his abilities, and rumors have a habit of feeding upon one another and end up out of control. The stories about Jesus were false but infectious, and it became necessary to deal with them at the source.

But we know that there is another dynamic to the biblical narrative. The demand "let him come down from the cross, and we will believe in him" (Matt 27:42) suggests the story of the temptation in the wilderness, where Satan visits Jesus in the desert and tempts him three times. As MacKinnon frequently pointed out, this is the last temptation (according to the Lucan version of the story):

> And he took him to Jerusalem, and set him on the pinnacle of the temple, and said to him, "If you are the Son of God, throw yourself down from here; for it is written, 'He will give his angels charge of you, to guard you,' and 'On their hands they will bear you up, lest you strike your foot against a stone.'" And Jesus answered him, "It is said, 'You shall not tempt the Lord your God.'" And when the devil had ended every temptation, he departed from him until an opportune time. (Luke 4:9–13)

Casting himself down from the temple, like tearing himself down from the cross, would mean putting God to the test. Those who say, as in the quotation from Matt 27:42 above, "let him come down now from the cross, and we will believe in him" are like the Pharisees demanding a sign (see Matt 16:16). We can interpret this as a demand for a proof of Jesus's authority, a cut-rate route to belief or, worse than that, a way of misunderstanding the whole nature of the divine scheme, which works not by demonstrations of power that compel belief, but by outpourings of love that invite belief (and accept rejection, the dark side of love, which makes us prefer the comfort of subjection to an irresistible power that kicks us into heaven whether we like it or not).

Even so, what may appear surprising to us is the fact that the authorities have the wit to realize this. For when the raising (more accurately, the resuscitation) of Lazarus took place, one might have thought it would give Jesus's opponents a chilling sense of his invincibility (or perhaps comfort them with the thought that even the Romans could hardly deal with someone who had powers of this sort). But it does not. Instead, they have the capacity to recognize that he cannot use his power as a way of making people believe in him. Paradoxically, his omnipotence is his weakness, precisely the revelation of God that he feels himself charged to make clear as a human being in the flesh. They see at the very moment when in one sense he makes his powers most clear (by bringing a man back from the dead) exactly where his weakness lies. And he knows this—and scuttles off into hiding.

The problem of miracles is generally discussed in terms of their "scientific" plausibility, but as part 3 suggested, that is not necessarily the most problematic aspect of miracles. Given passages like the temptation in the wilderness, we can see the danger that miracles might do less to reveal than to conceal Christ's message. If the whole point of the kenotic approach is to stress the way in which God is revealed through weakness, an act of power won't do; only love will do. And for just that reason, Jesus of Nazareth is vulnerable despite his ability to bring people back from the dead.

And not only is Jesus of Nazareth vulnerable—we are vulnerable too. We know that however much we may sentimentalize the relationship between God and humanity by supposing that "he's got the whole world in his hands," it is manifestly clear that this does not mean the prevention of suffering, torture, and agonizing death. Flew was right to labor this point in "Theology and Falsification," as we saw in part 1.[15] Treat God as just like a human parent, and it would be impossible to think that God shouldn't be arrested for neglect. A human mother would not let a child suffer in the way God lets God's children suffer. As Frank Weston put it in *The One Christ* when considering the way in which a small child ascribes unlimited powers to its mother: "Perfect love requires omnipotence that it may never fail the beloved; so thinks the child."[16]

But this is not the way it is with God. The divine parent lets the children die, including, points out Dorothy Sölle on the basis of her reading of

---

15. Flew and MacIntyre, *New Essays*, 98–99.

16. Weston, *One Christ*, 121. The whole of ch. 5, "The Self-Abandoned Logos," is particularly important.

Moltmann's *The Crucified God*, God's own Son. She calls it a sort of "divine child abuse."[17]

Miracles (as I tried to argue in *Signs of God*) are most problematic not when one asks whether they can happen but when one asks why, if they can happen, they don't happen more often. The answer—if there can be one—is that this has to do with a tension between the desire to act and the recognition of the destructive effect such action would have upon the divine purpose of succeeding by love. Perhaps that tension becomes visible in the story of Lazarus itself, where the shortest verse in the Bible tells us that "Jesus wept" (John 11:35). What is the logic of all this? Lazarus is in the grave. Jesus weeps, and around him they say how much he must have loved Lazarus—except that this love seems to have no practical benefit, because Lazarus remains inside the tomb rotting. And this seems to concern them too—it is not a question of ready acceptance that in the midst of life we are in death. So we read that some, naturally enough, say that loving Lazarus is not enough. In a world of suffering, one needs someone capable of doing more than share it (a Jesus behaving like a grief counselor); they want something done about it. And Jesus seems to accede to this. He pulls Lazarus back from the grave, resuscitates him, forces him to die twice, you might say.

The tension between the desire to act and the recognition that action invites misunderstanding is above all reflected in Jesus's own life. One may suggest that in the story of the raising of Lazarus he is driven to act. And yet despite this, his enemies glimpse in the way he acts that he can still be disposed of, because the very self-imposed limitations of his ministry mean that he cannot simply destroy those who oppose him. In the face of this extraordinary display of power, those watching begin to plot to get rid of him. How? Why did they think they had a chance of succeeding? If he can resuscitate the dead, is he going to find it difficult to come down from the cross and walk away? But his enemies have an insight into Jesus's own dilemma here. Yes, he can call the angels down, but he's stuck, stuck because of the kenotic imperative. He has to submit to torture and death. Hence his enemies believe that they can start to discuss disposing with him at the very moment where he might seem to be indestructible.

And he was surely himself deeply uncertain of his own way forward. The danger of self-deception, of not seeing how one was putting self first, of basking in the comfort of being chosen, exalted, preferred, the self-righteousness of the one who sacrifices himself so nobly ("The last temptation is the greatest treason: / To do the right deed for the wrong

---

17. See Youngs, *Way of Kenotic Christ*, 35. Youngs quotes Sölle, referring to a sort of "divine child abuse" in her book *Suffering*.

reason."—MacKinnon often quoted these words of Becket from T. S. Eliot's *Murder in the Cathedral*), and then the final journey, the temptation to do exactly what those who saw him bring Lazarus out of the grave wanted, a demonstration of power, a horse rather than an ass, exactly what his enemies realized he couldn't do without betraying himself; how that must have given an edge to their mockery. Finally, the collusion in one more tortured victim and then the final sense of abandonment and being invaded again by the sense that he may have misunderstood what was going on inside him all along.

In most fairy tales there has to be an Aslan or a Gandalf to ensure that in the end things come right. When it comes to the final battle, Mordor proves destructible after all. This desire that Might, however much it sets itself against Right, must in the end lose out against what proves to be superior force, is fundamental to the world of Lewis or Tolkien. What about the biblical world? Must not Moses be stronger than Pharaoh? Do we take from Mark 3:27 that Christ must be stronger than Satan? "But no one can enter a strong man's house and plunder his property without first tying up the strong man; then indeed the house can be plundered." Must not Jesus prove stronger than those who put him to death?

In one sense, we must answer yes to this. Can we really go with those who have the disciples coming together and deciding that they will perpetuate the wisdom of a good man who died, despite the fact that he was killed? Will they say that "he is risen" in the sense that his teachings or goodness live on in the determination of his disciples to remain true to the cause? I find this totally unpersuasive. The men who fled while the women stayed at the foot of the cross had to be reinvigorated by the message that his body had gone. He had to have risen from the dead. But this didn't necessarily remove the sense of failure from his life.

MacKinnon often mentioned the story of the gushing woman who said to the duke of Wellington that it must be a wonderful thing to win a military victory. "Madame," the duke replied, "a victory is the worst thing in the world, saving only a defeat."[18] Whether Wellington really had such sensitivity to the horrors of wars won or lost is open to question, but the allusion MacKinnon made was clear. The resurrection is a victory of sorts, but the circumstances in which it was won are as tragic and destructive as a battlefield of dying soldiers lit up by night flares so that they could lose their last possessions to scavengers (who would not bother to throw dice in order to decide who kept them) after Waterloo. The resurrection, he was suggesting, had been made into another triumphal procession through the

---

18. Quoted in McDowell, *Philosophy*, 283.

streets of Rome, where the victors celebrated what had happened as the best possible outcome, sweeping away all the elements of tragedy as they passed by in triumph. We might think of Walter Benjamin reminding us, in his famous *Theses*, that history is written from the perspective of the victors:

> Whoever has emerged victorious participates to this day in the triumphal procession in which current rulers step over those who are lying prostrate. According to traditional practice, the spoils are carried in the procession.[19]

Benjamin was thinking of the triumphal processions under the Rome *imperium*, which followed a victory over some rebellious "barbarian" part of the empire. He meant that rulers not only destroy their foes but then proceed to control the story according to which these foes deserved or invited their fate. They destroy their enemies and then retell the story of their destruction as if it was a necessary evil ("You do not understand that it is expedient for you that one man should die for the people, and that the whole nation should not perish"—John 11:50) or a result of provocation ("We heard him say, 'I will destroy this temple that is made with hands, and in three days I will build another, not made with hands'"—Mark 14:58). In this way they destroy their enemies all over again.

The point of MacKinnon's quotation from the duke of Wellington, that a victory is the worst thing of all, save only a defeat, is that this was not a desirable ending to his life—though I realize that to say this is to sweep to one side theories of penal substitution, which would suggest that a condition of the atonement was that by being punished in the place of sinners Christ satisfied the demands of justice and made it possible for God "justly" to forgive sin. The approach here is to suggest that no such punishment was necessary, so that the tragic nature of the cross is not undermined by claims that it was somehow a necessary condition of our redemption. Rather, we would suggest that Jesus is mocked, crucified, killed, and then forced to emerge from the grave in a display of power that threatened to undermine his own message. Angels were not allowed to break his fall as the devil tempted him, but it seems that they were allowed to put him together again like a tortured Humpty-Dumpty after he had been thrown off the mountain he must never throw himself off.

Despite—and perhaps even because of—his vision of God, Jesus remains uncertain throughout his life about the role he is required to play. Even the uncertainty with which this book began, the uncertainty that can reach as far as doubting God's existence, may have been able to affect

---

19. Benjamin, *Illuminations*, thesis 7, 245–55.

one who, though he was driven to conclude that in him, a mere human, God was defining the nature of deity, could have wondered whether that conclusion was possible—or the delusion of a madman. All his life he was haunted by the idea that it is the prince of demons who has the power to cast out demons. Could that be a possible interpretation of all that he was able to do as a healer? Brought before the council and asked whether he was the Christ—"You say that I am" (Luke 22:70)—was he providing the diplomatic answer or was his reply tinged with his own uncertainty? And willing that the cup be taken from his lips—"Your will, not mine, be done" (Luke 22:42)—beneath that all-too-human weakness lay a doubt concerning whether he really understood what was happening to him. Was the last cry on the cross—"My God, My God, why hast thou forsaken me?" (Matt 27:46)—merely a form of identification with sinful humanity in its state of rejection, or a wish to understand how he could have been driven to believe that he was carrying God within himself when God was being tortured to death and there was no end in sight except death? The kenotic idea is at the heart of Jesus's ministry but precisely as kenotic it has to be arrived at by a human being as he tries to make sense of his life, not by a divine parachutist descending from the comfortable heavenly realms above and always bearing in mind that he is on a temporary secondment to unpleasant places, like a Eurocrat sent out of the Brussels bubble to represent the European Union in some hot spot overseas.

However powerfully the death of Christ may be interpreted as a death of God, or a death within God, there is in the end no alternative but a display of power. In the end, the conclusion was a "triumph" that threatened to destroy the message that it was intended to uphold. If he had died in his bed at ninety, he would still have been raised from the dead, but not as a display of power over his enemies.

Christian symbolism understood this. In its symbolism it commemorates the suffering and death through the crucifix. Its central figure is portrayed hanging from a cross, not walking out of a tomb.

"Say nothing to anyone," Jesus begged many of those whom he cured—because the whole Christian story was otherwise destined to become nothing more than a display of irresistible power. "Do not touch me" (John 20:17), he insists to Mary Magdalene when she recognizes that it is not the gardener. What Mary Magdalene encounters in the garden is not a wounded Lazarus brought back to life but a body no longer in the same state—and desperate not to be misunderstood as celebrating a great victory.

In the end, the power of love could be established only by riding on the back of an act of power. The self-giving and embrace of weakness that are seen to be intrinsic to the nature of God finds themselves forced to employ, through the act of resurrection, a display that threatens to undermine the message of Christianity. One may regret, with the theology of liberation, the way in which a persecuted Christian minority turned within three centuries into a persecuting church, but that final triumphant conclusion to the Christian story, *Christus Victor*, was always likely to distort the message. The failings of the institutional church were erected upon the failings of Christ's own ministry. If the church had to succeed by force that was only because, in the last instance, the same had to be said of Christ himself. The fact that the religion that emerged among the followers of Christ, however much they "preached Jesus and the resurrection" (Acts 17:17–18), focused its commemoration of Christ's life upon the cross, could be said to reflect an awareness of the danger posed by that triumphant conclusion to the Christian story.

MacKinnon's Warning

My concern with McCormack, then, is a sense that his ontologically receptive Logos is not quite as self-effacing as it might seem. He tells us that the receptivity of the Logos is the ground of the unified subject that is Jesus of Nazareth.[20] He is determined to use ontological receptivity as a characteristic which ensures that when the Logos assumes humanity he will not turn Jesus of Nazareth into an instrument, but at the same time—and this is the passive-aggressive aspect of McCormack's ontological receptivity—the receptive Logos still keeps his hands on the steering wheel in the incarnation, even when it is Jesus of Nazareth whose hands are on the wheel.

Kenosis, McCormack tells us,

> is just this: that ontological receptivity on the part of the eternal Son that makes the humility and obedience of Jesus to be his "own"—not merely in a figurative possessive sense but in a sense that makes it clear that the subject of that human attitude and activity is also the eternal Son.[21]

Is this not still a takeover by the Logos when he makes the humility and obedience of Jesus to be his "own"? McCormack scare quotes try to dilute the takeover. Yet is the power to receive, which is lauded as the essence of the divine being, a means by which the Logos can exercise a more indirect control over the humanity? Is Jesus of Nazareth being smothered by the divine love?

20. McCormack, *Humility of Eternal Son*, 258.
21. McCormack, *Humility of Eternal Son*, 19.

McCormack makes a further move that he expresses by saying that the *logos incarnatus* is grounded in the *logos incarnandus*. The incarnation is there before the foundation of the world (Eph 1:4) in the sense that it brings to concrete expression the eternal nature of God. It is here that I think MacKinnon's warning applies. We might recall MacKinnon's use of Gerard Manley Hopkins's famous allusion to a few drops cast off by the eternal process of divine selving, a kind of ecstatic afterthought, so that the world appeared less as the product of a conscious divine decision, still less as a response to any divine need, than as a simple overflow or by-product of the blissful agony of being God. It might be said that this applies to the creation, but might it not apply just as much to the incarnation, which was also an expression of God's natural exuberance? It was Jesus's fate to be caught up in this exuberance and then, when he had finally allowed himself to be caught up in it, to find that it was fated to destroy him. The cry of dereliction from the cross, "My God, My God, why have you forsaken me?," is a recognition of where he had been led by total receptivity as he struggled to understand how the divine life that had overflowed into the life of a Galilean, that blissful agony of selving, had led him to the cross.

There lurks here the danger of Christomonism,[22] which might be applied to Barth as well as to McCormack. There is a danger of promoting humanity to center stage. Just as the idea of human beings as the summit of the evolutionary scale is misplaced, so is the idea of creation as in any sense a necessity for God, of humanity being a necessary part of creation or, as the fall makes clear, the salvation of men and women being part of God's eternal design. As an omnipotence of love, God has to countenance failure for Godself and the possibility of human beings destroying themselves by failing to respond to God's love. This is the potential tragedy implicit in salvation history, and it is the potential tragedy implicit in salvation history that forms the heart of what I have called MacKinnon's warning.

There was resistance to the idea of divine vulnerability in McCormack himself, reflected in his reaction to Moltmann's question about why he could not acknowledge divine mutability. To recall his words once again, he replied that it introduced an element of the arbitrary into God's work ad extra, of "ad hoc reaction to events as they unfold."[23] All too often, he complained, "the promised future seems to hang in the air, without adequate foundation. And that does indeed undermine hope."[24] I suggested that for all his emphasis upon ontological receptivity, McCormack wants to make

---

22. See Roberts's essay on Barth, in Toon and Spiceland, *One God in Trinity*, 84.
23. McCormack, *Humility of Eternal Son*, 194.
24. McCormack, *Humility of Eternal Son*, 194.

sure that God is suitably armor-plated in relation to the created order. The Son is willing to receive and apparently yields control in the reciprocity of divine love to the human being who is assumed—and yet he must achieve a complete victory over evils. Arguably what happened to Jesus of Nazareth showed that this was to expect too much.

The tragedy of Christ's life and death, as MacKinnon saw it, points toward a less confident but perhaps more realistic assessment. It was demonstrated in the life of Jesus. If we believe that in his life God was providing a definitive revelation, the realization of that had first to come to Jesus himself. He had to know that he was not deluded (as many of his enemies thought he was). Miraculous powers had been given him, but he wouldn't have thought that this marked him out as unique. He had to reflect, go into the wilderness, pray, be tempted. None of this would have involved being aware of a unique past. It would have involved long years of reflection between the preaching in the temple and the start of his ministry. To claim that it was the Spirit of God driving him forward, that in his obedience to the Father he was acting as the Son of God, that his existence was so clear an expression of the life of the unknown and unknowable God that it could be represented as internal to it, was an act of faith—and it certainly gave no guarantees about either his own future or that of the world in which he found himself.

MacKinnon's eclectic mind ranged over many subjects. He could give a guest lecture to historians, and one would see how people who wondered at first what some amateur theologian was doing trying to tell them about the Bolshevik Revolution of 1917 were forced to recognize that he had read much more widely in their subject than they had. His writings reflected that eclectic mind, too, writings often full of philosophical insights and examples from literature. To reread *The Problem of Metaphysics* some forty years after it was written is to encounter the depth of reflection on the significance of works by Shakespeare and Sophocles, for instance, that is reminiscent of Balthasar's multivolume *Theo-Dramatik*. For those of us with much less talent and commitment to arduous learning, one imagines that the sort of reflection MacKinnon made on the inevitable opportunity cost of any decision to do one thing rather than another (he was reflecting on the ministry of Jesus, and suggesting that the limitations of human existence went beyond the particularities of age, gender, race, and location to the basic facts of having to live day by day) may have borne some relation to his own difficulties in assimilating such a vast range of topics and presenting them in a coherent manner. He used to say that he wanted those studying under him not to be the sort of theologians who brought theology into disrepute with philosophers. That was not a light requirement, but what he demanded of himself went far beyond those two disciplines.

He had a particular interest in the danger of nuclear weapons and wrote about it frequently. Such a concern is hardly out of date at a moment when the likelihood of our blowing or burning ourselves up is not small. Despite an impish sense of humor, MacKinnon was intensely serious and had a strong aversion to shallow optimism. The worship of God had to be understood against the background of a distinct possibility of failure, even the failure of God. Farrer's quote at the time of the fall of Paris, that "rational theology will not tell us whether this has or has not been an unqualified and irretrievable disaster to mankind," remains as valid today as it was when he wrote in the middle of the last world war.[25] To quote an essay written by MacKinnon in 1989:

> We are committed in the name of deterrence, to policies that dismiss as insignificant the likelihood of irretrievable damage to our genetic inheritance. We announce ourselves as prepared to take this risk: of course, glossing our commitment by claiming that the announcement is made in order to ensure that it shall never be implemented. But do we deceive ourselves into supposing that this publicly announced willingness has the force of a magic charm that will somehow ensure that we never have to fulfil our undertaking? Or have we not rather taken the first step on the dangerous path of a posturing heroism, ending when we see ourselves as justified in a leap into the abyss, precipitating hardly conceivable consequences not for ourselves but for mankind? Do we not fear a little, the spell upon our imagination, of the vision of ourselves cast by intractable circumstance for the role of those who will achieve the coming of the unknown? We have, after all, in this century paid a terrible price to those who were entranced by conviction of their own heroic destiny.[26]

In the coming months, these words may prove more prescient than we would like. In the meantime, however much ontological receptivity reflects a divine willingness to be determined through the response of an individual human being, and however much that human being has been elevated to become the focal point of God's own eternal being, such elevation means neither that the mystery of God has been put to one side nor that the possibility of catastrophic failure has been overcome.

25. Farrer, *Finite and Infinite*, 300.
26. McDowell, *Philosophy*, 165. See, more generally, an essay written as the first signs appeared of the collapse of communism: "On Comprehending the Threat," in McDowell, *Philosophy*, 161–71.

Conclusion

Since the reader has been forced to suffer concluding summaries to every chapter, this final conclusion will be short.

Part 1 suggested that we ourselves travel through life in a state of uncertainty—even about whether God exists. Like Pascal, we make a bet, and all bets have uncertain outcomes.

Part 2 looked at the order God brought when chaos was upon the face of the deep. It suggested that it was an order with a built-in flexibility that allowed the created universe to develop in ways of its own.

Part 3 moved on to the impact of God's voluntarily chosen weakness upon the moral as opposed to the natural order. It considered the implications of the fact that God allows human beings to develop in ways of their own choosing, the implicit danger of such an allowance being reflected in the traditional idea, based on the story of the fall, that such powers in human hands were stolen rather than given. By giving consent, God opens up the possibility of failure, including God's own. It is a weakness that does have its hard side, since it may entail a self-chosen inability to save those to whom God has to say, "I never knew you." The God of power is bludgeoned into universalism by the argument Heinrich Heine used on his deathbed, speaking in French: *Bien sûr, il me pardonnera; c'est son métier* (Of course God will forgive me; that's his job). The God of love cannot be bludgeoned, since God has chosen to have the future defined by the response of God's creatures. For precisely this reason, Jesus travels through the Gospels at once preaching love and suffusing his message with an unremitting harshness that reminds us that our moral choices are serious.

In part 4 the book tried to look more closely at the God who embraces risk, suffering, and even failure. What does it mean to call God Creator? What does it mean to call God at one and the same time transcendent and immanent? What does it mean to speak of God as a triunity or a Trinity of three persons? Some of these ideas are applied in part 5 in order to explore the way in which the uniqueness of Christ can be understood.

The attempt to arrive at an understanding of God prepared the way for the discussion of Christology in part 5. It examined the problems for Christology of seeing kenoticism in terms of a heavenly backstory that requires the Word to parachute out of heaven and arrive changed in the far country. It also suggested that we have to turn our understanding of Christ inside out so that rather than fitting him into a preexistent scale of goodness or location in time and place, we recognize that what we've misunderstood as context derives from the very reality it is trying to place. Though I recognize that there is much in Torrance's notion of Christ "carving out a space-time track in the cosmos"[27] which can be criticized, I think that his exploration of parallels between science and theology remains important and shows how theologians are able to make use of scientific insights and not merely hide from them.

The last section of part 5 was an exploration of the risk, suffering, and failure displayed in the life of Jesus and, with a particular emphasis upon McCormack's recent *The Humility of the Eternal Son*, an exploration of how his concept of "ontological receptivity" may help us to understand the way in which the life of Christ is at one and the same time the life of a human being and internal to the life of God. However, the final chapter suggested that even McCormack, with his emphasis upon ontological receptivity, where, as he puts it, "the person-forming activity of the Logos is realized *humanly*"[28]—i.e., through the freely willed activity of the human Jesus—cannot avoid some hidden strings behind the life of Christ (as there are in Barth), strings that ensure that however much the Logos gives it is never allowed to lose control over what happens. Challenged by Moltmann's conception of the divine mutability, McCormack admitted that "the promised future seems to hang in the air, without adequate foundation. And that does indeed undermine hope."[29] MacKinnon might suggest that it does not undermine hope, but it does undermine an easy optimism that in the end all will be well. The universe was not created simply in order to provide suitable accommodation for what are sometimes presumed to be its only important members, human beings. That provides some perspective for the fact that they may not even be able to survive their stay in it.

In the idea of kenosis a vulnerability works down from the Creator to influence creation and challenge any false confidence it may have in its role as the raison d'être of existence. As for the one whose incarnation was meant to display a commitment to humanity, that commitment should not be misinterpreted as a guarantee of success, whether for those who live and die or for the world of which even the lucky ones, who enjoy the ecstasy of consciousness for several decades, have but a fleeting glimpse as they pass through. The possibility of failure—even the failure of God—is implicit in the kenotic approach, and it is one of the great virtues of Donald MacKinnon as a theologian that he never shied away from this. He used often to quote the very last lines of Sophocles's *Women of Trachis* as translated by Sir Richard Jebb:

---

27. Torrance, *Space, Time and Incarnation*, 85.
28. McCormack, *Humility of Eternal Son*, 258.
29. McCormack, *Humility of Eternal Son*, 194.

> And you, maiden, do not be left at the house. You have seen immense, shocking death, with sorrows great in number and strange. And in all of them there is nothing that is not Zeus.[30]

The reflection in the last line, that in all the sorrow and death described earlier in the play "there is nothing that is not Zeus," suggests the sort of conclusion toward which Jesus is driven by the recognition that where his own sufferings were concerned "all of this is God." The God of love is a fearsome thing, a God whose wrath is inseparable from God's love, a God prepared to fail and in accepting God's failure to accept our own. The perichoresis of persons living in mutual dependence within the Godhead is the foundation for seeing the Logos sustained in being only through dependence upon Jesus of Nazareth. But there is also a sense in which that dependence applies even to the relations between God and ourselves, as we strive to reenter that divine perichoresis from which we were once banished. We now face the sharp touch of that divine self-giving, which chooses to live only through our responses and whose weakness is such that God may be forced to say to us, "I never knew you."

The kenotic God stands before us (to fall into the use of pronouns for a moment) with the threat of her own self-chosen weakness undeniable. Not only does she not summon legions of angels to save Jesus of Nazareth, but she empties herself even of the power to save us. There is no all-powerful patriarch to bargain with. In any case, a patriarch might have grown tired of the world and closed its independence down. She loved it and gave herself to it, making it the determinant of its own future. Faith, rather than certainty, made a world that could develop in ways not even God could fathom, whose creation involved human beings who emerged with a power to share in the management of the world and perhaps to destroy it. Unsurprisingly, humankind, which as T. S. Eliot recognized cannot bear too much reality, recoils from the consequences of God's self-limitation and seeks to replace her with the security of a divine tyrant. But he exists no more. Only the tragic reality of the crucifixion, with a dark side represented by the fate of Judas, remains before us. The transcendence of the tragic is what we have to come to terms with, not as a denial of the God of love, but as the demand that love will always make of us.

---

30. Quoted in "Transcendence of the Tragic," in MacKinnon, *Problem of Metaphysics*, 122.

Bibliography

Adams, Marilyn McCord. *Christ and Horrors: The Coherence of Christology.* Current Issues in Theology 4. Cambridge: Cambridge University Press, 2006.
Allison, Dale C. *The Historical Christ and the Theological Jesus.* Grand Rapids: Eerdmans, 2009.
Altizer, Thomas J. J., and William Hamilton. *Radical Theology and the Death of God.* Indianapolis: Bobbs-Merrill, 1966.
Anselm of Canterbury. *Proslogion.* Translated by M. J. Charlesworth. Notre Dame, IN: University of Notre Dame Press, 1979.
Aquinas, Thomas. *Summa contra Gentiles.* Translated by Anton C. Pegis et al. Notre Dame, IN: University of Notre Dame Press, 1975.
———. *Summa Theologiae.* London: Eyre and Spottiswoode, 1964–80.
Arendt, Hannah. *Eichmann in Jerusalem.* London: Penguin, 1963.
Athanasius. *The Orations of St. Athanasius against the Arians According to the Benedictine Text: With an Account of His Life by William Bright.* Translated by William Bright. Eugene, OR: Wipf and Stock, 2005.
Augustine. *Confessions.* Translated by Henry Chadwick. Oxford: Oxford University Press, 1991.
———. *On the Trinity.* Translated by Gareth B. Matthews. Cambridge: Cambridge University Press, 2002.
Ayer, Alfred. *Language, Truth and Logic.* New York: Dover, 1952.
Ayres, Lewis. *Nicaea and Its Legacy: An Approach to Fourth-Century Trinitarian Theology.* Oxford: Oxford University Press, 2004.
Baillie, D. M. *God Was in Christ: An Essay on Incarnation and Atonement.* London: Faber and Faber, 1961.
Baker, J. A. *The Foolishness of God.* London: Collins, 1970.
Balthasar, Hans Urs von. *The Action.* Vol. 4 of *Theo-Drama: Theological Dramatic Theory.* San Francisco: Ignatius, 1994.
———. *Dare We Hope That All Men Are Saved?* San Francisco: Ignatius, 1989.
———. *The Dramatis Personae: Man in God.* Vol. 2 of *Theo-Drama: Theological Dramatic Theory.* San Francisco: Ignatius, 2004.
———. *Mysterium Paschale: The Mystery of Easter.* San Francisco: Ignatius, 2000.
———. *Prolegomena.* Vol. 1 of *Theo-Drama: Theological Dramatic Theory.* San Francisco: Ignatius, 2004.
———. *The Word Made Flesh.* Vol. 1 of *Explorations in Theology.* . San Francisco: Ignatius, 1989.

Barlow, Dilly, narrator. "Parallel Universes." *BBC Horizons*, February 14, 2002. https://www.bbc.co.uk/science/horizon/2001/parallelunitrans.shtml.

Barth, Karl. *Anselm: Fides Quaerens Intellectum: Anselm's Proof of the Existence of God in the Context of his Theological Scheme*. London: SCM, 1960.

———. *Church Dogmatics*. Edited by Thomas F. Torrance and Geoffrey W. Bromiley. 13 vols. Edinburgh: T&T Clark, 1956–75.

———. *The Epistle to the Romans*. Translated by Edwyn C. Hoskyns. London: Oxford University Press, 1968.

———. *Protestant Theology in the Nineteenth Century*. Grand Rapids: Eerdmans 2002.

Bartsch, Hans Werner, ed. *Kerygma and Myth: A Theological Debate*. London: SPCK, 1962.

Bechtel, Lynn. "Genesis 2:4b—3:24: A Myth about Human Maturation." *Journal for the Study of the Old Testament* 67 (1995) 3–26.

———. "Rethinking the Interpretation of Genesis 2:4b—3:24." In *A Feminist Companion to Genesis*, edited by Athalya Brenner, 108–28. Sheffield, UK: Sheffield Academic, 1998.

Benjamin, Walter. *Illuminations*. Edited with introduction by Hannah Arendt. Translated by Harry Zorn. London: Pimlico, 1999.

Birch, Charles, et al., eds. *Liberating Life: Contemporary Approaches in Ecological Theology*. Eugene, OR: Wipf and Stock, 2007.

Boethius. *The Consolation of Philosophy*. Translated by Richard H. Green. New York: Dover, 2012.

Bonhoeffer, Dietrich. *Act and Being: Transcendental Philosophy and Ontology in Systematic Theology*. Dietrich Bonhoeffer Works 2. Minneapolis: Fortress, 1996.

———. *Letters and Papers from Prison*. Edited by Eberhard Bethge. London: SCM, 1971.

Brenner-Idan, Athalya. *A Feminist Companion to Genesis*. Sheffield, UK: Sheffield Academic, 1998.

Brouwer, Rinse H. Reeling. "The Divine Name as a Form of Kenosis in Both Biblical Testaments." In *Kenosis: The Self-Emptying of Christ in Scripture and Theology*, edited by Paul T. Nimmo and Keith L. Johnson, 59–76. Grand Rapids: Eerdmans, 2022.

Brown, David. *Divine Humanity: Kenosis and the Construction of a Christian Theology*. Waco: Baylor University Press, 2011.

———. *The Divine Trinity*. London: Duckworth, 1985.

———. "Trinitarian Personhood and Individuality." In *Trinity, Incarnation and Atonement: Philosophical and Theological Essays*, edited by R. J. Feenstra et al., 40–75. Notre Dame, IN: University of Notre Dame Press, 1989.

Brown, Robert McAfee. "Review of Wayne Meeks's *The First Urban Christians*." *New York Times*, April 3, 1983. https://www.nytimes.com/1983/04/03/books/the-everyday-life-of-early-christians.html.

Browning, Robert. "Bishop Blougram's Apology." In *The Poems and Plays of Robert Browning*, 226–48. New York: Modern Library, 1961.

Buckley, James, and Gregory L. Jones, eds. *Theology and Eschatology at the Turn of the Millennium*. Hoboken, NJ: Wiley-Blackwell, 2002.

Bulgakov, Sergius. *The Lamb of God*. Grand Rapids: Eerdmans, 2008.

Bultmann, Rudolf. *Essays Philosophical and Theological*. Translated by James C. G. Greig. London: SCM, 1955.

———. "Jesus Christ and Mythology." In *Kerygma and Myth: A Theological Debate*, edited by Hans Werner Bartsch, 1–41. London: SPCK, 1972.
Butler, Joseph. *The Analogy of Religion, Natural and Revealed*. Edited by David McNaughton. Oxford: Oxford University Press, 2021.
———. *Fifteen Sermons and Other Writings on Ethics*. London: Griffin and Tegg, 1841.
Carnley, Peter. "The Poverty of Historical Scepticism." In *Christ, Faith and History*, edited by S. W. Sykes and J. P. Clayton, 165–90. Cambridge: Cambridge University Press, 1972.
Carroll, Sean. *The Particle at the End of the Universe*. New York: Penguin, 2013.
Chesterton, G. K. *Orthodoxy*. San Francisco: Ignatius, 1995.
Chown, Marcus. *Quantum Theory Cannot Hurt You: A Guide to the Universe*. London: Faber and Faber, 2007.
Clayton, Philip, and Arthur Peacocke, eds. *In Whom We Live and Move and Have Our Being: Panentheistic Reflections on God's Presence in a Scientific World*. Grand Rapids: Eerdmans, 2004.
Coakley, Sarah. "Does Kenosis Rest on a Mistake? Three Kenotic Models in Patristic Exegesis." In *Exploring Kenotic Christology*, edited by C. Stephan Evans, 246–64. Oxford: Oxford University Press, 2006.
———. "Kenosis and Subversion: On the Repression of 'Vulnerability' in Christian Feminist Writings." In *Swallowing a Fishbone? Feminist Theologians Debate Christianity*, edited by Daphne Hampson, 82–111. London: SPCK, 1996.
———. "Kenosis: Theological Meanings and Gender Connotations." In *The Work of Love: Creation as Kenosis*, edited by John Polkinghorne, 192–210. Grand Rapids: Eerdmans, 2001.
———. "What Does Chalcedon Solve and What Does It Not? Some Reflections on the Status and Meaning of the Chalcedonian 'Definition.'" In *The Incarnation: An Interdisciplinary Symposium on the Incarnation of the Son of God*, edited by Stephen T. Davis et al., 143–63. Oxford: Oxford University Press, 2002.
Corner, Mark. *Death Be Not Proud: The Problem of the Afterlife*. Religions and Discourse 46. Bern: Lang, 2010.
———. *Does God Exist?* Eugene, OR: Wipf and Stock, 2015.
———. "Religious Belief and the Shadow of Uncertainty." *New Blackfriars* 65 (May 1984) 212–23.
———. *Signs of God: Miracles and Their Interpretation*. Aldershot, UK: Ashgate, 2005.
Coulson, C. A. *Science and Christian Belief*. London: Oxford University Press, 1955.
Dante. *The Divine Comedy*. Edited by David H. Higgins. Translated by C. H. Sisson. Oxford World's Classics. Oxford: Oxford University Press, 1998.
Darwin, Charles. *The Origin of Species by Means of Natural Selection or The Preservation of Favoured Races in the Struggle for Life*. Edited by J. W. Burrow. London: Penguin, 1968.
Darwin, C. R. "Letter from C. R. Darwin to J. D. Hooker." Cambridge University Library, March 29, 1863. https://cudl.lib.cam.ac.uk/view/MS-DAR-00115-00189/1.
Davies, Paul. *The Demon in the Machine*. London: Penguin, 2020.
Dawkins, Richard. *The Blind Watchmaker: Why the Evidence of Evolution Reveals a Universe without Design*. New York: Norton, 2015.
Descartes, René. *Meditations and Other Metaphysical Writings*. Translated by Desmond M. Clarke. London: Penguin, 1999.

Devlin, Christopher, ed. *The Sermons and Devotional Writings of Gerard Manley Hopkins*. Oxford: Oxford University Press, 1967.
Eliot, T. S. *Four Quartets*. London: Faber and Faber, 1968.
Evans, C. Stephen. *Exploring Kenotic Christology*. British Columbia: Regent College Publishing, 2009.
Farrer, Austin. *Finite and Infinite: A Philosophical Essay*. Westminster: Dacre, 1943.
Ferguson, David. "Kenosis and the Humility of God." In *Kenosis: The Self-Emptying of Christ in Scripture and Theology*, edited by Paul T. Nimmo and Keith L. Johnson, 194–212. Grand Rapids: Eerdmans, 2022.
Flew, Antony, ed. *Body, Mind and Death*. New York: Macmillan, 1964.
Flew, Antony, and Alasdair MacIntyre. *New Essays in Philosophical Theology*. London: SCM, 1955.
Forrest, Peter. "A Philosophical Case for Kenosis." *Religious Studies* 36 (2000) 127–40.
Forsyth, P. T. *The Person and Place of Jesus Christ*. Repr., Eugene, OR: Wipf and Stock, 1996.
Fromm, Erich. *The Fear of Freedom*. London: Routledge, 2001.
Gregory of Nazianzus. "Epistle 101 to Cledonius." In *Christ: Through the Nestorian Controversy*, edited by Mark DelCogliano, 388–98. Vol. 3 of *The Cambridge Edition of Early Christian Writings*. Cambridge: Cambridge University Press, 2022.
Grillmeier, Aloys. *From Chalcedon to Justinian I*. Translated by Pauliner Allen and John Cawte. Vol. 2, pt. 1 of *Christ in Christian Tradition*. Atlanta: John Knox, 1987.
———. *From the Apostolic Age to Chalcedon (451)*. Translated by John Bowden. Vol. 1 of *Christ in Christian Tradition*. Atlanta: John Knox, 1975.
Hampson, Daphne. *Theology and Feminism*. Oxford: Blackwell, 1990.
Hartshorne, Charles. *Omnipotence and Other Theological Mistakes*. New York: State University of New York Press, 1984.
Hawking, Stephen. *A Brief History of Time*. London: Bantam, 1988.
Hawking, Stephen, and Leonard Mlodinow. *The Grand Design*. London: Bantam, 2010.
Hebblethwaite, Brian. *Evil, Suffering and Religion*. London: SPCK, 2000.
———. "Some Reflections on Predestination, Providence and Divine Foreknowledge." *Religious Studies* 15 (1979) 433–48.
Hebblethwaite, Brian, and Edward Henderson. *Divine Action: Studies Inspired by the Philosophical Theology of Austin Farrer*. Edinburgh: T&T Clark, 1990.
Heidegger, Martin. *Being and Time*. Translated by John Macquarrie and Edward Robinson. Oxford: Blackwell, 1962.
Heiden, Konrad. *Der Fuehrer: Hitler's Rise to Power*. London: Victor Gollancz, 1944.
Hick, John. *Death and Eternal Life*. Louisville: Westminster, 1994.
———. *Evil and the God of Love*. London: Palgrave Macmillan, 2010.
Hodgson, Leonard. *The Doctrine of the Trinity*. London: Nisbet, 1951.
Hopkins, Gerard Manley. *Sermons and Devotional Writings*. Edited Christopher Devlin. London: Oxford University Press, 1959.
Humboldt, Alexander von. *Cosmos: A Sketch of a Physical Description of the Universe*. Baltimore: John Hopkins Press, 1997.
———. *Letters*. New York: Rudd and Carleton, 1860.
Irenaeus. *Adversus haereses (Against the Heresies)*. In vol. 1 of *The Ante-Nicene Fathers*, edited by Alexander Roberts and James Donaldson. New York: Scribner's, 1903.
Jammer, Max. *The Philosophy of Quantum Mechanics: The Interpretation of Quantum Mechanics in Historical Perspective*. New York: Wiley & Sons, 1974.

Jantzen, Grace. *God's World, God's Body*. London: Darton, Longman and Todd, 1984.
Jüngel, Eberhard. *God as the Mystery of the World: On the Foundation of the Theology of the Crucified One in the Dispute between Theism and Atheism*. Translated by Darrell L. Guder. Grand Rapids: Eerdmans, 1983.

———. *God's Being Is in Becoming: The Trinitarian Being of God in the Theology of Karl Barth*. Grand Rapids: Eerdmans, 2001.

———. "The Last Judgment as an Act of Grace." *Louvain Studies* 15 (1990) 389–405.

Kafka, Franz. *Metamorphosis*. Translated by Willa Muir and Edwin Muir. Tel Aviv: Schocken, 1987.
Kähler, Martin. *The So-Called Historical Jesus and the Historic Biblical Christ*. Edited and translated by Carl E. Braaten. Philadelphia: Fortress, 1988.
Kaltwasser, Cambria. "Kenosis and the Mutuality of God." In *Kenosis: The Self-Emptying of Christ in Scripture and Theology*, edited by Paul T. Nimmo and Keith L. Johnson, 231–48. Grand Rapids: Eerdmans, 2022.
Kant, Immanuel. *Critique of Pure Reason*. Translated by Norman Kemp Smith. London: Macmillan, 1973.

———. "What Is Enlightenment?" In *Toward Perpetual Peace and Other Writings on Politics, Peace, and History*, edited by Pauline Kleingeld, translated by David Colclasure, 17–23. Rethinking the Western Tradition. New Haven, CT: Yale University Press, 2006.

Kee, Alistair, and Eugene Thomas Long. *Being and Truth: Essays in Honour of John Macquarrie*. London: SCM, 1986.
Kelly, J. N. D. *Early Christian Creeds*. London: Longman, 1972.
Kierkegaard, Søren. *Concluding Unscientific Postscript*. Translated by David F. Swenson and Walter Lowrie. Princeton, NJ: Princeton University Press, 1974.

———. *Fear and Trembling. The Sickness Unto Death*. Translated by Walter Lowrie. Princeton, NJ: Princeton University Press, 2013.

———. *Philosophical Fragments*. Translated by Howard V. Hong and Edna H. Hong. Princeton, NJ: Princeton University Press, 1985.

Kille, D. Andrew. *Psychological Biblical Criticism*. Minneapolis: Fortress, 2001.
Knox, John. *The Church and the Reality of Christ*. New York: Harper and Row, 1952.
Komline, Kantzer. "Augustine, Kenosis and the Person of Christ." In *Kenosis: The Self-Emptying of Christ in Scripture and Theology*, edited by Paul T. Nimmo and Keith L. Johnson, 97–121. Grand Rapids: Eerdmans, 2022.
Küng, Hans. *Eternal Life? Life after Death as a Medical, Philosophical, and Theological Problem*. Eugene, OR: Wipf and Stock, 2002.
Laplace, Marquis de. *A Philosophical Essay on Probabilities*. Translated by F. W. Truscott and F. L. Emory. New York: Wiley and Sons, 1902.
Lampe, G. W. H. *The Resurrection: A Dialogue Arising from Broadcasts by G. W. H. Lampe and D. M. MacKinnon*. Edited by William Purcell. London: Mowbray, 1966.
Lederman, Leon, and Dick Teresi. *The God Particle*. New York: Houghton Mifflin, 1993.
Lessing, Gotthold. "On the Proof of the Spirit and of Power." In *Lessing's Theological Writings*, edited by Henry Chadwick, 51–56. Stanford, CA: Stanford University Press, 1956.
Lewis, C. S. *A Grief Observed*. London: Faber and Faber, 1966.
Locke, John. *An Essay Concerning Human Understanding*. Edited by Peter H. Nidditch. Oxford: Oxford University Press, 1979.

Lorenz, Edward Norton. "Predictability: Does the Flap of a Butterfly's Wings in Brazil Set Off a Tornado in Texas?" Paper for the American Association for the Advancement of Science, December 29, 1972.

MacKinnon, Donald M. *Borderlands of Theology: And Other Essays*. Edited by George W. Roberts and Donovan E. Smucker. Eugene, OR: Wipf and Stock, 2011.

———. *The Problem of Metaphysics*. Cambridge: Cambridge University Press, 1974.

———. *Themes in Theology: The Three-Fold Cord*. Edinburgh: T&T Clark, 1987.

MacKinnon, Donald M., and J. D. Holmes. "Introduction." In *University Sermons*, by John Henry Newman, 9–25. London: SPCK, 1982.

McCall, Bradford. *A Modern Relation of Theology and Science Assisted by Emergence and Kenosis*. Eugene, OR: Wipf and Stock, 2018.

McCormack, Bruce Lindley. *The Humility of the Eternal Son: Reformed Kenoticism and the Repair of Chalcedon*. Cambridge: Cambridge University Press, 2021.

McDowell, John C. *Hope in Barth's Eschatology: Interrogations and Transformations beyond Tragedy*. Routledge Revivals. London: Routledge, 2019.

———. *Philosophy and the Burden of Theological Honesty: A Donald MacKinnon Reader*. London: T&T Clark International, 2011.

McFague, Sallie. *Models of God: Theology for an Ecological Nuclear Age*. Minneapolis: Fortress, 1987.

McGuckin, John. "Origen of Alexandria on the Kenosis of the Lord." In *Kenosis: The Self-Emptying of Christ in Scripture and Theology*, edited by Paul T. Nimmo and Keith L. Johnson, 77–96. Grand Rapids: Eerdmans, 2022.

McKinney, Richard W. A., ed. *Creation, Christ and Culture: Studies in Honour of T. F. Torrance*. London: Bloomsbury, 2016.

Meeks, Wayne. *The First Urban Christians: The Social World of the Apostle Paul*. New Haven, CT: Yale University Press, 1983.

Midgley, Mary. *Beast and Man*. Routledge Classics. London: Routledge, 1995.

———. *Evolution as a Religion: Strange Hopes and Stranger Fears*. Routledge Classics. London: Routledge, 2002.

———. *Wickedness*. Routledge Classics. London: Routledge, 1984.

Milton, John. *Paradise Lost*. Introduction by John Leonard. Penguin Classics. London: Penguin Classics, 2000.

Moltmann, Jürgen. *The Crucified God: The Cross of Christ as the Foundation and Criticism of Christian Theology*. 40th anniv. ed. Minneapolis: Fortress, 2015.

———. *In the End—The Beginning: The Life of Hope*. Translated by Margaret Kohl. Minneapolis: Fortress, 2004.

———. *Theology of Hope*. London: SCM, 2002.

———. *The Trinity and the Kingdom of God*. London: SCM, 1981.

Monod, Jacques. *Chance and Necessity*. New York: Knopf, 1971.

Moore, G. E. "Is Existence a Predicate?" *Aristotelian Society Supplement* 15 (1936) 175–88.

Murphy, Nancey. *Bodies and Souls, or Spirited Bodies?* Cambridge: Cambridge University Press, 2006.

———. "Divine Action in the Natural Order: Buridan's Ass and Schrödinger's Cat." In *Chaos and Complexity: Scientific Perspectives on Divine Action*, edited by Robert Russell et al., 263–303. Vatican: Vatican Observatory, 1996.

Newman, John Henry. *The Dream of Gerontius*. London: Longmans, 1909.

———. *Essay in Aid of a Grammar of Assent*. Edited by I. T. Ker. Oxford: Oxford University Press, 1985.

———. *University Sermons*. London: SPCK, 1982.
Nichols, Terence L. *The Sacred Cosmos: Christian Faith and the Challenge of Naturalism*. Christian Practice of Everyday Life. Repr., Eugene, OR: Wipf and Stock, 2009.
Nietzsche, Friedrich. *The Gay Science*. Translated by Walter Kaufmann. New York: Vintage, 1974.
———. *The Genealogy of Morals*. Translated by Walter Kaufmann and R. J. Hollingdale. New York: Vintage, 1967.
———. *The Will to Power*. Translated by Walter Kaufmann and R. J. Hollingdale. New York: Vintage, 1968.
Nimmo, Paul T., and Keith Johnson, eds. *Kenosis: The Self-Emptying of Christ in Scripture and Theology*. Grand Rapids: Eerdmans, 2022.
Oakes, Edward T. "'He Descended into Hell': The Depths of God's Self-Emptying Love on Holy Saturday in the Thought of Hans Urs von Balthasar." In *Exploring Kenotic Christology*, edited by Stephen C. Evans, 218–45. Vancouver, BC: Regent College Publishing, 2009.
Oord, Thomas Jay. *Open and Relational Theology*. Grasmere, ID: Sacrasage, 2021.
———. *The Uncontrolling Love of God: An Open and Relational Account of Providence*. Downers Grove, IL: IVP Academic, 2015.
Paley, William. *Natural Theology or Evidences of the Existence and Attributes of the Deity*. Edited by Matthew D. Eddy and David Knight. Oxford: Oxford University Press, 2008.
Pannenberg, Wolfhart. *Jesus, God and Man*. London. SCM, 2002.
Pascal, Blaise. *Pensées*. Penguin Classics. London: Penguin Classics, 1995.
Peacocke, Arthur. *Creation and World of Science: The Re-Shaping of Belief*. Rev. ed. Oxford: Oxford University Press, 2004.
———. *Paths from Science towards God: The End of All Our Exploring*. Oxford: One World, 2001.
———. *Theology in an Age of Science*. Oxford: Blackwell, 1990.
Philosophy Overdose. "Russell-Copleston Debate on God's Existence (1948)." YouTube, June 9, 2021. https://www.youtube.com/watch?v=MVLKURgffto.
Pike, Nelson. "Divine Omniscience and Voluntary Action." *Philosophical Review* 74 (1965) 27–46.
Plantinga, Alvin. *God and Other Minds: A Study of the Rational Justification of Belief in God*. Ithaca: Cornell University Press, 1990.
———. *The Nature of Necessity*. Oxford: Clarendon, 1979.
Plato. *The Republic of Plato*. Translated by Frances Cornford. Oxford: Oxford University Press, 1941.
Polkinghorne, John. *Belief in God in an Age of Science*. New Haven, CT: Yale University Press, 1998.
———. *Quantum Physics and Theology: An Unexpected Kinship*. London: SPCK, 2007.
———. *Serious Talk*. Philadelphia: Trinity, 1995.
———, ed. *The Work of Love: Creation as Kenosis*. Grand Rapids: Eerdmans, 2001.
Pollard, William. *Chance and Providence: God's Action in a World Governed by Scientific Law*. London: Faber and Faber, 1958.
Popper, Karl. *Unended Quest: An Intellectual Autobiography*. 2nd ed. Routledge Classics. London: Routledge, 2005.
Rahner, Karl, ed. *Encyclopedia of Theology: The Concise Sacramentum Mundi*. Translated by J. Griffiths et al. London: Burns & Oates, 1975.

———. *Foundations of Christian Faith: An Introduction to the Idea of Christianity*. Translated by W. V. Dych. New York: Crossroad, 1986.
Roberts, Richard H. "Karl Barth." In *One God in Trinity*, edited by Peter Toon and James D. Spiceland, 78–94. London: Bagster, 1980.
———. "Theological Rhetoric and Moral Passion in the Light of MacKinnon's Barth." In *Christ, Ethics and Tragedy: Essays in Honour of Donald MacKinnon*, edited by Kenneth Surin, 1–14. Cambridge: Cambridge University Press, 1989.
Robinson, John A. T. *Honest to God*. London: SCM, 1963.
———. *In the End, God: A Study of the Christian Doctrine of the Last Things*. London: James Clarke, 1950.
Rosenzweig, Franz. *The Star of Redemption*. Translated by William W. Hallo. Notre Dame, IN: University of Notre Dame Press, 1985.
Rowland, Christopher. *Christian Origins: The Setting and Character of the Most Important Messianic Sect of Judaism*. 2nd ed. London: SPCK, 2002.
———. *Radical Prophet: The Mystics, Subversives and Visionaries Who Strove for Heaven on Earth*. London: Tauris, 2017.
———. *Revelation*. London: Epworth, 1993.
Russell, Bertrand. *The Problems of Philosophy*. Oxford: Oxford University Press, 1967.
Russell, Robert. "Does 'the God Who Acts' Really Act? New Approaches to Divine Action in the Light of Science." *Theology Today* 54 (1997) 43–65.
Russell, Robert, et al., eds. *Chaos and Complexity: Scientific Perspectives on Divine Action*. Vatican: Vatican Observatory, 1996.
Saunders, Nicholas. *Divine Action and Modern Science*. Cambridge: Cambridge University Press, 2002.
Schwöbel, Christoph. "The Generosity of the Triune God and the Humility of the Son." In *Kenosis: The Self-Emptying of Christ in Scripture and Theology*, edited by Paul T. Nimmo and Keith L. Johnson, 267–89. Grand Rapids: Eerdmans, 2022.
Shelley, Percy Bysshe. *Selected Poems and Prose*. London: Penguin, 2017.
———. *The Selected Poetry and Prose of Shelley*. Introduction and notes by Bruce Woodcock. Wordsworth Poetry Library. Ware, Hertfordshire: Wordsworth Editions Limited, 2002.
———. *Shelley's Poetry and Prose*. Edited by Neil Fraistat and Donald Reiman. Norton Critical Edition. New York: Norton, 2002.
Sölle, Dorothee. *Suffering*. Philadelphia: Fortress, 1975.
Sonderegger, Katherine. "Cyril of Alexandria and the Sacrifice of Gethsemane." In *Kenosis: The Self-Emptying of Christ in Scripture and Theology*, edited by Paul T. Nimmo and Keith L. Johnson, 122–36. Grand Rapids: Eerdmans, 2022.
Stead, Christopher. *Divine Substance*. Oxford: Clarendon, 1977.
Surin, Kenneth, ed. *Christ, Ethics and Tragedy: Essays in Honour of Donald MacKinnon*. Cambridge: Cambridge University Press, 1989.
Swinburne, Richard. *The Evolution of the Soul*. Oxford: Clarendon, 1997.
Sykes, S. W. "The Strange Persistence of Kenotic Christology." In *Being and Truth: Essays in Honour of John MacQuarrie*, edited by Alistair Kee and Eugene T. Long, 349–76. London: SCM, 1986.
Sykes, S. W., and J. P. Clayton, eds. *Christ, Faith and History*. Cambridge: Cambridge University Press, 1972.
Tennyson, Alfred. *In Memoriam*. New York: Norton, 2003.
Theissen, Gerd. *The First Followers of Jesus*. London: SCM, 1978.

———. *The Gospels in Context: Social and Political History in the Synoptic Tradition.* Minneapolis: Fortress, 1992.

———. *The Shadow of the Galilean: The Quest of the Historical Jesus in Narrative Form.* Minneapolis: Fortress, 1987.

———. *Social Reality and the Early Christians.* Minneapolis: Fortress, 1992.

Tillich, Paul. *Systematic Theology.* 3 vols. Chicago: University of Chicago Press, 1951, 1957, 1963.

Time. "Religion: Witness to an Ancient Truth." *Time,* April 2, 1962. https://content.time.com/time/subscriber/article/0,33009,873557-4,00.html.

Toon, Peter, and James D. Spiceland, eds. *One God in Trinity.* London: Samuel Bagster, 1980.

Torrance, Thomas F. *Divine and Contingent Order.* Edinburgh: T&T Clark, 1998.

———. *Space, Time and Incarnation.* London: Oxford University Press, 1969.

———. *Space, Time and Resurrection.* Edinburgh: Handsel, 1976.

Towler, Robert. *The Need for Certainty: A Sociological Study of Conventional Religion.* London: Routledge and Kegan Paul, 1984.

Vanstone, William. *Love's Endeavour, Love's Expense: The Response of Being to the Love of God.* London: Darton, Longman and Todd, 2007.

Volf, Miroslav. "The Final Reconciliation: Reflections on a Social Dimension of the Eschatological Transition." In *Theology and Eschatology at the Turn of the Millennium,* edited by James Buckley and L. Gregory Jones, 89–113. Hoboken, NJ: Wiley-Blackwell, 2002.

Watts, Susan. "Are We Closer to a 'Theory of Everything'?" *BBC News,* September 8, 2010. https://www.bbc.co.uk/blogs/newsnight/susanwatts/2010/09/how_far_have_we_got_in_the_sea.html.

Webb, Clement C. J. *Problems in the Relations of God and Man.* London: Nisbet & Co., 1911.

Welch, Claude, ed. *God and Incarnation in Mid-Nineteenth Century German Theology.* Oxford: Oxford University Press, 1965.

Wesley, John. *Earnest Appeal to Men of Reason and Religion.* London: Whitfield, 1796. https://wesleyscholar.com/wp-content/uploads/2018/10/Appeals-to-Men-of-Reason-Religion-1796.pdf.

Weston, Frank. *The One Christ: An Enquiry into the Manner of the Incarnation.* London: Longmans, Green and Co., 1914.

Whitehead, Alfred N. *Religion in the Making.* New York: Meridian, 1960.

Wiles, Maurice. *God's Action in the World.* London: SCM, 1986.

Williams, Bernard. "Tertullian's Paradox." In *New Essays in Philosophical Theology,* edited by Antony Flew and Alasdair MacIntyre, 187–211. London: SCM, 1955.

Williams, Rowan. *Arius: Heresy and Tradition.* London: SCM, 2001.

———. *Christ the Heart of Creation.* London: Bloomsbury, 2018.

———. "Trinity and Ontology." In *Christ, Ethics and Tragedy: Essays in Honour of Donald MacKinnon,* edited by Kenneth Surin, 71–92. Cambridge: Cambridge University Press, 1989.

Wittgenstein, Ludwig. *On Certainty.* Edited by G. E. M Anscombe and G. H. von Wright. Oxford: Blackwell, 1974.

Wollheim, Richard, ed. *Hume on Religion.* London: Fontana, 1963.

Youngs, Samuel J. *The Way of the Kenotic Christ: The Christology of Jürgen Moltmann.* Eugene, OR: Cascade, 2019.

Index

adoptionism. *See* Christology
agnosticism, 5
analogia entis, (analogy of being), 151
Anselm of Canterbury, 147, 237-38
Apollinarianism/Apollinarius, 170, 184, 190
Aquinas, Thomas, 56, 94, 150-52, 158-59, 189-90, 237
Arendt, Hannah, 97-98, 237
Aristotle, 97, 149, 150-51
Arius, 157, 171-72
Athanasius, 170, 172-73, 237
Augustine, 90, 92, 94, 103, 126-30, 132, 137, 142, 146, 154, 157-58, 179-80, 237
Ayer, Alfred, 7-11, 237

Baillie, Donald, xv-xvi, 161, 164, 207, 237
Baker, John Austin, xiv, 159-60, 237
Balthasar, Hans Urs von, 89, 188-89, 212, 217, 232, 237, 243
Barth, Karl, 30, 46, 93, 160-61, 164-65, 167, 178, 208-10, 219-21, 231, 235, 238
Basil of Caesarea, 89-90, 92
Bechtel, Lynn, 104-6, 238
Benjamin, Walter, 228, 238
Boethius, Anicius, 80, 238
Bonhoeffer, Dietrich, 45-46, 116, 131, 141, 152-53, 153n19, 238
Bradley, F. H., 8
Brown, David, xiii-xv, 101, 156, 158-60, 175, 186-88, 191-93, 208, 238

Browning, Robert, 20, 25, 238
Bulgakov, Sergius, 190, 238
Bultmann, Rudolf, 14, 50, 50n1, 68-69, 74-75, 238
Butler, Joseph, 21, 26, 98, 239

Carnley, Peter, 15, 239
Carroll, Sean, 142-44, 239
certainty, 4, 21, 32, 236
  of commitment, 20, 25-26
  not given by history, 13-18
  mathematical, 19
  and knowledge, 28-29, 245
  the need for, 31, 245
  and religious experience 30, 63
  scientific, 48
  See also uncertainty
chance, nature of, 50
chaos theory, xvi, 46, 49-50, 59-63, 65, 67, 72, 74, 131
Chesterton, G. K., 77, 239
Chown, Marcus 42, 239
Christology, ix, 121, 164, 202
  adoptionist, 190
  Alexandrian and Antiochene approaches, 169-70
  continuity of identity, 172-78
  eschatology, 198-200
  failure of Christ, 223-30
  "from above" and "from below," 180-82, 194
  Homoousios, 171
  the human subject in Christology, 186-88

INDEX

Christology (continued)
    kenotic Christology, 133, 161, 203, 218, 221, 234 (*see also* Kenosis)
    Logos-flesh and Logos-man Christologies, 170
    ontological receptivity and Christology (*see* ontological receptivity)
    tertium quid, danger of, 173–74
    theotokos 184–85
    two natures in one person, 169–72
Christomonism, 231
Coakley, Sarah, 182–84, 195, 221, 239
Compton's demon, 66, 71
concrete universal, 212, 217
Copleston, Frederick, 5–6, 21–22, 31, 243
Creation, 122–33, 164
    continuous 125–27, 145
    and kenosis, xvi–xvii, 37, 62–63, 74, 82–83, 99, 110, 116n29, 119, 132, 160, 234–36
    out of nothing, 127–29
    and pantheism, 136–37
    and *tikkun*, 219–20
    relation to time and space, 121, 129–34, 212
Cyril of Alexandria, 173–74, 182, 184–85, 187, 201–3, 205, 244

Dante, 90–91, 94, 100, 239
Darwin, Charles, 39–40, 43–44, 47, 51–53, 55, 58, 61, 73, 239
Dawkins, Richard, 48, 55–56, 114, 119, 239
Deism, 122–24, 129, 132, 135–36, 152
Descartes, 128, 147, 239

Einstein, Albert, 42, 66, 66n5, 68, 83, 130
Eliot, T. S., 101, 227, 236, 240
eschatology. *See* Christology
evolution, theory of, 43–48, 50–59, 61–63, 74, 82–83, 114–15, 119, 123, 155–56, 231, 239, 242
extra calvinisticum, 161–62

faith, xiv, xvi, 1, 3–6, 10–12, 14–15, 30–33

and doubt, 14–15, 18–21, 25–26, 30–31, 33
justification by, 10
and history, 13–16
leap of, 15–16, 22–24
the Fall, xvi, 102–16, 120, 199, 231, 234
Farrer, Austin, xi–xii, 120, 233, 240
Fergusson, David, 189
Flew, Antony, 24–26, 52, 91, 93, 109, 225, 240, 245
Forrest, Peter, 175–78, 240
Forsyth, P. T., 99, 240
Fromm, Erich, 97, 101, 240

General Divine Actions (GDA), 65, 120
Gess, Wolfgang. xiv–xv, 218
God
    as Being, 146–53
    as Creator, 122–33
    as the "God particle" (*see* Higgs boson)
    as Light, 138–42, 152
    as omniscient, 56–57, 79–83, 91, 102, 179, 243
    as transcendent and immanent, xvii, 121, 132–34, 135–53, 154, 164–65, 206, 234
    as Trinity (*see* Trinity)
    See also Deism, Pantheism, and Panentheism
God of the gaps, 43–44, 59–75
Gregory of Nazianzus, 90, 92, 170, 170n1, 182, 240
Gregory of Nyssa, 156, 156n3, 182–84, 195, 212
Grillmeier, Aloys, 171, 174n7, 175, 240

Halley's comet, 45, 144
Hampson, Daphne, 203, 239, 240
Hartshorne, Charles, 83, 83n14, 240
Hawking, Stephen, 41–42, 42n10, 49, 72–73, 123–25, 129, 132, 145, 240
Hebblethwaite, Brian, xiii, 80–83, 240
Heidegger, Martin, 107, 142, 148–51, 153, 240
Heine, Heinrich, 234
hell, problem of, 85–101, 212, 243

INDEX

Hick, John, 90–92, 100, 103n2, 103–6, 108–10, 112, 115, 240
Higgs boson (God particle), 43, 50, 138, 140–46, 151, 153
Hodgson, Leonard, 155–56, 240
homoousios. See Christology
Hopkins, Gerard Manley, 116, 116n10, 120, 231, 240
Humboldt, Alexander von, 39–40, 240
Hume, David, 52, 86–87, 100, 245
Huxley, Thomas Henry, 47, 58

incarnation, 121, 173, 187, 200, 208–10, 230–35
 concrete universal, 217
 and Creation, 212
 and eucharist, 215–16
 and kenotic imperative, 12, 137, 157, 181, 211, 218
 and reincarnation, 175–77, 194, 196
 Space, Time and Incarnation, 130n7, 212–15
 and Trinity, 157, 162–65, 188–91, 196
Irenaeus, 103, 103n2, 110, 115, 240

Jantzen, Grace, 136–37, 241
Jüngel, Eberhard, 89, 190, 241

Kafka, Franz, 174, 181, 241
Kähler, Martin, 14, 241
Kaltwasser, Cambria, 220–21, 241
Kant, Immanuel, 1, 110, 147–48, 147n12, 180, 201, 241
kenosis, ix, xii-xvii, 12, 32–33, 64, 74–75, 84, 106, 107n11, 108–9, 116, 119, 136, 169, 175, 181–84, 188–91, 197, 203–4, 211–12, 218–20
 and Creation, 37, 74, 80, 122–34
 and the failure of Christ, 223–30
 feminist reservations about, 184–85, 203–4
 hard side of, 85–102
 kenotic imperative, 12, 37, 150, 171–72, 226
 and pantheism, 136–37
 the "sky-dive," 178–81, 186, 197

and vulnerability of God, 136, 159–64, 194, 208, 220–23, 230–32, 234–36
Kierkegaard, Søren, 23, 26, 32, 178, 178n15, 241
Knox, John, 14, 241
Küng, Hans, 92–93, 95, 241

Laplace, Pierre-Simon, 44n13, 44–45, 59–60, 62, 241
Lederman, Leon, 43, 144–46, 241
Lessing, Gotthold, 13–14, 241
Lewis, C. S., 95, 227, 241
liberation theology, 14–15, 20, 26, 32, 230
Locke, John 176, 176n12, 181, 191, 241
logical positivism, 7, 48

McCormack, Bruce, xiii, xiiin5, 184–91, 196, 201, 204, 207, 218, 220, 222–23, 230–31, 235, 242
McDowell, John, 93, 242
McFague, Sallie, 136–37, 242
McGuckin, John, 179, 242
MacKinnon, Donald, ix-x, xvii, 93, 102, 102n1, 116, 116n29, 157–60, 160n13, 163–64, 167, 188–91, 193–94, 196, 201, 204, 214–19, 224, 226–28, 230–36
Marcellus of Ancyra, 170–71
Meeks, Wayne, 15, 238, 242
Midgley, Mary, 47, 53–58, 63, 97–98, 98n20, 242
miracles, 3–4, 16n7, 16–18, 64, 67–68, 74–75, 120, 122, 131, 133, 194, 197, 201, 205, 207, 211, 225–26, 232, 239
Milton, John, 96, 98, 107–15, 242
 Paradise Lost, 107–15
Mitchell, Basil, 25–26, 32
Moltmann, Jürgen, xii, xvi, 137, 159, 172, 196, 219, 222, 226, 231, 235, 242, 245
Monod, Jacques, 54–59, 70–71, 83, 114, 119, 242
Moore, G. E., 28, 148–49, 242
Murphy, Nancey, 72, 92, 242
Nestorius, 173, 174n7, 175, 182–85

Newman, John Henry, 19–20, 26–28, 28n1, 33, 33n7, 93–94, 100–1, 242
　The Dream of Gerontius, 93–94, 100–1
Newton, Isaac, 44, 46, 62, 125, 130
Nietzsche, Friedrich, xii-xiii, 114–15, 243

ontological argument, 147–50
ontological receptivity, xiii, xiiin5, xvii 186–88, 191, 201, 207–8, 220, 222–23, 230–35
Origen, 91, 179–80, 242

Paley, William, 8–9, 51–54, 122–23, 243
panentheism, 138, 141, 152, 239
Pannenberg, Wolfhart, 161, 206, 243
pantheism, 135–37, 152
Pascal, Blaise, 22–23, 26–27, 32, 234, 243
Peacocke, Arthur, 56, 69, 239, 243
perichoresis, 158, 163, 188–90, 196, 219, 236
Plantinga, Alvin, 6, 6n3, 27, 147, 243
Plato, 139, 149, 172, 196, 243
Polkinghorne, John, 49, 62, 66, 69–71, 74, 239, 243
Pollard, William, 67–68, 70–71, 243
Popper, Karl, 83, 243
pre-Socratics, 143–46, 151, 153
purgatory, 86–87, 92–95, 100
Pusey, Edward, 90–92

quantum theory, xvi, 42, 46–47, 49, 50–51, 59–75, 79, 82, 119–20, 124, 131, 142, 239, 240, 243

Rahner, Karl, 141–43, 243
relativity, 46–47, 49, 66, 130, 213–14
religious experience, xvi, 29–30, 119
Rice, Richard, 81
Roberts, Richard, ix-x, 231n22, 244
Robinson, John, 69, 88–89, 131, 136, 141, 206, 240, 244
Rosenzweig, Franz, 108–9, 196, 219–20, 244

Rowland, Christopher, 195, 198–201, 201n14, 244
Russell, Bertrand, 5–6, 21–22, 31–32, 147–48, 243, 244
Russell, Robert, 71, 244

Saunders, Nicholas, 64–68, 72–73, 79, 244
scandal of particularity, 212–15
Schwöbel, Christoph, 189, 244
shekhina, 196, 204, 219–20
Shelley, Percy Bysshe, 4, 244
Sölle, Dorothy, 225–27, 226n17, 244
Sonderegger, Katherine, 201–5, 244
Sophocles, 232, 235–36
Special Divine Actions (SDA), 44, 51, 65, 71–72, 74–75, 120, 122, 131
Stanislavsky, Konstantin, 186, 191, 208
substantial relations. *See* Trinity
Sykes, Stephen, 161, 203, 239, 244

Tennyson, Alfred Lord, 52–53, 244
Theissen, Gerd, 15–16, 244
Theodoret, 184–85
theotokos. See Christology
Thomasius, Gottfried, xv, xvn14, 218
Tikkun ha-Olam (Repair of the World), 107, 150, 219
Tillich, Paul, 104, 131, 245
Tindal, Matthew, 122
Torrance, Tom, 46, 49, 130–31, 212–15, 234–35, 238, 242, 245
Towler, Robert, 31, 245
Tracy, Thomas F., 71–72
transcendence and immanence. *See* God
Trinity, xvii, 121, 154–65, 185, 188, 191–92, 196, 204, 208, 231, 234, 237, 238
　Aquinas and "substantial relations," 158–59, 189–90
　and Christology, 161–63
　"economic" and "immanent" Trinity, 155
　and *hypostasis*, 174–75
　and Incarnation, 157

uncertainty, ix, xv-xvii, 1, 3–4, 6, 13–18, 19–26, 27–32, 37, 59–63, 64, 71, 73–74, 119–20, 167, 170–72, 181, 193–94, 197, 204–6, 207, 211–12, 217, 226, 228–29, 234, 239

Vanstone, William, 101, 159–60, 245
Volf, Miroslav, 89, 245

Wesley, Charles, 160, 245
Wesley, John, 11, 30, 63
Weston, Frank, xiv, 225, 225n16, 245
Whitehead, Alfred N., 210, 216, 245
wickedness, 85–89, 96–98, 100, 242. *See also* hell, problem of
Wilberforce, Bishop Samuel, 43, 47
Wiles, Maurice, 120, 245
Williams, Bernard, 10, 245
Williams, Rowan, 167, 219, 245
Wittgenstein, Ludwig, 28–30, 245
Wren-Lewis, John, 70, 79

www.ingramcontent.com/pod-product-compliance
Lightning Source LLC
Chambersburg PA
CBHW030823230426
43667CB00008B/1343